THE MUSÉE D'ORSAY

THE COLLECTIONS IN 365 WORKS

THE MUSÉE D'ORSAY

THE COLLECTIONS IN 365 WORKS

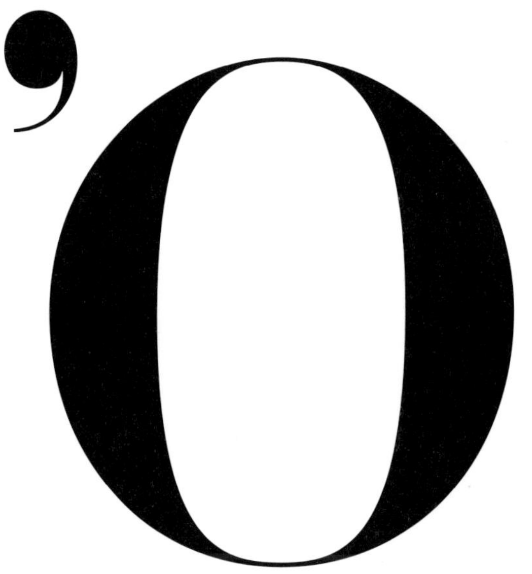

Musée d'Orsay

SKIRA

185. PARIS — Panorama

la nouvelle Gare d'Orléans
C. M.

« THE NEW ORSAY »

PAST AND PRESENT

Paul Perrin
Head of Curatorial and Director of Collections at the Musée d'Orsay

Located in a former train station with a rich international collection of masterpieces from the period 1848-1914, the Musée d'Orsay is a unique institution.

It was one of the first major cultural sites to be located in a disused utilitarian building. The Gare d'Orsay and its luxurious 400-room passenger hotel were built by architect Victor Laloux (Grand Prix de Rome 1878) for the 1900 Paris World Fair on the ruins of the former Cour des Comptes, which had been burned down by the Commune in 1871. The only railroad station in the center of the capital, standing opposite the Hôtel de Salm (which housed the administration for the Legion of Honor) in the former aristocratic quarter on the Left Bank, not far from the Louvre, there was no doubt as to the Gare d'Orsay's monumental character.

The metal substructure, on a similar scale to the Eiffel Tower, is completely masked on the outside by a somewhat eclectic stone façade and from within by a large coffered vault reminiscent of an antique basilica. "The station is superb and looks like a palace for the fine arts," wrote the painter Édouard Detaille. It was an unconsciously perceptive observation.

Opposite page Alexandra Lebon, *Gare d'Orsay: the large interior clock in gilded stucco (western tympanum glass roof)*, 2023, photograph
Previous page Panorama toward the new Gare d'Orléans [Gare d'Orsay], early 20th century, postcard

After operating for forty years, rail traffic slowed, and after World War II, only the suburban lines were operating. In the 1960s, when 19th-century architecture was widely denigrated, plans began to be made to demolish the edifice and construct, on the banks of the Seine, a brand-new modernist-style hotel. However, the scandal sparked by the destruction of Baltard's *Les Halles* glass and iron market structure aroused interest in protecting these then unloved 19th-century buildings and, just in time, the Gare d'Orsay was listed as a historic monument in 1973.

Once saved, the idea was floated that the station might serve as the home for a new national museum dedicated to a brief but remarkably intense

Above Interior of Gare d'Orsay, early 20th century

period in the history of French and, more broadly, Western art, from 1848 to 1914, thereby providing a link between the Louvre and the Musée National d'Art Moderne, that had recently been installed in the new Pompidou Center. With its huge glass roof, ballroom and giant clocks, the station itself is a distillation of the 19th century, an echo of its revolutions in industry and transport, of the vogue for travel and of the development of leisure and tourism. It is also a reminder of the technical innovations made possible by scientific progress, the exploitation of natural resources and the invention of new forms of energy (the station was served by electric locomotives), the new urban temporality and the death of the cyclical time of agriculture and religion, and finally, it is a symbol of World Fairs, globalized commercial, financial and diplomatic relations and the colonial phenomenon, of the triumph of Paris as the capital of the arts and entertainment, and so on. In short, it embodies a certain glorious and all-conquering "modernity" associated with the idea of the "progress" of civilization that still largely colors our picture of the 19th century.

In 1977, President Valéry Giscard d'Estaing officially approved the creation of the Musée d'Orsay. The project continued to the end of his term in 1981, and was then handed over to his successor François Mitterrand, by whom it was officially opened in December 1986. An initial architectural competition was launched for the renovation and conversion of the station into a museum and was awarded to the ACT Architecture team (Renaud Bardon, Pierre Colboc, Jean-Paul Philippon); a second competition later appointed Italian architect Gae Aulenti to design the interior and the museographical elements. Eschewing any form of pastiche, the transformation sought to highlight the structure and decorative elements of Laloux's masterpiece and yet distance itself from it through bold contrasts and a modern, monumental aesthetic. For the visitor, wandering through the museum's spaces amounts to a *promenade architecturale,* to adopt Le Corbusier's expression.

Despite its visible emphasis on painting and sculpture, the museum does not only house "fine arts"; it is a truly multi-disciplinary space, where the visual and decorative arts, architecture, as well as photography and cinema—the new media of the 19th century—come together. In the 1980s, the museum brought together collections from the former Musée du Jeu de Paume (Impressionism), the Louvre (Realism, Academism, Symbolism) and the Musée National d'Art Moderne (Post-Impressionism), along with many other

Above Jim Purcell, *Hanging Thomas Couture's painting "Les Romains de la décadence" (The Romans of the Decadence)*, 1986, silver gelatin negative

acquisitions, as well as returned loans and works formerly in storage. These have enabled the museum's strong points to be reinforced (the Musée d'Orsay's impressionist and post-impressionist collections are the richest in the world), and the creation of major collections of photography (from the pioneers to the Pictorialists), and of Architecture and Decorative arts (ranging from the World Fairs' wonders of eclecticism to all the various forms of Art Nouveau). The collections have also been greatly enriched with works by artists from a range of countries, making the museum the only one in the world able to present such a vast panorama of artistic creation in Europe and North America from the 19th to the early 20th centuries. The collection currently contains around 140,000 items, including 5,000 paintings, 5,000 sculptures and medals, 3,500 *objets d'art*, 500 pastels and almost 65,000 drawings (decorative and architectural items in addition to so-called "artists' drawings"), around 50,000 photographs, not to mention some extraordinary documents and archive holdings, and artists' correspondence.

While the selection presented in this book is of necessity small, it is nonetheless representative. It covers every technique, generation and style, including acclaimed masterpieces and fresh discoveries, French art and foreign schools, items acquired by the Beaux-Arts administration during artists' lifetimes, and more recent acquisitions that together allow the Musée d'Orsay to display an increasingly diverse (and feminine) image of 19th and early 20th-century art.

Such a varied collection reflects the many questions that were being raised in artistic circles during this period: what is Beauty now in the age of "modernity" and machines? Should the objective be the invention of new designs, or is it better to revitalize tradition by drawing on the past or turning to other cultures? Should reality, technical progress and the material opulence accruing from "progress" be cele-brated or should the goal be to restore the power of the imagination, the inner world and the ideal? What purpose do works of art serve? Pure aesthetic pleasure ("art for art's sake") and the enjoyment of an elite, or education and the improvement of the society in which the majority live ("social art" and "art in everything")? To consolidate the power of the rich and powerful, or to depict the existence of the lowest on the social ladder? To contribute to the development of new "nations," or to further the emancipation of the individual?

In light of the works selected for this book, it is clear that 19th-century artists offer a wide range of often diametrically opposed answers to these questions. To the point that the art world of the period resembles a battlefield, with antagonistic factions, debates and scandals, schisms and "secessions," conservative forces and "avant-gardes" (a word borrowed from the military lexicon); invention and originality is to be found as much on the side of the "moderns" as that of the anti-modernists. Paradoxically, in what was an age of conflict (artistic, philosophical, social, gender, etc.), many artists pursued an ideal of synthesis and unity, of Eden or the Golden Age, of regaining harmony with nature, of the total work of art (*Gesamtkunstwerk*) and correspondances between the arts.

More than ever, these are issues that seem to resonate with our times. No doubt all of us, as visitors or readers, will find plenty in these works to provoke thought and stir emotions, perhaps leading us to question contemporary society, in part heir to the positive and the negative aspects of the 19th century, but also allowing us to escape into past and imaginary worlds.

Above Jim Purcell, Musée d'Orsay: overview of the nave, 1986, gelatin silver print
Next page The Impressionists gallery, 2012

Honoré Daumier
Félix Barthe

Painted unbaked clay
6¾ × 6 × 5½ in. (17.2 × 15.3 × 13.9 cm)
Acquired from the Le Garrec heirs in 1980
with the help of M. Michel David Weill
and the Fondation Lutèce

Between 1832 and 1835, at the request of Charles Philipon, founder of the satirical newspapers *La Caricature* and *Le Charivari*, Daumier modeled some forty satirical busts (*bustes-charges*) in unbaked clay and painted them in oils; the thirty-six that have survived are all now kept at the Musée d'Orsay under the name *Celebrities of the Juste Milieu*. These are energetic caricatures of political figures from the reign of Louis-Philippe, but also depict friends of the artist in Republican circles. While these small busts have a field day with the then fashionable pseudo-science of phrenology (the study of skull formation as a sign of character), they also break with the satirical sculptures of the period by their being polychrome. Daumier used these busts as models for the lithographs he drew for Philipon's two papers. Made when he was only twenty-four, they demonstrate the young artist's freedom of invention. Philipon bought the whole set of models, thereby helping to preserve an outstanding ensemble that, given its fragility, had not been expected to last. They form a portrait gallery in which deputies, peers, and friends of the artist are depicted with a psychological incisiveness that is sometimes cruel but always funny, and that reaches beyond simple caricature. É. P.

François Rude
Genius of the Fatherland

Plaster
7 ft. 4¼ in. × 6 ft. 5¼ in. × 2 ft. 11½ in. (2.24 × 1.96 × 0.90 m)
Acquired in 1898

Dominating *The Departure of the Volunteers* of 1792, the colossal bas-relief that runs across the Arc de Triomphe, *Genius of the Fatherland* has become one of the great popular icons of French history under the name of *The Marseillaise*. Originally intended to celebrate Napoleon's Grande Armée, the Arc de Triomphe was left unfinished for some twenty years after his fall. Completed and inaugurated under King Louis-Philippe in 1836, it became a rather surprising hotchpotch designed to project "national reconciliation". Rude, the son of a stove-maker who supported the Revolution as early as 1789, went into exile after the Bourbon restoration of 1815, but was commissioned by Adolphe Thiers (then Minister of Trade and Public Works) to sculpt one of the high reliefs for the monument. He came up with a winged genius, an allegory of the Fatherland, its mouth open in a great, silent cry, leading a group of volunteers ready to sacrifice themselves to save the nation and its freedoms: The Marseillaise was their song. The romantic sculptor par excellence, Rude expressed urgency and patriotic passion by means of violent contrasts of shadow and light, achieving a *terribilità* never before attained in a public monument, and casting a long shadow over French sculpture in the second half of the nineteenth century. The work was controversial, and dismissed by some as a "raging shrew," but this *Genius of the Fatherland* soon became an icon of the French Republic. É. P.

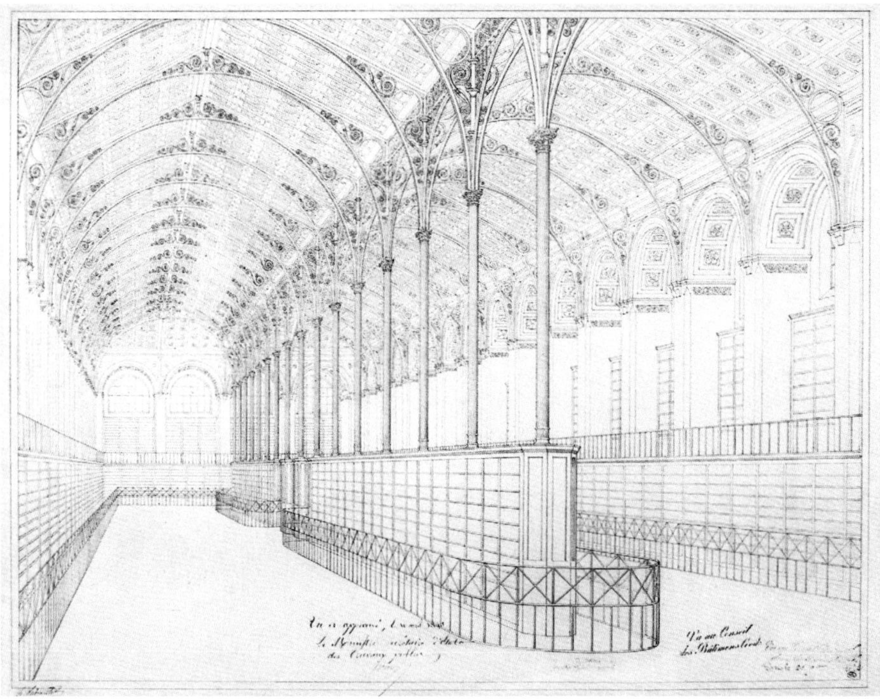

Henri Labrouste
Perspective View of the Sainte-Geneviève
Library Reading Room

Graphite, pen, and ink
17¾ × 23¼ in. (45 × 59 cm)
Acquired in 1981

A winner of the Prix de Rome, Henri Labrouste belonged to the generation of romantic artists who set out to respond to technological devel-opments and societal needs. In this respect, designing a library—an amenity that catered to the growing social practice of reading and called for nonflammable materials—was a particularly stimulating challenge. Henri Labrouste was named architect of the Bibliothèque Sainte-Geneviève in 1838. It was his responsibility to oversee the transfer of the prestigious Genovefan fathers' collection to a new building. His plans were approved in 1839 and construction work started in 1843. Behind the austere, simply decorated façade recalling the Renais-sance palazzos of Florence, he built a structure in metal—thought then to be fireproof—which helped reduce the number of abutments in the reading room, and thus maximized available space and increased luminosity. Combining technical innovation and aesthetics, Labrouste used delicate decorative motifs inspired by antique ornamentation to enhance the plastic beauty of the metal elements. This building, in which the stone envelope contrasts with the cast iron construction inside, marks a very modern step away from the classical architectural principles of formal and structural homogeneity. A. T.-B.

Hector Horeau
An Opera for the City of Paris

Watercolor
9½ × 14 in. (24 × 35.5 cm)
Acquired in 2007

Known as the Opéra Le Peletier, the theater of the Royal Academy of Music was built in 1821 by François Debret. Located in Rue Le Peletier, it was ravaged by fire in 1873; construction of the "New Opera" began in 1861 and the building was inaugurated in 1875.

The replacement of Debret's inadequate audi-torium had been envisaged since the early 1840s, and among the many designs eventually submitted was this one by Hector Horeau, a highly imaginative architect whose ideas tended to be developed and implemented by others. He suggested an opera house ope-ning onto Rue de Richelieu, its façade evoking a great circular portico, affording easy access to pedestrians and giving onto the galleries surrounding the whole building, which offe-red shelter for approaching coaches. Simply decorated with pilasters on the first floor, the Corinthian order on the second, and statues on the attic, the portico opened onto a bright, high-ceilinged foyer that created a theatrical ambience around visitors. Beyond that were the auditorium, the stage and, in a small buil-ding partly connected to the stage, the rooms used by the administration. The ceiling over the entrance and foyer was in glass, while the stage was surmounted by a dome on a quadrangular base open at the sides. Horeau presented his project in the competition held in 1860, which was won by Charles Garnier. C. M.

William Henry Fox Talbot
China on a Shelf

Salted paper print after a paper negative
5½ × 7 in. (13.9 × 18 cm)
Gift of the Kodak-Pathé Foundation, 1983

The man of science from Lacock Abbey, a member of the Royal Society, was the designer who was to establish the technical specificity of photography: the negative-positive process which he called "calotype" (for the negative), and for which he filed a patent in 1841. Practiced in Great Britain, notably by Hill and Adamson, the calotype spread more especially to France between 1843 and 1860.

Talbot brought out *The Pencil of Nature*, a publication that involved highlighting the new possibilities offered by photography, with six fascicles published between 1844 and 1846. The book is made up of an introduction followed by twenty-four photographs, with a commentary relating to the value of applying photography to this or that particular purpose. Thus "photogenic drawings," architectural views, urban views, works of art, and collections of objects, as well as still lifes and genre scenes, are all featured in these pages. The portrait, being the area of special interest to the daguerreotypists, does not feature here.

For this plate (number III in the album's first fascicle), Talbot has carefully arranged a collection of pieces of china on some shelves. Talbot insisted on photography's special ability to reproduce such an arrangement of different items in a single shot and mentions a possible forensic application for photography ("The mute testimony of the picture"). J. L.

Léon Riesener
Full-face, half-length Portrait of Eugène Delacroix

Daguerreotype
2¼ × 1¾ in. (6 × 4.3 cm)
Acquired with the help of the Commission Nationale de Photographie

This striking portrait of Eugène Delacroix is by his cousin Léon Riesener. In March 1842, the painter was unwell, and he went to rest with the Rieseners, who lived in Frépillon near Montmorency in northern France. Léon Riesener was himself a painter, and after Delacroix died, he described their relationship. "He was not my master in painting, but in that, as in everything else, he was my oracle."

The two men were close companions and shared a keen interest in photography; Delacroix was a founder member of the Heliographic Society, along with Eugène Durieu, with whom he worked on calotypes of nudes in 1854, which he showed to his cousin Riesener. With reference to his stay at Frépillon, Delacroix wrote to one of his friends: "I am having my daguerreotype done; I'll have some anyway. I am also busy arranging some drawings in *Le Magasin pittoresque* format for the woodcuts I want to make."

In this very small daguerreotype, Riesener captures Delacroix's personality with great subtlety. In so doing, he produced one of the four earliest known portraits of the painter (including another notable daguerreotype kept at the Musée du Petit Palais), who is shown posing nobly in a carefully elegant posture. His distant gaze in this close-up view contributes to the power of this photograph. J. L.

Auguste Préault
Ophelia

Bronze relief
2 ft. 5½ in. × 6 ft. 6¾ in. × 7¾ in. (0.75 × 2.00 × 0.20 m)
Acquired in 1876

The dark, passion-riven world of Shakespearean tragedy provided remarkable subject matter for French romantic artists of the 1830s—the "*Hernani* generation," as it was named, after the drama by Victor Hugo. Préault was a great theater-lover and attended the premiere of *Hamlet* performed by an English troupe at the Théâtre de l'Odéon on September 11, 1827. He was fascinated by the ravishing Harriet Smithson's performance as Ophelia, which inspired this sculpture of the young woman driven to a watery death by her despair. The romantic aesthetic is evident in the handling of the agonized body which, swept away by the current, bends and twists, the head thrown violently to one side like a dead Christ. But what is strikingly new is the sketchy treatment of the volumes, as if to illustrate Préault's famous aphorism, "I am not for the finished—the finite—but for the unfinished: the infinite." Only the arms, head, and legs emerge from the formless magma of the water, rendered in small, taut folds with which the young woman's hair and tunic merge. This unfinished quality was a major obstacle to an acceptance of Préault's work in official circles. The plaster version of *Ophelia* was rejected by the Salon in 1849, and it was not until 1876, when Romanticism was already yesterday's news, that the State commissioned a bronze version. O. F.

Gustave Courbet
The Wounded Man

Oil on canvas
2 ft. 8 in. × 3 ft. 2½ in. (81.5 × 97.5 cm)
Acquired in 1881

Alongside *Man in Despair*, *The Wounded Man* is one of the most poignant of the score of self-portraits that the artist painted during his years of training. It reveals an eclectic meditation on the art of his predecessors—from the Nordics to the Venetians—and an assimilation of Romanticism in its declining years. Here Courbet already shows the assertive temperament and the self-assured talent on which he built his reputation, while at the same time revealing a degree of introspection in this abandoned face with closed eyes. The original composition, painted in 1844, showed the artist enjoying a siesta outside with his lover, who was leaning against his shoulder; but this was probably abandoned after his companion, Virginie Binet, broke off with him in 1851. Instead the artist adopts the posture of a wounded hero, the sword replacing the woman. So the artist is making an intimate confidence through this metaphor of the defeated duelist and the rejected lover. When Courbet stopped producing self-portraits, he wrote in 1854 to his collector friend Alfred Bruyas: "I have made many portraits of myself in my life, in keeping with the changes in my mental situation I have, in a word, written my life." Up to the *Portrait of the Artist at Sainte-Pélagie*, painted at the end of his life when he was in prison for his part in the Paris Commune uprising of 1871, the artist's omnipresence in his work is expressed in other ways, notably through allegory. Courbet was so attached to this work that he took it with him into exile in Switzerland. X. R.

Jean-Léon Gérôme
The Cock Fight

Oil on canvas
4 ft. 8¼ in. × 6 ft. 8¼ in.
(1.43 × 2.04 m)
Acquired in 1873

Gérôme made his first major impression at the Salon of 1846 with *The Cock Fight*, heralding the advent of the neo-Greek movement, the latest development in neoclassicism, remarkable for its precision finish, quality of line, and its use of light colors. This original approach was inspired above all by the resumption—after Napoleon I's military success in Naples—of the excavations at the ancient sites of Pompeii and Herculaneum. These fascinated painters, sculptors, and architects alike with their elegance and bright polychrommy. The battle between the birds, like the opposition between the young bodies and the Sphinx of the fountain, is doubtless a veiled reference to the artistic combat triggered by a group of young artists around Gérôme—people like Hamon and Picou, who brought a breath of fresh air to the historical genre. Looking at this painting, Baudelaire poured scorn on this "meticulous school," while Théophile Gautier celebrated the "prodigious feats of draftsmanship, action, and color" that sealed Gérôme's reputation. The artist's career was crowned with every honor and marked by unbroken commercial success both throughout Europe and in the United States. X. R.

Gustave Courbet
Young Man Sitting, Study:
Self-portrait known as "At the Easel"

Charcoal on paper
17½ × 13½ in. (45 × 34 cm)
Acquired in 2003

Like Rembrandt, Van Gogh, and Picasso, Courbet was fascinated by his own image, and his intellectual, physical, and artistic development is punctuated by painted and drawn self-portraits, methodically exploring his self. The Musée d'Orsay holds three self-portraits, one showing the painter smoking his pipe, from 1871, and this one. The image of the artist at work is significant: it shows him to be fully and consciously an artist, his pose laying claim to the heritage of the Old Masters, echoing Renaissance and classical stereotypes, but also the figure of Ingres. The chiaroscuro recalls Rembrandt, while the dramatization and sub-jectivity are appropriated from his predecessors in the romantic generation. The upward view imparts élan and dynamism to the figure, in contrast to his meditative face with its half-closed eyes. The power of conception and the principles of composition of this drawing are as striking as in the painted self-portraits from before 1850. This charcoal drawing intensely conveys the searching of a man who, throughout his life, continued to question his status and experience as an artist. This outs-tanding sheet is characteristic of the power of Courbet's drawings, which were rare. I. J.

Auguste Clésinger
Woman Bitten by a Snake

Marble
1 ft. 11½ in. × 5 ft. 10¾ in. × 1 ft. 10 in.
(0.60 × 1.80 × 0.56 m)
Acquired in 1931

This marble was, along with *The Romans of the Decadence* by Thomas Couture (p. 31), the most talked-about work at the Salon of 1847, where it sparked an artistic and social scandal. As indicated by the cellulite that appears at the top of the thighs of this marble, Clésinger had worked with a cast taken directly from the body, in this case the body of a demimondaine, the Parisian beauty Apollonie Sabatier, who was Baudelaire's muse and had her own salon. Known to her friends as "La Présidente," Sabatier brought the artist undreamt-of success. The use of casts made directly on the body was violently contested in the nineteenth century:

it was taken as a sign of artistic laziness and lack of probity. Clésinger carefully cultivated excellent relations with Théophile Gautier, who orchestrated the scandal. For Delacroix, the piece was no more than a "daguerreotype in sculpture." However, these generous forms, whose realism so aroused the prudishness of visitors to the Salon, are associated with more conventional elements, such as the idealized and less expressive face, and the base covered with flowers like the bronze mount of a clock, making *Woman Bitten by a Snake* a perfect example of eclecticism in sculpture. É. P.

Louis Adolphe Humbert de Molard
Louis Dodier as a Prisoner

Daguerreotype
4½ × 6 in. (11.5 × 15.5 cm)
Gift of the Braunschweig family in
memory of Francis Braunschweig
through the Société des Amis
du Musée d'Orsay, 1988

Baron Humbert de Molard was a brilliant expo-nent of photography, who seems to have taken on this new art early in 1843, during the "pri-mitive" period of photography, as it is known. It was more especially near Lagny (just east of Paris) and at the family home, Le Manoir d'Argentelles in Normandy, northern France, that he constructed his genre scenes by calling upon those close to him, one being his steward, Louis Dodier. Humbert de Molard captures aspects of this country life he was so attached to; as an established daguerreotypist and calo-typist, he brings on stage the actors in this pro-vincial theater. He devised veritable *tableaux vivants* with men at table, a girl with her bird-cage, a beggar, a game of cards, or a pig being cut up. Louis Dodier sat for Humbert de Molard on a number of occasions, and there are three versions of this *Louis Dodier as a Prisoner*, pro-duced in 1847.

Using a low-angle shot and lighting that brings out every nuance, he contrives to heighten the presence of this sitter with the particularly intense gaze. The scene resembles something out of the romantic literature and painting that was then in vogue; the artist's favorite actor and accomplice, Louis Dodier, is a willing player in the drama. J. L.

Félix Duban
Interior View of the Sainte-Chapelle

Graphite and watercolor
19½ × 13¾ in. (49.6 × 35.2 cm)
Gift of M. Tropey in memory of M. Bailly, 1893

Seeking to unite the nation around a shared past, the July Monarchy set up a special administration in charge of preserving and promoting France's historic monuments. Begun in 1836 under the direction of Félix Duban, the restoration of the Sainte-Chapelle was a key moment in the development of this consciousness of the national heritage. Seconded by Jean-Baptiste Lassus and Eugène Emmanuel Viollet-le-Duc, the architect offered a respectful recreation of the past based on the scrupulous study of archeological remains and historical sources. His research led him to choose bright colors, dominated by red and blue, and to precisely reproduce the statuary, as shown in this drawing. Its archaeological precision aside, this composition also reflects Duban's personal sensibility and fascination with polychromy, inspired by the antique paintings of Pompeii. With its two sculpted and painted fragments, this drawing evokes the spirit of the architect's famous *Fantasies*, poetic reconstructions of antique interiors. They remind us that Duban always sought to give his architecture a dreamlike dimension. A. T.-B.

Maison Froment-Meurice
Dressing table of the Duchess of Parma

Partly gilt silver, gilt copper, painted enamel on copper, blue glass, emeralds, and garnets
3 ft. 11¼ in. × 6 ft. 2 in. (1.20 × 1.88 m)
Acquired with the help of the Société des Amis du Musée d'Orsay, 1981

This ensemble was commissioned by a subscription among French legitimist gentlewomen for the wedding of Louise-Marie-Thérèse de Bourbon, the granddaughter of Charles X, and the Prince de Lucques, the future Duke Charles III of Parma, in November 1845. Its decoration constitutes a nostalgic and idealized vision of the Middle Ages as a time of steadfast loyalty to God and King, while exalting traditional France and the bonds of wedlock. The lilies and roses of France intertwine with ivy, a symbol of conjugal fidelity. Sent to London in 1851 for the Great Exhibition, and later given to the duchess, this prestige item evokes a mix of Western and Oriental civilizations and, stylistically, spans the periods from St. Louis to Louis XIV. The jewelry boxes, their form recalling the reliquaries made in the Meuse region in the thirteenth century, are decorated with portraits of twenty French women of notable piety, courage, and literary talent, including Blanche de Castille, Joan of Arc, and Clémence Isaure. The ewer and the bowl reference Islamic and Renaissance sources, while the candlesticks hark back to bronze models from the seventeenth century. The overall stylistic heterogeneity prefigures the eclecticism that dominated the decorative arts during the Second Empire. Y. B.

Thibault

The Barricade in the Faubourg du Temple before the Attack, Sunday June 25, 1848

Daguerreotype
4½ × 6 in. (11.7 × 15 cm)
Acquired with the help of the Patrimoine
Photographique, 2002

Nothing is known about the author of this daguerreotype, who has captured a particularly critical moment during the days of the Paris insurrection in June 1848. However, this daguerreotypist seems to have been in touch with the editors of the newspaper *L'Illustration*, founded in 1843 and modeled on *The Illustrated London News*. After a break in publication because of the disturbances, an issue of the paper was brought out with inset reproductions of two shots of the barricade, one dated June 25, the other June 26, following the assault by General Lamoricière's troops. They both carried the mention, "after a daguerreotyped plate by M. Thibault." The version "before the assault" was published from the daguerreotype currently kept at the Musée Carnavalet. The daguerreotype shown here, identical—apart from the odd detail—to the Paris museum's version, is thus a part of a reportage on these dramatic events (the Musée d'Orsay also possesses a version dated the day after the attack). Taken from above a street cleared of any human presence (the population having been ordered to stay indoors), the viewpoint offers an outstanding overall vision of this theater of urban revolution, of a Paris marked by bloody battles that caused some three thousand casualties in the period June 22–26, 1848. J. L.

Ernest Meissonier
The Barricade

Watercolor, gouache, and pencil on paper
10¼ × 8¼ in. (26 × 21 cm)
Acquired in 1997

Ernest Meissonier is known for his depictions of military scenes from the seventeenth century, and his evocations of the Napoleonic legend. This drawing chronicles what he called "important things"—both a tragic moment in French history and something he experienced at first hand: the bloody repression that followed the closure of the National Workshops, which had been such a beacon of hope for Parisian workers. On June 25, 1848 Meissonier, on duty as a captain of the National Guard, was responsible for defending the Hôtel de Ville and Rue de la Mortellerie. Looking back in a letter dated 1890, he wrote: "I was still terribly affected by the event I had just witnessed, and believe me … those things penetrate your soul. When you reproduce them, it is not just to make a work of art, it is because you have been stirred in the depth of your guts and because that memory must never die." Meissonier executed quick sketches in pen and watercolor, boldly heightened here with blue gouache, which further accentuates the horror of the scene. He presented this work to Delacroix and the Musée d'Orsay acquired it in 1997, when it joined a sizeable collection gifted to the French state by the artist's widow. It is a first study for the painting with the same title now held at the Louvre (Department of Paintings). I. J.

Honoré Daumier
The Republic or The Republic Feeds Her Children and Instructs Them

Oil on canvas
28¾ × 23½ in (73 × 60 cm)
Gift of Étienne Moreau-Nélaton, 1906

The proclamation of the Second Republic on February 24, 1848 generated great euphoria, particularly in the art world: a new fine arts department was set up and the Salon was opened up to all artists. It was in this "spirit of 1848" that competitions were organized to allocate State commissions. Daumier, the author of numerous political cartoons under Louis-Philippe, produced his first work as a painter as an entry to a competition to compose a figure to symbolize the Republic. His sketch was among the twenty shortlisted by a panel of judges including Ingres and Delacroix. Daumier's composition offers a strong, reassuring appearance for the new regime, heir to the First Republic, as the tricolor flag recalls. However, the overly revolutionary Phrygian cap has made way for a laurel wreath, which evokes victory, peace, and immortality at the same time. He replaces the traditional representation of Christian charity with the image of the Republic as a mother figure, monumental and enlightened, who "feeds her children and instructs them." Despite the enthusiastic reception, Daumier—no doubt uncomfortable with the mandatory large format—never painted the final painting for the competition, and thus the episode ended in failure. I. P.

Thomas Couture
The Romans of the Decadence
or **Roman Orgy**

Oil on canvas
15 ft. 5 in. × 25 ft. 4 in.
(4.72 × 7.72 m)
Acquired in 1847

From its lofty position in the middle of the center aisle of the Musée d'Orsay in 1986 (where it still hangs today), *The Romans of the Decadence* became the embodiment of the rediscovery of neoclassical painting from the 1970s onward. Back in the nineteenth century, it was mockingly called *pompier* ("fireman") art, because of the perceived similarity between the helmets of the ancient divinities and the headgear of contemporary firemen. The huge canvas, a State commission exhibited at the Salon of 1847, illustrated the *Satires* of the Roman poet Juvenal (first-second century AD). Although it looked like the great official machine par excellence, it nonetheless revealed the fresh approach that artists were showing with regard to traditional sources of inspiration. The composition is characteristic of the eclecticism of the day, mixing monumental architecture inspired by Veronese with a more Michelangelesque treatment of the convulsing bodies, and taking in the Romanticism of Delacroix, who was then at the height of his powers. The work is complex both in its technique and in its subject matter: an orgy, which certainly resonated with the political turmoil before the Revolution of 1848. Above all it reflected a state of mind specific to the times—people were torn between a faith in technical progress and economic development, and the dread of the vice and decline that threaten any great civilization. X. R.

Jean-François Millet
The Haymakers' Rest

Oil on canvas
2 ft. 11 in. × 3 ft. 9½ in
(0.89 × 1.16 m)
Acquired in 1848

The advent of the Second Republic coincided with early public recognition for Millet's painting. Probably with support from his friends at the fine arts department, Millet sold *The Winnower*, which was exhibited at the 1848 Salon, to the politician Alexandre Auguste Ledru-Rollin for a decent price; the following year the painter won his first official commission. The artist initially opted to depict a religious scene, but later decided to work on a fresh canvas, *The Haymakers' Rest*. The 1,800 francs paid to him by the State enabled the artist to move to Barbizon, where he remained until his death. By painting a profane subject instead of the originally planned biblical composition, the painter indicated his preference for contemporary country themes and continued in the vein started with *The Winnower*. Familiar with the rural world (to which his own family belonged), Millet here depicts haymakers enjoying a moment's respite in the shade of a haystack. This silent gathering around a woman having a drink is echoed in the background, where a peaceful line of cattle drink by the river, the work in the fields setting the daily rhythm for man and beast alike. Millet returns to this theme of peasants resting in a number of works, including a pastel of 1866, *La Méridienne*, interpreted by Vincent van Gogh in a 1889 painting kept at the Musée d'Orsay. I. P.

Ernest Hébert
La Mal'aria

Oil on canvas,
4 ft. 5¼ in. × 6 ft. 4 in. (1.35 × 1.93 m)
Acquired in 1851

Typical of the eclecticism rife at the Salon of 1850–51, which featured Gustave Courbet's *A Burial at Ornans* (p. 39) and Félix Barrias's *The Exiles of Tiberius* (p. 42), *La Mal'aria* is the work of a painter on the way to becoming one of the prominent artists under the Second Empire. Having met with success as early as 1839 with *Tasso in Prison*, and having won the Prix de Rome, Hébert came home from his residency in Rome more fascinated by contemporary Italy and its pictur-esque scenes than with a repertoire of forms derived from admiration for the ancient remains and the glories of the Renaissance. For this Grenoble-born cousin of the novelist Stendhal, Italy was somewhere he loved to stay;

he enjoyed two lengthy directorships at the Académie de France in Rome from 1867 to 1873, and from 1885 to 1891. The fruits of Hébert's long career—he also made an apse in mosaic for the Paris Pantheon—are preserved in two museums, one in Paris and the other at La Tronche (Isère), in the house he lived in regularly and where he died. Despite Hébert's classical training at the École des Beaux-Arts, *La Mal'aria* shows his romantic inclination in the depiction of a malaria-infested marshland area, returning to the symbolism of the boat carrying people from the world of life to the world of death, echoing the skiffs of Eugène Delacroix, which were to become a favorite motif of the Symbolists at the turn of the century. X. R.

Manufacture nationale de Sèvres, Louis Désiré Barré, painter
"Egg" vase, size 2

Hard-paste porcelain and gilt bronze
3 ft. 5¼ in. × 1 ft. 4¼ in. (1.05 × 0.41 m)
Mobilier National collection, on permanent
loan to the Musée d'Orsay since 2009

The flower painter Louis Désiré Barré joined the Sèvres porcelain manufactory in 1846. Here, meticulously depicted bouquets based on the Dutch flower-painting tradition are replaced by a simpler composition, structured by bramble branches bearing fruit. Four kinds of flowers—nasturtium, convolvulus, bellflower, and various types of passionflower—are distributed over the two sides of each vase. The naturalistic rendering shows the painter's skill at depicting their transient appearance in minute detail. The use of brambles to connect flowers or organize a bouquet or frieze is characteristic of the years from 1848 to 1855. The rich gilding is by Pierre Doré. The gilt bronze mount with ram's heads, ornamental floral motifs, and scrolls with birds at their center is the work of Louis Honoré Boquet, an independent engraver and bronze mounter who had a workshop within the manufactory from 1819 onward. The advent of the Second Republic in February 1848 brought upheaval in the organization at Sèvres, which had previously been governed by the royal household. This pair of vases was presented in an exhibition of work by the national manufactories held in 1850, among other works chosen to justify the existence of these State-run workshops. Y. B.

Théodore Rousseau
An Avenue in the Forest of L'Isle-Adam

Oil on canvas
3 ft. 3¾ in. × 2 ft. 8¼ in. (1.01 × 0.82 m)
Bequeathed by M. Alfred Chauchard, 1910

This landscape, in a vertical format idealizing "the trees shooting up like columns in a Gothic cathedral," was painted on the spot by Rousseau in the spring of 1846, during a stay at L'Isle-Adam with the painter Jules Dupré. The atmosphere of the scene is peaceful and bucolic; a girl—sitting in a sunlit clearing—watches over some cows grazing. This serene, luminous view of nature is different from the romantic and tormented vein of the landscapes painted by Rousseau under the July Monarchy, pictures that were regularly rejected by the Salon judges, who saw his submissions more as sketches than finished paintings. On the other hand, the painter received encouragement from the likes of Théophile Gautier, Eugène Delacroix, and George Sand. The republican regime looked on him more favorably, awarding him a medal for *An Avenue*, which was featured at the 1849 Salon. Rousseau, who admired the seventeenth-century Dutch landscape artists and English painter John Constable, contributed to the revival of the landscape genre in France. After moving to Barbizon, he sought with other artists to convey his observations of nature through the prism of the individual temperament, the impression, and not just through accurate rendering. This way of tackling the landscape left a deep mark on the future Impressionists. I. P.

Rosa Bonheur
Plowing in Nevers or The First Dressing

Oil on canvas
4 ft. 4¼ in. × 8 ft. 6¼ in. (1.33 × 2.60 m)
State commission, 1848

This painting was an official commission made after the Salon of 1848, where Rosa Bonheur won a medal. The Ministry of the Interior wanted a work representing cattle in a meadow. The artist observed the scene depicted here when out walking during a stay in the *département* of Nièvre. The term *sombrage* refers to the plowing of the field before the vines are planted. Powerful teams of animals are needed to deeply turn the earth (here the oxen work in sixes). The viewpoint used here—slightly from below, with a wide angle—heightens the vividness of this meticulously described scene, as does the large format of the canvas. The painting was a great success at the Salon of 1849 and was compared to the writings of George Sand, another woman who, in her novel *La Mare au diable* (*The Devil's Pool*, 1846), spoke of plowing as a subject worthy of painting.

In depicting work in the fields, Bonheur offers a peaceful, reassuring and unchanging vision of the rural world. To this can be added an almost ethnographic interest in agricultural practices and regional identity, represented here by the "portraits" of Charolais-Nivernais cattle.

Originally meant for the fine arts museum in Lyon, the painting proved so popular that it was kept in Paris at the Musée du Luxembourg (then a museum of works by living artists), where it remained on display until 1920. I. P.

Camille Corot
A Morning or The Dance of the Nymphs

Oil on canvas
3 ft. 2½ in. × 4 ft. 3½ in. (0.97 × 1.30 m)
Acquired in 1851

Corot here uses the codes of the historical landscape taught by his masters, Achille-Etna Michallon and Jean-Victor Bertin, by populating his forest interiors with nymphs. However, he distances himself from the classical tradition by not depicting a clearly identified subject, but a mythological reverie, born out of crossing the memory of an evening at the Opéra with a study executed in Rome some twenty years previously. The composition recalls a theater stage and wings, while the vaporous atmosphere evokes the vague contours of a recollection. The painting was well received by the critics. Théophile Gautier praised this "small whitish, misty canvas, shivering in the chilly dawn breeze," in which the artist "recalls nature, the way one recalls a well-loved tune." Some later criticisms highlighted the singularity of the artist's late manner. Baudelaire admired Corot's "unfailing rigor of harmony," while regretting that he was "not really devilish often enough." Likewise, the writer Émile Zola recognized the grace of his "diaphanous creatures," but preferred the "powerful reality" of his studies: "If M. Corot were willing once and for all to kill off the nymphs that populate his woods, and replace them with peasant women, I would be excessively fond of him." I. P.

Barthélemy Thalamas
Metaphorical Portrait

Daguerreotype
4¼ × 3¼ in. (10.9 × 8.2 cm)
Acquired in 2003

This daguerreotype occupies a somewhat marginal position in the tradition of the postmortem portrait. The dead person is not photographed, but is represented by a painted portrait and a death mask, two methods used for keeping a faithful representation of a loved one before the advent of photography. The picture raises a number of questions. Was the photographer unable to get to the house while the body of the deceased was still resting there? Were the portrait and the mask made while the man was alive, or after his death? Did he die long before this photograph was taken, and was this image inspired by the availability of the new medium of photography? However, the presence of the inanimate images alongside the woman, who is shown presenting them with such gravity and tenderness, leaves no room for doubt: they are there to bear witness to the strength of her bond to this man, a bond whose nature is, however, difficult to establish: in the portrait he seems to be wearing a priest's clothes.

Although it is untypical, this daguerreotype played the same role as most postmortem images. The point is to support visual memory just when this is beginning to fade, to confirm the reality of the loved one's existence, and to make their absence easier to bear. J. B.

Gustave Courbet

A Burial at Ornans
or A Painting of Human Figures,
the History of a Burial at Ornans

Oil on canvas
10 ft. 4 in. × 21 ft. 11 in. (3.15 × 6.68 m)
Gift of Mlle Juliette Courbet, 1881

A manifesto for Courbet's realist aesthetic, this painting caused a sensation at the Salon of 1850-51 because it raised a trivial, contemporary genre scene without narrative to a level and a format previously reserved for religious, mythological, or history painting. In the distance are the cliffs surrounding the painter's native town, grounding the work in a land whose stony roughness is conveyed here by the very texture of the paint, applied by knife. The inhabitants, who actually took turns to pose in the artist's studio, are faithfully represented, actual size. These "crude" figures shocked the Parisian public. This frieze-like cortège, at once classical and egalitarian, attains the same dignity as the heroes of classical painting, which it thus defies. The painter here places himself in the prestigious lineage of the Le Nain brothers, the seventeenth-century painters being rediscovered at the time by the critic Champfleury. Confronting waning Romanticism, Courbet's bold statement launched a new artistic movement, with its lack of action and refusal to turn its protagonists into heroes. For the painter, this assemblage of humble figures stood as a historic event, linking political and artistic upheavals. X. R.

William Bouguereau
Dante and Virgil in Hell

Oil on canvas
9 ft. 2½ in. × 7 ft. 4¾ in. (2.80 × 2.25 m)
Acceptance in lieu, 2010

If an artist failed within the academic system at the start of his career, there was always the option of creating a good impression by pulling off some bold stroke in public view at the Salon. Following two failed attempts to win the Prix de Rome, the young Bouguereau remembered how Eugène Delacroix had burst onto the scene at the age of twenty-four, thanks to his *Barque of Dante* at the Salon of 1822. For the 1850 Salon, he chose another episode from the *Inferno*: Canto XXX by the Italian poet Dante. In this, exploring the eighth circle of Hell, Dante and Virgil watch the eternal combat between the heretic and alchemist Capocchio, caught in the fangs of Gianni Schicchi, who had adopted the identity of a dead man to claim his inheritance. No source of dark European Romanticism is overlooked in Bouguereau's efforts to capture the public's imagination, with the outrageously muscular and shiny form of Schicchi in the manner of Michelangelo and Fuseli, the demon with bat's wings derived from illustrations in frenzied dark tales, the bunch of damned souls and the red glows in the background taken from English artists William Blake and John Martin. All this is under the melancholy gaze of the two poets, a motif borrowed from the Dutch painter Ary Scheffer. However, Bouguereau still had his sights on the Prix de Rome competition, and sought to reassure the harsh professors at the Institut; so he duly performs his academic exercises, creating the drape (Virgil) and the academic nude (Capocchio). This strategy paid off, with Bouguereau winning the coveted first prize that same year, tied with Baudry. C. F.

Jean-Baptiste Louis Gros
Detail of the Panathenaia Frieze, Parthenon, Athens

Daguerreotype
4¼ × 5¾ in. (11 × 14.5 cm)
Gift of M. Roger Thérond, 1985

A painter and draftsman, Baron Gros started creating daguerreotypes as early as 1840. In 1851 he was a founder member of the Heliographic Society, serving briefly as its first president. Being a diplomat, he traveled a lot. From January to June 1850, he was in Greece as a plenipotentiary minister, interceding on the issue of the Anglo-Greek dispute over the "Elgin Marbles," which had been removed from the Parthenon by Lord Elgin and transferred to London in 1816.

That May, for ten days the diplomat took some time off and, for his own enjoyment, set about photographing the ancient sites, producing some eighty daguerreotype plates. In an article published in the newspaper *La Lumière* in February 1851, the art critic Francis Wey highlighted the great value of these photographs for archeological research.

This view of a detail of a Parthenon frieze is outstandingly sharp and shows great technical skill, a recurring feature of Baron Gros's work (he built up a huge reputation for himself on account of the exceptional quality of his daguerreotypes, earning the nickname "the Napoleon of the plates"). This peerless photographer also left a set of views of his travels abroad (in London and Bogotá) and of Paris as well (*Gare de l'Est*, c. 1850, Musée d'Orsay). J. L.

Félix Joseph Barrias
The Exiles of Tiberius

Oil on canvas,
8 ft. 3½ in. × 13 ft. 7¾ in. (2.53 × 4.16 m)
Acquired in 1851

Inspired by the *Lives of the Twelve Caesars* by the historian Suetonius, *The Exiles of Tiberius* shows a frieze of people banished by Tiberius, the tyrant who ruled Rome from 14 to 37 BCE. Evoking the faces on ancient coins, the strict profile of the republican senator in his toga, bidding farewell to the land he is abandoning, conveys a sense of austerity and moral rectitude. In front of him, the dejected, hooded woman in black is like a personification of grief. Like David in his *Sabine Women*, the painter demonstrates his talent by offering a variety of facial expressions. In spite of the classical restraint, the vigor of the oarsmen instills a kind of romantic élan into the composition, setting up an echo of Géricault's *Raft of the Medusa*. The boat thus partakes in the symbolism of the passage from life to death, one of the great themes running through nineteenth-century art, from Eugène Delacroix to Odilon Redon. As is often the case, a learned subject is used to speak of contemporary events: in this instance, the confiscation of the ideals of the Second Republic, proclaimed in 1848, by the political reaction that led to Napoleon III's coup d'état in 1851. Barrias taught Degas; this work, painted at the Académie de France in Rome, winner of an award at the official Salon of 1850–51, is his masterpiece. X. R.

Eugène Guillaume
The Gracchi

Bronze
33½ × 35½ × 24 in. (85.2 × 90.2 × 60.7 cm)
Acquired in 1853

The son of a magistrate and a student of Pradier, Guillaume won the Prix de Rome for sculpture in 1845. It was during his Roman sojourn that he made the works that would bring him both fame and regular commissions, *The Reaper*, *Anacreon*, and *The Gracchi*, all of which are held at the Musée d'Orsay. Deeply influenced by antique sculpture, content with a somewhat austere neoclassicism, Guillaume is a perfect example of the kind of official sculptor who thrived under French regimes after 1848. In *The Gracchi*, Guillaume used his solid grounding in Roman sculpture and literature to cater to the taste of a learned elite with a concern (at least superficially) for moral edification. Tiberius and Caius Gracchus belonged to one of Rome's most eminent patrician families. Made a tribune of the plebeians in 133 BCE, Tiberius embarked on a series of ambitious reforms that went against the interests of his own caste. He was killed during an uprising encouraged by a number of senators and patricians, just as his brother Caius was when he decided to press ahead with reform of the Roman Republic. The example of the Gracchi's virtue deeply marked Roman history and helped shape French revolutionary and republican ideas. Guillaume worked freely from models of republican funer-ary sculpture he had studied in Rome to produce a group that offers gravity and elegance in a powerful and perfectly mastered composition, which deservedly won him considerable immediate success. É. P.

Pierre Puvis de Chavannes
Young Black Man with Sword

Oil on canvas
3 ft. 5¼ in. × 2 ft. 4¾ in. (1.05 × 0.73 m)
Acquired in 2009

In 1850, Pierre Puvis de Chavannes was twenty-six years old and keen to feature among the reformers of art. He found himself at a crossroads, with a choice between taking the recent and difficult path of Gustave Courbet's realism, or following the trail blazed for twenty years by Delacroix and Chassériau. Receiving unanimous acclaim from critics like Théophile Gautier and Charles Baudelaire, while also attracting an open-minded bourgeois clientele, the orientalist brand of Romanticism allowed young Puvis to express his talent as a colorist without straying too far from the lessons of Classicism. Indeed, at the root of *Young Black Man with Sword* was the academic exercise of the studio nude study.

Puvis filled it out with colorful historicizing, romantic props, also slipping into the background a twilight landscape with some smoking ruins. However, choosing a young African was a really bold stroke: the richness of color and shadow on the skin is done with great virtuosity, and the pose recalls the lasciviousness associated with the East as well as the armed impudence of Caravaggio's *Amor Vincit Omnia* (1601–02). It is especially daring when one considers that slavery had only been abolished two years previously in France, in 1848, and the French West Indies were still prone to violent disturbances, with some colonists refusing to allow the emancipation of their black slaves. C. F.

Eugène Delacroix
The Lion Hunt

Oil on canvas
2 ft. 10 in. × 3 ft. 9¼ in. (0.86 × 1.15 m)
Acquired in 1984

As Maurice Denis said, "Remember that a painting, before being a battle horse, a nude woman or any anecdote, is essentially a plane surface covered with colors assembled in a certain order." His words could have been written expressly about the painting Delacroix was inspired to produce by the lion hunt pictures of Peter Paul Rubens, the prince of Flemish baroque art. The work shown here is a preparatory sketch, bearing witness to Delacroix's creative process. It is conceived as a force field, a clash of eddying primary colors, vectors of different kinds of energy. The yellow expresses the animal fire of the rearing horse and raging lions, while red signals the courage and strength of the men, but also their sanguine energy as hunters. Finally, the occasional patches of blue sky bring moments of rest—a cold, calm counterpoint in the bloody, wild maelstrom. So radically expressive is Delacroix's use of color here that his hunters seem to augur the abstract modernity of Kandinsky's horsemen. However, we should not forget that in 1854 the sketch was still an arena for private experimentation, something to show friends and connoisseurs, but not to be exhibited to the public. C. F.

James Pradier
Sappho

Marble
3 ft. 10½ in. × 2 ft. 2¼ in. × 3 ft. 11¼ in.
(1.18 × 0.67 × 1.20 m)
Acquired in 1852

Being well known and highly regarded from 1820, Pradier received commissions from every regime: the Restoration and the July Monarchy enabled him to produce some major works, notably for the Chamber of Deputies in 1830, for the Place de la Concorde in 1836, and the pediment of the Palais du Luxembourg in 1840. The female figure is the central theme in his work. However, his style is not reducible simply to the introduction of pleasant sensuousness into the ancient repertoire, as the painfully restrained and silently palpitating drama of Sappho makes abundantly clear. Of course, the figure combines the nobility of marble and the dignity of the subject matter, but the clarity of the construction, the wildness of the gesture, and the meditative intensity of expression suddenly give it a presence and interiority: the ancient poetess Sappho, in despair, is contemplating suicide.

Everything here shows how Pradier was always an ambiguous artist with a whole range of talents: recognized by the Académie at an early age, he nevertheless explored the paths of Romanticism, as in this subject taken from literature. He was close to Victor Hugo, who spoke out to support him on several occasions.

Sappho was on display at the Salon in 1852 when the sculptor died suddenly; the statue was covered with a black veil and the artist was posthumously awarded the exhibition's medal of honor. É. P.

Théodore Chassériau
The Tepidarium: the room where the women of Pompeii came to rest and dry themselves after bathing

Oil on canvas
5 ft. 7¼ in. × 8 ft. 5½ in. (1.71 × 2.58 m)
Acquired in 1853

The subtitle reveals the painter's archeological ambition: after bathing, the Roman women dry themselves around a large bronze brazier, collecting their clothes from the compartments. Despite the erudition of the furniture accumulated in the foreground (copied from the archeology museum in Naples) and the faithfully reconstructed scenery of the baths of Venus Genitrix at Pompeii, the atmosphere owes less to Chassériau's visit to the Bay of Naples in 1840 than to his trip to Algeria in 1846. Indeed, the shimmering fabrics and sparkling jewels, the sticky, languishing bodies in an enclosed space, assisted by Moorish servants, and the woman with the nude torso in the foreground going through the motions of a belly-dance, are more evocative of the sultry atmosphere of the harem than the civic hygiene of the Roman thermal baths. Orientalism is the subterfuge used by Chassériau to reproduce the lost colors and heat of ancient Rome, frozen by the neoclassical aesthetics of Jacques-Louis David. He got this idea from the older artist Delacroix who, during a visit to Morocco in 1832, had discovered antiquity far from the discolored ruins of the Roman forum, still very much alive in the fierce beauty of the tribal chiefs and the women carrying amphorae. But Chassériau was also influenced by his teacher, Ingres, who had warmed up the ancient nude through the sensuality of his odalisques; in return, Ingres was probably prompted by *The Tepidarium* to paint the unbelievable swarm of foreshortened female forms in his *Turkish Bath* (1862, Musée du Louvre). C. F.

Charles Cordier
Chinese Man; Chinese Woman

Half-length bust in bronze, gilt bronze, and enamel;
pagoda and openwork corner piece,
36 × 21½ × 17 in. (91.5 × 55 × 43 cm); 38 × 21½ × 18 in.
(96.5 × 55 × 46 cm), acquired in 2023

Early works by Charles Cordier, these two busts constitute the artist's earliest foray into sculpture in color. One of the pioneers of polychrome statuary during the Second Empire, Cordier had always been drawn to modern subjects, which reflect a desire to devote his work to the "ubiquity of beauty" and the representation of all humanity. Unlike many of his contemporaries, Cordier did not proclaim the supposed superiority of Europeans. On the contrary, he defended the idea that each civilization possesses its own unique beauty, which he sought to express through his art. For the 1853 Salon, Cordier presented two elaborate portraits of Chinese figures, with accessories in keeping with the expectations of the period: the woman, with a pagoda behind her, sports long nails, while her expression of surprise is made still more disturbing by the use of blue stone for her pupils. The man holds a pipe, in an allusion to opium, and, like his female counterpart, has eyes of blue stone. The embroidered costumes worn by both are rendered with a remarkable attention to detail.

Cordier embraced diversity and saw his subjects as forming part of a complete image of humanity. The success of these Chinese figures is confirmed by the number of versions of single busts made in different sizes and materials: monochrome bronze, gilt bronze, and hard-paste porcelain. É. P.

Charles Nègre
The Stryge

Salted paper print from a dry waxed paper negative
13¼ × 9¼ in. (33.5 × 23.6 cm)
Acquired in 2002

A representation of Nègre's friend, the photographer Henri Le Secq, in a setting worthy of their shared taste for medieval architecture; a visual evocation of the "bird's-eye view of Paris" described by Victor Hugo in *Notre-Dame de Paris* (1831); a touch of humor in the juxtaposition of a monstrous figure—the famous gargoyle sculpted after a drawing by the architect Eugène Viollet-le-Duc (who owned a signed print of this image)—and an elegant fellow in frock coat and top hat; a photographic depiction of the "heroism of modern life," like a retort from this former student of Paul Delaroche, the great specialist in history painting, to Charles Baudelaire's 1845 injunction to painters to "make us see … how great and poetic we are in our cravats and our patent-leather boots": so many reasons that helped turn this masterpiece—whose modern title is taken from a contemporary etching by Charles Meryon (a protégé of Le Secq)—into an icon of nineteenth-century photography. T. G.

Joseph Paxton
Perspective View of the Château de Ferrières

Pencil, ink, and watercolor on
paper with white highlights
16¼ × 29 in. (41 × 73.5 cm)
Acquired in 2010

The Duke of Devonshire's "gardener," Joseph Paxton, rose to international fame thanks to the success of the Crystal Palace, the huge iron and glass structure he conceived for the Great Exhibition of 1851, which was built in a matter of months. Two years later, this demonstration of British industrial supremacy prompted the rich banker James de Rothschild to approach Paxton to rebuild his château at Ferrières, and thus to express his great economic success in stone. Paxton had just designed Mentmore Towers for the banker's English cousin, Mayer de Rothschild, which James wanted to emulate.

This perspective view of the main (northwest) façade is from Paxton's first design, based with some precision on the English Renaissance architecture of Wollaton Hall, his inspiration for Mentmore. But James de Rothschild strongly disliked this style, and was no doubt the one who urged the architect to go closer to the prestigious models of French classical architecture. Eugène Lami was also an important influence on Ferrières, which was the illustrious English architect's only construction on French soil. A. T.-B.

Max Berthelin
Palais de l'Industrie: cross section

Pen, ink, and watercolor
12¼ × 26½ in. (31.1 × 67.3 cm)
Acquired in 1979

The idea of a peaceful, international comparison of trade, industry, and the fine arts was realized by the Great Exhibition of London in 1851. The Crystal Palace, built by Joseph Paxton, became a symbolic monument, an expression of modernity by virtue of its transparency, grand dimensions, innovative construction, and speedy assembly—it was built in six months, thanks to the standardized elements used for the structure and decoration. This building, designed for the Paris Exposition Universelle of 1855, was made to last. The Palais de l'Industrie, standing at the end of the Champs-Élysées, was built by the architect Jean-Marie-Victor Viel and the engineer Alexis Barrault, and rather awkwardly combined a triple metal hall with a façade in stone, complete with triumphal entrances. The interior comprised a central great hall, 157 feet (48 m)

wide and 328 feet (100 m) long, with no braces to break up the space (there were twenty-two of them in the Crystal Palace), surrounded by a gallery nearly 100 feet (30 m) wide, making it, at the time, the biggest public building in metal. Unfortunately, the entrance was from the side, so visitors were unable to enjoy the height and light of the great central vault. The Palais was home to the Salon until its destruction in 1898, when it was replaced by the Grand and Petit Palais, built for the 1900 Exposition Universelle. Max Berthelin had been responsible for "extraordinary works" at the municipality of Paris since 1852. Like Victor Baltard, he was interested in iron architecture, as can be seen from this study of the internal structure of the Palais de l'Industrie, even though the building was far from being finished. C. M.

Félix Tournachon, known as Nadar
Charles Baudelaire

Salted albumen print from a wet
collodion glass negative
8½ × 6½ in. (21.2 × 16.4 cm)
Acquired in 1991

Baudelaire's contempt for photography is too legendary not to have been exaggerated or misunderstood. After all, in 1865, when the author of the polemical pamphlet on "The Modern Public and Photography" (1859) wrote to his mother that "Paris is more or less the only place where people can do what I desire, that is to say, an exact portrait, but with the fuzziness of a drawing," he was surely thinking of the many photographs taken of him by his friend Nadar.

The most serene and intimate image of Baudelaire caught by any photographer, this print—the only one known—eloquently demonstrates Nadar's qualities as a portraitist who sought to convey his sitter's psychology. It is by his "feel-ing of light" that caresses here "eyes that one can never forget" and by his "moral understanding" of the subject that this former caricaturist and art critic could, as a photographer, overcome the reticence of the most difficult among his sitters from the intellectual and artistic elite. In one of his rare written allusions to a friendship that would also inspire Nadar's last book (*Charles Baudelaire intime: le poète vierge* [An Intimate Portrait of Charles Baudelaire: The Virgin Poet], 1911), Baudelaire wrote: "Nadar is the most astonishing expression of vitality. … I was jealous of him because he was so successful with everything that is not abstract." T. G.

Charles Hugo
Victor Hugo on the Rock of the Exiles

Salted paper print after
a collodion glass negative
4 × 2½ in. (10.3 × 6.3 cm)
Gift of Mme Marie-Thérèse and
M. André Jammes, 1984

Victor Hugo had been in exile on Jersey since August of 1852, at an address in Marine Terrace. Up until 1855, when he left for the neighboring island of Guernsey, he launched into photography with the help of his sons Charles and François-Victor, and his friend Auguste Vacquerie. Through this fruitful collaboration, some four hundred images came out of the Jersey photography studio. In a diary entry dated January 21, 1853, Adèle Hugo wrote: "This summer we are going to tour the island; the gentlemen will be taking all the finest views; my father will write some verse, and it will all go into a charming book that we shall be selling one day next year." The book did not come out, but this output forms a major group; in it Victor Hugo is both the actor and stage director of his own legend, and his entourage and other outlaws like himself all join in. Hugo was fascinated with the technical possibilities of photography, and also planned to use it to illustrate his own writings, but he personally was no photographer. Hugo also disseminated his self-portraits far and wide. In this photograph showing *Victor Hugo on the Rock of the Exiles*, the poet uses a mineral setting and allows himself to be pictured in this posture alone, his gaze directed elsewhere, toward the infinite; thus, faced with exile, he takes his place in history. J. L.

Jean Auguste Dominique Ingres
The Spring

Oil on canvas
5 ft. 4¼ in. × 2 ft. 7½ in. (1.63 × 0.80 m)
Bequeathed by Comtesse Duchâtel, 1878

Throughout the nineteenth century, this painting of *The Spring* by Ingres was held to represent perfection, to be a classical nude worthy of the masterpieces of ancient Greek sculpture. The insertion of the figure in a narrow stone niche, like the nymphs sculpted in bas-relief by Jean Goujon in 1548, and which the young Ingres copied in 1800, is testament to the artist's ambition to instill life into the goddesses of antiquity, as Raphael had done in his paintings 350 years earlier. For Théophile Gautier, at least, he succeeded: "M. Ingres knows as well as the Greeks do the melodies of form, the eurhythmy of poses and the metrics of this admirable human body—the most beautiful garment that the ideal can wear." The painting's interest certainly does not lie in the setting: this was done by two students, who worked to complete a study left unfinished by Ingres many years before, during a stay in Florence in 1820. As for the subject, "The Spring," its meaning is obscure. Placed on a smooth mirror, the nymph releases braids of metallic water, which seem strangely solid and silent, without splashes or drips. Time stands still. What we see is the innocent sensuality of a creature with flesh that is uniform, modeled around a figure fantasized by a painter who was unconstrained by anatomical realism. C. F.

Jean-Valentin Morel, Louis-Constant Sévin
Hope Cup

Bloodstone jasper, silver-gilt base, embossed gold mount, opaque and transparent enamel, 25¾ × 19¾ × 8¾ in. (65.5 × 50 × 22 cm)
Acquired in 2024

More than two feet high, Jean-Valentin Morel's *Hope* cup is a masterpiece unparalleled in nineteenth-century lapidary art. Seated astride Pegasus, Perseus wields his spear at the dragon, which hurls its last ounce of strength into the battle, while Andromeda, chained to her rock, awaits deliverance. By pronouncing her more beautiful even than the Nereids—depicted on the foot of the cup—Andromeda's mother, Queen Cassiopeia, had stirred the wrath of Poseidon, who dispatched a sea monster that could be halted only by sacrificing the princess. The reverse side of the scene shows Perseus brandishing the head of Medusa, whom he has just beheaded—an apotropaic mask that reappears in the form of a cameo bristling with enamel snakes on the front of the piece.

This extraordinary tour de force took Morel some three years to complete. Surrounding himself with the most talented artists of the time, he revived a forgotten technique for polishing jasper. Acclaimed by critics at the 1855 Paris Exposition, it joined the collection of Henry Thomas Hope, a member of a particularly wealthy family of London bankers who also owned the famous Hope Diamond, now in Washington DC (Smithsonian Institution). The motto, *at spes non fracta* ("but hope remains intact"), borne by two cherubs seated on the edge of the cup, is a clear allusion to the imagery of the piece and the name of its patron. A. A.

Georges Alphonse Bonifacio Monbro
Bottom of wardrobe

Ebony, gilt bronze, champlevé enamel and painted
enamel on copper, and colored stones
4 ft. 4 in. × 2 ft. 9¾ in. × 1 ft. 5¾ in.
(1.32 × 0.86 × 0.45 m)
Acquired in 1980

Monbro was a cabinetmaker, antique dealer, and repairer of old furniture when in 1855 he exhibited this invaluable item as "bottom of wardrobe." In making this submission, he was offering a bold composition that aimed to define a new style based on his knowledge of the past. He was one of the main cabinetmakers to perpetuate a taste for furniture in the style of André Charles Boulle. This piece belongs in that vein because of the richness of its bronzes and the choice of ebony, and also hints at the survival or even revival of the Louis XVI style, through the presence of an oval enamel medallion painted in imitation Wedgwood. This item was one of a pair, and remains a high-class piece of workmanship, rare for the richness of the bronzes gilded and enameled by Achille Legost, a well-known enameler who was reputedly one of the top specialists in liturgical gold and silverwork. A supplier to the Mobilier de la Couronne under Louis-Philippe and Napoleon III, to Madame de Girardin, Eugène Sue, and others, Georges Monbro opened a branch in London. He specialized in the production of precious furniture influenced by eighteenth-century French styles, thus playing his part in reinterpreting these styles in some innovative combinations in terms of forms. Y. B.

Félix Duban
Architectural Fantasy in the Pompeian Style

Pencil and watercolor
15 × 19 in. (38 × 48 cm)
Acquired in 2006

Duban's *Fantasies* featured in a posthumous exhibition of his work at the École des Beaux-Arts, Paris, in 1872. These thirty or so "compositions" inspired both emotion and admiration. They were a revelation, for Duban had stopped exposing his work to critics after the frosty reception he received at the Salons of 1831 and 1833.

Although these works do contain recognizable archeological features (the wall painting here, for example, which probably represents Pomona, is a copy of a decorative panel found at Herculaneum), that is not the main interest of these pictures, which are devoid of human presence. The painted walls and surfaces, amphorae and cantharuses, stone beds covered with rich fabrics, statues, gardens decorated with fountains, wooded hills fading into the distance dominated by the silhouette of Vesuvius—everything here works toward a poetic, sensual vision of life in Pompeii; everything comes together felicitously in a space where air and light circulate freely, delicate and vibrant; everything serves to "open the doors of dream." This marvelous drawing, this gentle, sensual, and colorful piece of visual repose is the most famous of Duban's *Fantasies*. C. M.

Charles François Bossu,
known as Marville
Sky Study

Albumen print from a wet
collodion glass negative
6 × 8¼ in. (15 × 20.8 cm)
Acquired in 2011

Marville is best known as the official chroni-cler of the urban planification of Paris under Baron Haussmann. He was also one of the great "primitives" of photography, whose talent was revealed by the studies after nature published by Blanquart-Evrard in the early 1850s. Wor-king in the same vein, this print is one of a series of cloud studies that he photographed from his Parisian home, some of which he exhibited in Paris and London in 1857. Much was made of the interest of such an ensemble for artists who immediately saw its value as a document and not only as a work of art. For one thing, clouds could rarely be admired in photographs at the time, unless they were retouched (sensi-tized plates responded in different ways to the various colors of the spectrum, with the result that a correctly exposed negative of a landscape often meant an overexposed sky, and photo-graphers therefore used to sacrifice the latter, either painting it black on the negative to pro-duce a uniformly white sky, or simply putting in false clouds). For another, it was among the first successes in the field of photography applied to the study of atmospheric variations, just between the painted studies of Valenciennes and Constable and the pastels series of Boudin, the "king of skies" who introduced Monet to outdoor painting. T. G.

Gustave Le Gray
The Brig or The Brig in Moonlight

Albumen print from a wet
collodion glass negative
12¾ × 16¼ in. (32.2 × 41.5 cm)
Acquired in 1985

Charles Marville's studies and Le Gray's famous *Brig* (originally shown in London in 1856) featured together in exhibitions that captivated the world of photography on both sides of the Channel in 1857. The two men demonstrated different ways of approaching the difficulty of capturing the sky using the new collodion process, which Le Gray, a matchless technician and active teacher, had invented. Indeed, it was enough for Le Gray to proudly subtitle his print "Marine with clouds obtained simultaneously" to cause a sensation, and even prompt incredulity. Quite apart from the technical feat of being obtained with a single negative, this seascape—made on the Normandy coast in 1856—constitutes a powerful and large photographic tableau. As a student of the painter Delaroche, Le Gray was steeped in pictorial tradition which he transposes here with a sensibility that evokes Courbet in terms of the width of the framing, the radical frontality, and emphasis on the horizon. This community of vision is confirmed by the spectacular series of *Waves* he photographed on the Mediterranean coast the following year. Because of the fugacity of the subject, the quest for the "Sublime of Art" in these works inevitably meant combining two complementary negatives—one for the sea, one for the sky—in the final print. T. G.

Gustave Courbet

The Artist's Studio
or The Artist's Studio: a real allegory summing up seven years of my artistic and moral life

Oil on canvas
11 ft. 10 in. × 19 ft. 7½ in. (3.61 × 5.98 m)
Acquired in 1920

The star feature of the Pavillon du Réalisme opened by Courbet on the fringe of the Exposition Universelle of 1855, this huge, mysterious canvas sums up the painter's realist ambition in an imaginary, symbolic composition. In this introspective work, Courbet asserts all the ambiguity of the notion of realism, to which he had no intention of confining himself. In an ironical remake of the *Last Judgment,* he placed to his right the friends who supported him, like the patron Alfred Bruyas, the philosopher Pierre-Joseph Proudhon, the critic Champfleury, the muse Apollonie Sabatier, and the poet Baudelaire, while on his left are certain social types of his day, embodying the values of a political world and an aesthetic that he considered outmoded. Among these poor people, a poacher might have the features of Napoleon III after confiscating the Republic. The artist, next to a model symbolizing Truth, occupies the place of Christ in religious painting, thereby turning this studio with evanescent walls into an endless mystery. The self-taught and self-sufficient Courbet was constantly challenging the academic system in every genre, whether it be in the portrait, the landscape, or the nude, whose plump figure is poles apart from the fine neoclassical ideal. The painting's execution contrasts with the unlikelihood of the situation, emphatically underlining that, however realistic Courbet's paintings are, they continue to have a symbolic scope and are testimony to the highest ambition with respect to history. X. R.

Ernest Christophe
The Human Comedy
or The Mask

Marble
8 ft. ½ in. × 2 ft. 9½ in. × 2 ft. 4¼ in.
(2.45 × 0.85 × 0.72 m)
Acquired in 1876

This *Human Comedy* owes its fame to "The Mask," a poem in Baudelaire's *Les Fleurs du Mal* (*The Flowers of Evil*) of 1857. The poet had seen the plaster model of the sculpture and appreciated the symbolism of the dolorous face that, from a certain angle, could be seen behind the smiling mask: "But one is just a mask, some kind of trick, The graceful, radiant smile was a disguise/So this must be the woman's real face, here/Under the shadow of the one that lies." Although no great admirer of the statuary of his times, Baudelaire seems to have been fascinated by Christophe's sculpture, which he praised in his *Salon of 1859*, although the work was not actually exhibited there. The powerful body and the allegories of anguish and duplicity in the unmasked face play into Baudelaire's themes of eternal, immobile Beauty. É. P.

Alfred Stevens
What Is Called Vagrancy

Oil on canvas
4 ft. 3½ in. × 5 ft. 11¾ in. (1.31 × 1.65 m)
Bequeathed by Léon Lhermitte, 1926

This almost tear-jerking evocation of urban poverty was a real coup for Stevens, who had received a traditional academic training at the Académie Royale des Beaux-Arts in Brussels (Jacques-Louis David was one of the school's directors). Presented at the Paris Exposition Universelle in 1855, *What Is Called Vagrancy* belongs in the realist vein, whose heritage was important to the Naturalism of the late nineteenth century. The pauperization of the working class was one of its great themes. Indeed it was Léon Lhermitte, painter of the modest *Paying the Harvesters* (p. 165), who bequeathed the painting to the Musée du Jeu de Paume, the ancestor of the Musée d'Orsay. The scene is set in the area around the edges of Paris where poverty was rife, and the arrest of the poor woman and her two children is meticulously dramatized by the inclusion of a worker and a bourgeois woman who seem to be distressed by the family's fate. The contrast between those who benefited from the Industrial Revolution and those sacrificed to it, underscored by the gloomy wall and the snowy weather, becomes a moral point, one not missed by the emperor, Napoleon III. Stevens was also stylistically bold, reducing the depth and simplifying the outlines in a modern approach close to that of the young Manet, who may well have remembered the frieze-like composition for his soldiers when painting his *Execution of Maximilian*. X. R.

Jean-François Millet
Gleaners

Oil on canvas
2 ft. 8¾ in. × 3 ft. 7¼ in. (0.84 × 1.10 m)
Gift of Mme Pommery, 1890

Born into a peasant family, Millet began exhibiting canvases inspired by life in the fields in 1848. The gleaners theme featured in a series of works about the summer months, especially August, that occupied him in the 1850s. This painting, exhibited at the Salon in 1857, shows three women scouring the earth with quick, precise actions (gleaning was allowed in the time before sundown) to pick up the ears of corn left by the harvesters. Their bent backs and absent expressions betray the arduous, repetitive nature of the task. Their poverty contrasts with the abundance in the background suggested by the crowd of harvesters around the huge haystacks. Among the many commentaries on this picture, it was seen as a political manifesto in favor of the rural proletariat. A journalist at *Le Figaro* detected the specter of social revolt and evocations of the revolutionary Year of Terror "in the leaden horizon" filled by "the pickets of popular riots and scaffolds of '93." In contrast to such political readings (which probably exceeded the painter's intentions), Castagnary praised the poetry of the painting which "reproduces … one of those true, grand pages of nature of the kind found in Homer and Virgil." The work was acquired in 1889 by the widow Mme Pommery, who donated it to the Louvre to compensate for the loss of *The Angelus* (p. 69), sold to the United States a few months earlier. I. P.

Oscar Gustav Rejlander
The First Negative

Albumen print from a collodion
glass negative
8¾ × 6 in. (22.4 × 15 cm)
Acquired in 2011

Born in Sweden and based in England, the painter and photographer Gustav Rejlander enjoyed his first success (and a whiff of scandal) in 1857 with *The Two Ways of Life*, a majestic allegorical study with a composition inspired by the tradition of *grande peinture*. Also that year he produced this scene evoking the origins of art itself, via Pliny the Elder's account of the invention of both drawing and sculpture: in order to preserve the image of her lover before he traveled to a foreign land, the daughter of the Corinthian potter Butades drew an outline around the cast shadow of her beloved's face.

Painters began depicting this episode evoking the birth of their art back in the eighteenth century. Steeped in the traditions of painting, Rejlander's ambition was to win recognition for photography as a full-fledged artistic discipline. Taking the British tragedian John Coleman as his model, in *The First Negative* he posits a similar origin for photography, thereby raising it to the level of the noble arts, in keeping with the goals of the High Art Society, of which he was one of the most prominent members. By making the art of fixing shadows fundamental to the photographic act, he was surely not unaware that "skiagraphy"—writing in shadow—was the name given by William Henry Fox Talbot to the photogenic process whereby he obtained his first negative back in 1835. M. R.

Félix Tournachon, known as Nadar, and Adrien Tournachon
Pierrot the Photographer

Salted paper print
11¼ × 8¼ in. (28.6 × 21 cm)
Gift of Mme Marie-Thérèse
and M. André Jammes, 1991

This portrait of the mime artist Jean-Charles Deburau, star of the Théâtre des Funambules, was part of a series titled *Têtes d'expression de Pierrot*. Félix Nadar asked the performer to pose in 1854: "I had him make his debut in 1848, after the death of his father [Jean Gaspard Baptiste, creator of the Pierrot character], in the leading role in a pantomime of the self" (as Pierrot Minister). Nadar conceived a series of photographs organized around a wide variety of Deburau's expressive tropes (Pierrot as thief, Pierrot laughing, suffering, miming dread, and so on).

The Pierrot series was a public and critical success at the Exposition Universelle in 1855, but the only person to benefit from it was Adrien, Félix's brother, who at the time called himself "Nadar *Jeune*." In a surprising game of mirrors, this *Pierrot the Photographer* becomes a portraitist exhorting the viewer, who has been invited into his studio, to pose for the camera. Debate continues even today as to the respective roles of the two brothers. Their relationship—it was Félix who paid for Adrien's training as a photographer in the studio of Gustave Le Gray, for example—turned nasty and ultimately there was a trial over ownership of the pseudonym "Nadar." This was won on appeal by the older brother, Félix, in 1857. J. L.

Paul Baudry
Fortune and the Young Child

Oil on canvas
6 ft. 4¼ in. × 4 ft. 10¼ in. (1.94 × 1.48 m)
Gift of Napoleon III, 1857

During their four years in residence at the Villa Medici, winners of the Prix de Rome were required to send back to Paris three works—a copy from a past master, a nude, and a historical composition—to be judged. For the subject of his last submission, Baudry chose one of the fables of La Fontaine (Book V, 11): by waking him up, the goddess Fortune saves the life of a carefree schoolboy who has dozed off on the lip of a well, telling him, "Had you fallen, I am the one who would have been blamed ... in other words, Fortune is always in the wrong." But Baudry's work does not take this meditation much further; these nudes in a landscape are first and foremost testimony to the enthusiasm he felt during his stay in La Serenissima in 1852, and on discovering the Renaissance masters Titian, Giorgione, and also Correggio and Leonardo, as is obvious from Fortune's smiling face. The work was badly received in Paris, where the members of the Académie felt that Baudry had stooped to presenting pastiche with no invention, unscrupulously plagiarizing the Venetian masters. But on discovering the work at the 1857 Salon, the public was not so harsh, repeating Théophile Gautier's phrase: "Not just anyone can steal." Throughout his career, Baudry kept up this dialogue with the Venetian masters started here, a dialogue that reached its high point when the artist was commissioned by Charles Garnier to paint the ceiling of the main foyer at the Paris Opéra. C. F.

Henry Peach Robinson
She never told her Love

Albumen gold-toned print from
a collodion glass negative
7¼ × 9½ in. (18.6 × 24.3 cm)
Acquired in 2008

Miss Cindall, who became one of Robinson's favorite models for his photographic tableaux, here lends her graceful traits to the figure of a young woman on her death bed, apparently consumed by her untold love, as explained by the line below the print, taken from Shakespeare's *Twelfth Night, or What You Will*: "She never told her Love." This work is one of the preliminary studies for the masterly composition *Fading Away*, which Robinson made using the "combination printing" technique he had learnt with Rejlander. Five different negatives are thus put together to form a scene in which this virginal beauty passes away surrounded by her loved ones. What kills her is not unrequited love but tuberculosis, a contagious disease which was also incurable at the time. The two photographs were presented jointly at the photography exhibition at the Crystal Place in 1858, winning Robinson acclaim and glory for the technical mastery and artistic ambition that went into them. Linked in this way, the works created a narrative (one providing the key to the other), showing the Victorian public that the affliction evoked in the final print was both moral and physical. Death restores lost innocence. M. R.

Charles Cordier
Sudanese man in Algerian costume

Bronze and onyx bust on small
Vosges porphyry pedestal
3 ft. 1¾ in. × 2 ft. 2 in. × 1 ft. 2½ in.
(96 × 66 × 36 cm)
Acquired by the household of Emperor
Napoleon III in 1857

In 1848 Charles Cordier sculpted a bust of the African model Saïd Abdallah, a former slave whose beauty and bearing made a powerful impression on him. This work made his name and encouraged him to devote his career as a sculptor to representing the variety of human physiognomies—to become an "ethnographer-sculptor." In 1856 he traveled to Algeria, where he modeled numerous busts. This one was exhibited at the Salon of 1857 under the title *The Negro from Sudan*. It is one of Cordier's first polychrome pieces and uses what was known as the "natural polychrome" technique, involving the combination of colored marble and patinated bronze. The face is in silvered bronze which was artificially oxidized to evoke the model's skin color. The garment and turban are carved from blocks of Algerian onyx-marble. Offering motifs that are often spectacular, this variety of alabaster was used in the ancient world, and the quarries had just been rediscovered. He put it to excellent use to convey the shimmering of the oriental fabrics. This interplay of colors was completely new for the time and secured Cordier's fame as a pioneer of polychrome sculpture under the Second Empire. É. P.

Jean-François Millet
The Angelus

Oil on canvas
21¾ × 26 in. (55.5 × 66 cm)
Bequeathed by Alfred Chauchard, 1910

Millet was stirred to do this painting by a childhood memory. "In the olden days, working in the fields, whenever my grandmother heard the bell ringing, she would make us all stop what we were doing to say the Angelus 'for those poor departed,' very devoutly, with hat in hand."

The painting indeed depicts two peasants who have stopped digging up potatoes to respond to the call to prayer from the church belfry visible in the background. Both have their heads bowed reverently and are praying fervently. Despite the painting's small format, the characters take on a monumental dimension, standing out against a vast expanse of countryside all the way to the horizon where the fields meet the skyline. They embody the reassuring type of the good peasant living a pious, hardworking life to an unchanging rhythm, to the point that Gambetta in 1873 described the painting as a "lesson in social and political morals."

The Angelus was a huge success and became the subject of some wild speculation. Although a subscription was launched in France, the painting was snapped up by an American buyer at a public auction in July 1889. A year later, Alfred Chauchard, the director of the Magasins du Louvre, contrived to buy it back for the then unheard-of sum of 800,000 francs, so that he could bequeath it to the Louvre. I. P.

Jules Breton
Calling in the Gleaners

Oil on canvas
2 ft. 11½ in. × 5 ft. 9¼ in. (0.90 × 1.76 m)
Gift of Emperor Napoleon III, 1862

In this scene Jules Breton gives a tribute to work in the fields worthy of the paintings of Millet. He does however offer a radically different interpretation of social relations in the rural world. The liveliness and vigor shown by the women in the foreground have nothing to do with the frailty and the pain expressed by the aching bodies of the *Gleaners* (p. 63). While the gleaners have to make do with the meager leftovers from the harvest, Breton's proletarians are lifting huge bundles of corn, which would explain their apparent prosperity. In spite of one or two elements such as their bare feet and worn garments, these women are obviously not the needy folk of the artist's birthplace, Courrières,

the less than delightful reality of which he has evidently embellished. The gentle light at day's end adds a poetical atmosphere to this largely mythicized moment of sharing among peasants. The political message of this staged scene earned the work success at the Salon of 1859, at the end of which Empress Eugénie bought the canvas, with the emperor later gifting it to the Musée du Luxembourg in 1862. Indeed, abundant harvests embodied the prosperity of the country upon which the regime was built, while concealing the social inequalities that earned Millet criticism from the conservative classes of society. X. R.

Paul Guigou
Washerwoman

Oil on canvas
32 × 23¼ in. (81 × 59 cm)
Gift of Paul Rosenberg, 1912

An admirer of Courbet, Paul Guigou had contacts with the future Impressionists in the 1860s, but spent most of his career painting his native Provence. Among his luminous landscapes and figure studies is this *Washerwoman*. She is kneeling on a box by the water, placing the linen to be washed in front of her. Near the arch of the bridge, other washerwomen are hanging out their washing. Guigou offers a realistic depiction of the women's accessories, such as the *tian*, an item typical of the region, and of their working conditions, which he had observed. In fact, he started painting outdoors at an early age, with his master Émile Loubon in Marseille, striving to capture the effects of the dazzling, contrasting light of the South. Here, this outlines the forms with great clarity, heightening the almost abstract character of this washerwoman, who is seen from behind with a big straw hat covering her shoulders. This ambitious painting stands out in Guigou's oeuvre for its size and the monumentality of the figure. In fact, it was never exhibited during his lifetime. This painting was discovered in the early twentieth century by Paul Rosenberg, the great dealer in works by Picasso, Braque, and Matisse, who gave it to the museum and worked for the posthumous recognition of this painter who for many years was unjustly neglected. S. Py.

Owen Jones
Project for a Crystal Palace in the Parc de Saint-Cloud: interior view

Pencil, watercolor, and colored pencil
1 ft. 6 in. × 3 ft. 11¼ in. (0.46 × 1.20 m)
Acquired in 1990 thanks to the Société
des Amis du Musée d'Orsay

An architect, decorator, and draftsman, Owen Jones came to attention in 1842 when, in collaboration with the Frenchman Jules Goury, he published a study of the Alhambra in Granada (*Plans, Elevations, Sections, and Details of the Alhambra*). But his most famous work, and the most significant for the development of decoration and interior architecture, was the splendid *Grammar of Ornament*, which he began publishing in 1856, and which served as a source of artistic renewal and inspiration for nearly half a century. Jones directed the construction of the Crystal Palace, designed by Joseph Paxton for the Great Exhibition of 1851 in London, and conceived its polychrome interior decoration. In 1860, the French government asked him to make plans for a large, permanent exhibition hall for French industry, complete with winter garden and park. He conceived a long gallery in metal and glass, ending in exedrae, topped by a dome (its shadow can be seen in this drawing). The Victoria and Albert Museum in London holds two drawings of this building. It was meant to stand on the site of today's Musée de Sèvres, construction of which put an end to Jones's project. However, the idea resurfaced again in 1871, after a fire in the palace at Saint-Cloud, inspiring a host of new designs. C. M.

Manufacture impériale de Sèvres, Jules Gély
Bertin vase, size 1 with light bouquets of lilies and poppies

Hard-paste porcelain and gilt bronze
3 ft. 2½ in. × 1 ft. 6½ in., 5 ft. 5 in. with the bouquets (98 × 47 cm [1.65 m])
Mobilier National collection, on permanent loan to the Musée d'Orsay since 2009

Created in 1850 and popular throughout the decades that followed, the Bertin form was one of the first new models to result from the new *coulage* production technique, developed at the Manufacture de Sèvres under the Second Republic. These vases also feature an innovative type of decoration in relief, commonly known as *pâte-sur-pâte* ("paste on paste"), first practiced at the factory in 1849. It consisted in applying dilute porcelain paste of variable consistency using a brush or knife. The technique was rediscovered by the sculptor Fischbag at the instigation of Denis Riocreux, first curator of the ceramics museum in Sèvres, who wanted to revive this style of decoration found on Chinese porcelain. The sculptor Jules Gély joined the manufactory in 1851, and began specializing in this kind of decoration. In 1861 he designed the decoration of four vases, each one evoking a season. These were exhibited at the London International Exhibition in 1862. The display also featured a changing or "chameleon" ground, invented in 1858, which showed pink under artificial light and gray in natural light. Two of the vases were sent to the Palais des Tuileries in 1866 as "gifts" and featured in the Paris Exposition Universelle in 1867. Enriched with "bouquets of light" not foreseen in the original design, these vases are now displayed as they were when they adorned the rooms of the French foreign ministry. Y. B.

Jean-Baptiste Carpeaux
Ugolino

Bronze
6 ft. 4¼ in. × 4 ft. 10¼ in. × 3 ft. 10¾ in.
(1.94 × 1.48 × 1.19 m)
Acquired in 1862

Born in Valenciennes into a modest family, Carpeaux won the Prix de Rome for sculpture in 1854. He made this group between 1857 and 1861, overstaying his welcome at the Villa Medici while also flouting the academic norms, which required no more than two figures plus a subject taken from antiquity or biblical history. Ignoring the reprimands, he preferred to "express the most violent passions." Deeply moved by the sculpture of Michelangelo, which he discovered during his stay in Italy, Carpeaux took inspiration from a canto in Dante's *Divine Comedy*, where the writer, guided through the Inferno by the Latin poet Virgil, meets Count Ugolino della Gherardesca, who describes his punishment to them. In the thirteenth century Ugolino had betrayed the Ghibellines and was locked up in a tower in Pisa with his sons and grandsons. Left to starve by his rival, he ate his progeny before he too succumbed to hunger. The nervous modeling of the body is testament to Carpeaux's careful study of the antique *Laocoon*, of Michelangelo, and of Géricault's *Raft of the Medusa*, as he set out to capture powerfully the father's grief and anguish and the stages of advancing death shown in the faces of the children. The resulting ensemble is one of the great masterpieces of Second Empire sculpture. É. P.

Eugène Emmanuel Amaury Pineu-Duval, known as Amaury-Duval
Madame de Loynes

Oil on canvas
3 ft. 3¼ × 2 ft. 8¾ in
(1.00 × 0.83 m)
Bequeathed by Jules
Lemaître, 1914

When Amaury-Duval painted her portrait, the Comtesse de Loynes was still just Jeanne de Tourbey. The daughter of working-class parents from Reims, she took advantage of her beauty and wit to conquer Paris and, through her lover Prince Napoleon, to open one of the most brilliant Second Empire literary salons. This was keenly attended by writers and critics such as Charles Sainte-Beuve, Hippolyte Taine, Alexandre Dumas, and also Gustave Flaubert, who admired her "panther-like graces and devilish wit." To do justice to such charms, Amaury-Duval called upon all the expertise he'd gleaned from portraits by his master Ingres; set in a jewel case of buttercup silk cushions, the brilliant black taffeta gown—extended by the deep purple drape and the jet-black hair—lend the downy face the opaline brightness of moonlight. The hypnotic gaze from the shaded gray eyes, framed by earrings in the neo-Greek style, celebrates the gift of this "admirable listener." But, comparable to the gaze of the Comtesse de Castiglione in her photographic self-portraits, this stage effect also introduces the intoxicating allure of the female sphinx, the enigmatic femme fatale, which enjoyed great success with the Symbolists at the end of the century. The critic Émile Cantrel observed that, "There is a world and a half-world in those eyes." C. F.

Léon Belly
Pilgrims Going to Mecca

Oil on canvas
5 ft. 3 in. × 7 ft. 11¼ in. (1.60 × 2.42 m)
Acquired in 1861

Compared to the romantic, dream-like accents of much orientalist painting, Belly's depiction of this caravan on its way to Mecca is highly realistic. The composition, which foreshadows the visual effects of cinema, really does give the impression that this compact group is moving toward the beholder. Like Uccello in his battle paintings of the Quattrocento, Belly uses perspective to create a sense of huge masses, endowing this crucial moment in the life of any Muslim—the pilgrimage to the Holy City of Islam—with real epic grandeur. At the same time, his rendering of details such as the intense reflections of the dazzling sun on the sand and the distorted shadows of the camels and riders is almost scientific in its precision. With this ambitiously large-scale rendering of an exotic subject, Belly was partaking in the movement to modernize history painting by means of meticulous depiction and a sense of anecdote, qualities also found in Gérôme. Painted after a journey to Egypt and shown at the Salon of 1861, this bold work's reward was to be bought by the State. No doubt official institutions appreciated its visual effects and the ecumenical detail of a man leading a donkey ridden by a woman with her baby, in a discreet reminder of the flight into Egypt by the Christian Holy Family. X. R.

Edgar Degas
Semiramis Building Babylon

Oil on canvas
4 ft. 11½ in. × 8 ft. 5½ in. (1.51 × 2.58 m)
Acquired in 1918

In his early years, Degas received a classical education that followed the canons inherited from ancient times and from the Renaissance. However, the artist preferred studying masterpieces closely in order to broaden his references beyond the academicism of the École des Beaux-Arts. While conforming to the precepts of history painting, with *Semiramis Building Babylon,* he demonstrates a synthesis of various different styles, ranging from the Greek Parthenon friezes to the frescoes of Luca Signorelli, which was his ambition even for his very earliest works. Already present in his portraits, his keen interest in the primitives is at the root of the interpretation he offers of the legend of the Mesopotamian queen. Wanting to find a contemporary visual rendering of the grandeur of bygone centuries, he perhaps also indulges in comparing the legendary queen with Emperor Napoleon III, who had embarked on a pharaonic construction program to turn Paris into a modern Babylon. The serenity of the scene can be felt, like Greek coins with faces in profile, while the soft, harmonious tones imitate the fresco for this string of characters along a frieze. The overall unity is at odds with the luxuriant Mesopotamia as fantasized by orientalist painters. Rather than the barely convincing work of a painter not up to the grand genre of history painting, *Semiramis* is a well thought-out and unclassifiable attempt by an already highly independent and original artist before he went on to focus on depicting modern life. X. R.

Edgar Degas
The Bellelli Family
or **Family Portrait**

Oil on canvas
6 ft. 6¾ in. × 8 ft. 2½ in. (2.00 × 2.50 m)
Acquired in 1918 with the help of the
Comte and Comtesse de Fels
and thanks to René de Gas

The composition of *The Bellelli Family* attests to a keen sense of portraiture, simultaneously respectful of the genre's codes and capable of a very contemporary sense of psychological depth. An indirect heir to Hippolyte Flandrin, via the teaching of academic painter Louis Lamothe, Degas's firm drawing underscores the roundness of the face of the young Giovanna and the primitive-style almond-shaped eyes of the mother. But the emphasis on the dramatic tension—which irrevocably distances the couple formed by his aunt and uncle, Laure and Gennaro Bellelli—shows the portrait to be infused with genre painting and history painting, which was undergoing a profound revival at the time. Degas effectively elevates his aunt's unhappiness, her dissatisfaction with married life, to the level of high tragedy, muted by the rigid bourgeois environment. The stifling atmosphere is conveyed, in part, by the heady motif of the wallpaper in the background. Degas makes the most of the synecdochic relation between the room and the scene taking place there, notably distorting space so as to give the impression that the husband is stuck to the fireplace, which itself is separate from the rest. The atmosphere of this painting, one of Degas's three biggest, anticipates the interiors painted by the Nabis in the 1890s. It was conceived from the outset as a masterpiece, reviving the group portrait in a monumental form, combining the reference to Rembrandt with the revelation of deep family wounds. X. R.

Edgar Degas
Thérèse de Gas

Oil on canvas
35 × 26¼ in. (89.5 × 66.7 cm)
Acquired in 1927

While, in his first portraits, Degas took those close to him as his models, he did have his preferences, as can be seen from the recurrence of certain figures. He seems to have had a particular fondness for the perfectly proportioned face of his eldest sister Thérèse. He first plotted its contours in a drawing, then painted this large-scale portrait, made shortly before she married her cousin, Edmondo Morbilli—indeed, Degas painted the young couple a little later in the same decade. In that portrait (c. 1865, Museum of Fine Arts, Boston), Thérèse has the same questioning, penetrating gaze as her brother in the self-portrait of *Degas and Évariste de Valernes* (Musée d'Orsay). His last portrait of her, from 1869, leaning against a mantelpiece

(*Portrait of Madame Edmondo Morbilli*, private collection) is clearly an homage to Ingres and his *Comtesse d'Haussonville* (Frick Collection, New York) and recalls Degas's youthful reverence for the work of his renowned predecessor. This first portrait of Thérèse, from the early 1860s, shows a less academic facet of his artistic loves: it is inspired by the Italian primitives he saw when traveling in Italy in the 1850s. In this smoothly painted portrait, Thérèse is set harmoniously into the cone firmly drawn by her ample black dress, but her stiffness and her "eyelashes [cut] like scissors" (as Degas put it) are closer to the frescoes of Italian Renaissance painters Fra Angelico and Signorelli. X. R.

Eugène Fromentin
Falconry in Algeria: The Spoils

Oil on canvas
5 ft. 4 in. × 3 ft. 10½ in. (1.63 × 1.18 m)
Acquired in 1863

Eugène Delacroix experienced a real revelation when he traveled to Morocco in 1831. He interpreted what he saw there as a vibrant ancient civilization that had kept all the rough edges of its origins. Much of his artistic career was devoted to keeping that dazzling memory alive. For Fromentin, the journey to Algeria was, in the same way, a journey back in time. In this painting of falcon hunting, however, what comes vividly to life is more the Middle Ages than antiquity. Proudly riding their thoroughbreds, two lords look on calmly after the hunt as the still-warm body of a hare is offered to the raptors. Leaving little room for picturesque or cruel details, placed between the hazy blue sky and the granular earth, this scene—painted seventeen years after the painter's first Algerian sojourn—is less a chronicle than the recollection of a European traveler filtered through dreams: the dreams of a romantic artist, nostalgic for a past when the aristocracy represented a genuine grandeur of soul, like that of the falcon wheeling high above Creation. "What a divine pleasure it must be … to ride over plains and through valleys, carrying this winged vassal on one's glove. One is master of the earth and sky," wrote the critic Paul de Saint-Victor when he saw this painting at the Salon of 1863. C. F.

Édouard Manet
The Luncheon on the Grass

Oil on canvas
6 ft. 10 in. × 8 ft. 8¼ in. (2.08 × 2.64 m)
Gift of Étienne Moreau-Nélaton, 1906

With *The Luncheon on the Grass*, Manet became famous. Initially called *The Bath*, the painting caused a mixture of scandal and hilarity at the 1863 Salon des Refusés. Victorine Meurent poses nude in the company of one of the artist's brothers and his brother-in-law, who seem to be chatting without taking any notice of another bather in the background. The juxtaposition of a realist female nude with these men in modern dress was just as shocking as the sharp execution, flouting academic conventions based on idealization and the fable; the finish, the perspective, and the modeling were equally unsettling. It was even more provocative because of Manet's obvious references to Titian and to the famous *Concert champêtre* in the Louvre, then attributed to Giorgione. By diverting tradition in favor of this risqué subject matter, which Manet himself described as a *partie carrée* (a partner-swapping foursome), and which he treats in a seemingly casual manner, deliberately flouting the rules, the painter indeed opts to measure himself against the greatest masters. Thus *The Luncheon on the Grass*, a composition full of artifices worked out in the studio, does not so much foreshadow impressionist plein-air painting as declare the sovereign freedom of the artist to pursue a radically novel personal painting style and world view. S. Py.

Alexandre Cabanel
The Birth of Venus

Oil on canvas
4 ft. 6¼ in. × 7 ft. 4½ in. (1.30 × 2.25 m)
Purchased by Napoleon III in 1863,
allocated to the Musées Nationaux in 1879

While this is one of the best-loved paintings among the general public, it has definitely been one of the most despised by art critics for a century. According to them, when it comes to a female nude, you have a straightforward choice: either you paint a goddess, in the style of Ingres, and the quest for universal beauty produces an assemblage of lines bordering on abstraction; or, like Manet, you look reality in the eye, and paint the first nude you come across in town, namely the prostitute from downstairs, candid and mercenary (*Olympia*). Cabanel's *Venus* is disturbing and irritating because it plays on both levels. His Venus is neither marmoreal nor untouchable; she has been turned into a pretty little pest of flesh and hair, lascivious and perverse, making that little sidelong glance of hers. That wave, as comfortable as a settee, and the candy cherubs, taken from rococo art, are merely derisory accessories to a mythological masquerade designed to delight the bourgeois audience while stroking their veneer of culture. That the picture was bought by Napoleon III was enough to turn this *Birth of Venus* into the emblem of the eclectic, fast-living, perverted high society of the Second Empire. However, liberated by the unjaundiced view of the surrealists, the contemporary eye can enjoy in this ancestor of the pin-up a mixture of vulgarity and unreality that never fails to raise the eternal question of what is good taste. C. F.

Édouard Manet
Olympia

Oil on canvas
4 ft. 3¼ in. × 6 ft. 2¾ in. (1.30 × 1.90 m)
Gifted to the State by public subscription
on the initiative of Claude Monet in 1890

In 1890, on behalf of the subscribers he had brought together, Claude Monet made a gift of *Olympia* to the French state, declaring: "Manet is seen here at the height of his glorious struggle, the master of his vision and of his craft." Yet the painting had triggered a tremendous furor at the Salon of 1865. While Manet here reverts to the traditional motif of the odalisque with the black slave, he rejects any flashy exotic elements and shows a prostitute receiving a splendid bunch of flowers, probably as a gift from a customer. The jewels, the black choker round her neck, the shawl and slippers all situate this woman in a state of undress—this is not a timeless nude—with her self-assured, brazen look, very much in the "here and now." Manet had his favorite model, Victorine Meurent, sit for this uncompromising nude, which is devoid of voluptuousness, poles apart from the academic canons, the idealization and nacreous flesh tints of Cabanel's *Venus*. Manet adds the provocative, allusive detail of the cat, a touch of irony with its question mark of a tail, but also an evil animal; it is substituted for the dog that appears in Titian's *Venus of Urbino*, of which *Olympia* is a modern formulation, just as it is a new *Maja desnuda*, in homage to Goya. Again, Manet shows how, when revitalized, tradition fuels what he calls "the spirit of contemporaneity." S. Py.

André Adolphe Eugène Disdéri
The Marchioness of Jalar: full length in eight poses

Albumen print after a collodion glass negative
7¾ × 9¼ in. (20 × 23.3 cm)
Acquired in 1995

The young Marchioness of Jalar went to Disdéri's studio on the Boulevard des Italiens. At this address, lavishly laid out to flatter his well-to-do clientele, the photographer had been receiving Second Empire high society since 1858. "M. Disdéri had a great project, that of founding an establishment to rival the huge establishments in London," E. Lacan commented in *La Lumière* in 1854. The idea was to show off one's social status and distribute one's picture (a full-length portrait) through the visiting card portrait (a print on albumen paper mounted on cardboard); this invention was a tremendous success, enabling a series of shots to be taken using the same negative. This "portrairuromania" [sic] lasted right into the mid-1860s before it was dethroned by the superior format, the album-card. It was also symptomatic of this urban society; its members strolled along the boulevards and appearances were extremely important. There can be no doubt that the photographer has encouraged the young woman, full of gentle self-assurance, going as far as a faint smile, to adopt several flattering poses to show her bearing, the fabrics, and the movement of her gown to best effect. The acquisition of a part of the Disdéri studio collection by the Musée d'Orsay has made it possible to have the use of the entire plate, before each shot was cut up and mounted separately. J. L.

James Tissot
Portrait of Miss L. L.
or Young Lady in a Red Jacket

Oil on canvas
4 ft. ¾ in. × 3 ft. 3¼ in. (1.24 × 0.99 m)
Acquired in 1907

As a fellow student of Degas, Tissot made a name for himself at the Salon of 1861, where he presented a series of scenes from the legend of Faust and Marguerite, in a picturesque style from the Renaissance period influenced by the Belgian painter Henri Leys. His reputation was sealed with a State purchase for the Musée du Luxembourg of *The Meeting of Faust and Marguerite* (now in the Musée d'Orsay). However, from the Salon of 1864 on, Tissot sought to present himself for commercial purposes as a portrait painter, exhibiting the *Portrait of Miss L. L.*—although the young woman in the Spanish-style red bolero was very likely a model. Though similar to the portraits of Ingres, and more particularly *Madame de Senonnes*, of which Tissot made a copy at the end of his life, the composition shows the influence of recent fashion engravings, while displaying almost photographic accuracy. This meticulous style, which gives the painter his characteristic modernity, was doubtless inspired by his father's business as a fashion dealer in Nantes. *Miss L. L.* was the artist's first masterpiece in terms of the variation of effects of material, thoroughly celebrating the sartorial vogue then at its peak thanks to the large stores. After this, the art of brilliantly rendering the most complex outfits made Tissot a hugely successful artist. X. R.

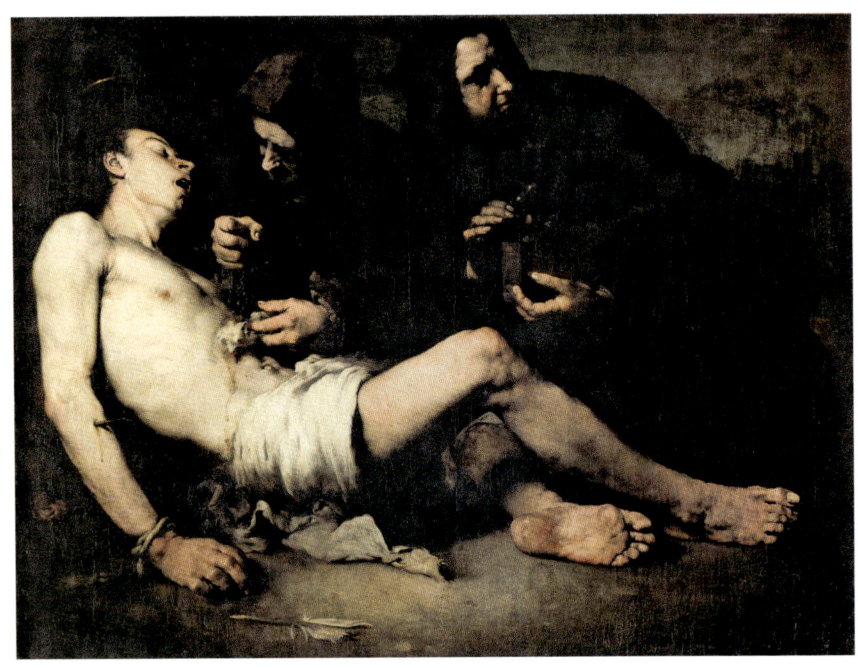

Théodule Ribot
The Martyrdom of St. Sebastian

Oil on canvas
3 ft. 2¼ in. × 4 ft. 3¼ in. (0.97 × 1.30 m)
Acquired in 1865

Ribot belonged to the generation of realist artists that won its spurs in the Salons of the 1860s and worked to renew the historical *grand genre* after its classical foundations had been shaken by the large-format paintings of Courbet in the preceding decade. Ribot was one of the few artists among his peers to take the risk of trying his hand at religious painting—another notable exception being Manet, who in the same year presented his *Jesus Mocked by the Soldiers* (Art Institute of Chicago). Most of his fellow artists preferred the romantic way of representing popular piety, as did Legros. Ribot was a student of the academic painter Auguste-Barthélemy Glaize and, like Manet, seems to have felt the need to burrow into the deep black found in the painting of the Spanish masters of the seventeenth century. Bought by the State at the Salon of 1865, his *St. Sebastian* is an exercise in admiration of the powerful chiaroscuros of José (Jusepe) de Ribera, but in an innovative, closer frame which endows the martyr's suffering with greater intensity. The choice of moment is original: rather than bristling with arrows, the saint is shown after his torture, being tended to by St. Irene. The modeling of the arch of the foot is a remarkable exemplar of realist detail, with the saint's prosaically dirty flesh possessed of a very contemporary truthfulness. X. R.

Ernest Meissonier
Campaign of France, 1814

Oil on wood
20¼ × 30¼ in. (51.5 × 76.5 cm)
Bequeathed by Alfred Chauchard, 1909

Although renowned for his genre scenes in the Dutch style of the seventeenth century, and for his scenes of gallantry evoking the French eighteenth century, Meissonier was above all famous for his highly precise representations of battles. Presented at the Salon of 1864, *Campaign of France, 1814* is part of an unfinished series chronicling the military exploits of Napoleon I, whose legend the Second Empire of Napoleon III lovingly burnished. However, like Delaroche before him, Meissonier was not afraid to show his hero struggling, so as to evoke the majesty of his determination even when doomed to failure. The lugubrious atmosphere of this snowy plain, whose infinite monotony is emphasized by the composition, echoes the disastrous Russian campaign, which was the beginning of the end for Napoleon. Although the format is that of an easel painting, Meissonier's rendering is extremely meticulous, as if indicating the effort to chronicle the event with the utmost rigor. This concern with exactitude is also evident in the studies of equestrian movements that the artist modeled in wax. Meissonier's historical realism thus led him to the kind of experiments later pursued by Degas, who was interested in his work at the beginning of his career. X. R.

Eugène Boudin
The Beach at Trouville

Oil on wood
10 × 19 in. (25.7 × 48 cm)
Donated by Dr. Eduardo Mollard, 1961

Looking to launch his art career, Eugène Boudin left the town of Le Havre at the age of thirty-seven, moving to Paris in 1861. There he mixed in a circle comprising painters like Troyon, Courbet, and the young Monet, whom he introduced to landscape painting. These artists, as well as Baudelaire, who met him at Honfleur, admired the skill and sensitivity with which he painted his skies. Boudin divided his time between the Normandy and Brittany coasts, where he would work from life in the fine weather, and Paris, where he would go over his studies in the studio, turning them into paintings. In order to attract a broader clientele, he gradually moved away from seascape painting toward a genre of his own invention: beach scenes. It was his idea to depict smart Second Empire society during the beach-bathing season, which was then very fashionable at resorts like Trouville or Deauville. His little "dolls," as he called them, earned him a degree of success at the Salon and among art lovers. While he continued to attach great importance in his paintings to rendering light effects in the sky and the exact shape of clouds, he also showed an interest in "the things and people of [his] day," thus adding a realist vein to his painting. It was mostly the works of Boudin that seemed less finished, notably his studies and pastels, which really drew the admiration of the impressionist artists alongside whom he exhibited in 1874. I. P.

Victor Hugo
The Bridge

Pen, brown ink, brown wash, and watercolor
highlights
12½ in. × 19½ in. (31.5 × 49.3 cm)
Bequeathed by Mme Alice Lockroy, 1929

A great traveler, Victor Hugo started exploring France and Europe in 1825, accompanied by family, friends, and mistresses. Between 1834 and 1837 he was particularly drawn to northern France and Belgium. His habit on these journeys was to keep written notes and make sketches, which he often included in letters to friends. His journey along the Rhine in 1840 gave rise to a book, *Le Rhin*, two years later. The sketches he made at such times were topographic, but they formed a repertoire in which reality was always tinged with imaginary elements. This drawing, which Hugo offered to his grandson Charles in 1866, is a memory of his German journey, an impressive, masterly sheet in which the picturesque and the fantastic attain a frantic, almost hallucinogenic strangeness. The initials V. H. on the façade of the house in the background may evoke the poet's anxiety and suffering when traveling in ancient towns that he loved, towns that were crumbling or metamorphosing. I. J.

Fannière frères
Beer service

Chased, carved silver, partly gilt
Pot: 9 × 7 × 5 in. (23 × 17.5 × 12.5 cm)
Goblets: 5½ × 3¼ in. (13.7 × 8.4 cm)
Tray: ¾ × 12½ in. (1.8 × 32 cm)
Acquired in 1986

Of all the great goldsmiths in Second Empire Paris, only the Fannière brothers were "at once draftsmen, modelers, casters, and engravers, which means that the models emerge fully conceived from their brains, their hands, and their workshop."

In a singular contrast with the impeccably finished neo-Renaissance pieces with which they had made their reputation, the beer service that the Fannières exhibited at the Union Centrale in 1865 was notable for its rustic naturalism. In fact, they were continuing a fine tradition in French silverware with the idea—already applied in the eighteenth century, and particularly under Louis XVI—of imitating a wooden receptacle, while applying an almost trompe-l'oeil plant ornamentation that also harked back to the virtuosity of rococo engraving.

The "very modern effect" that Burty saw in this piece no doubt derives from the early influence of Japanese art, which is apparent above all in the lively, picturesque treatment of the animal details (mouse, snail, lizard, spider, insects). The choice of the hops motif illustrates a principle that would be adopted by Art Nouveau craftsmen: decoration should be appropriate to the function. Y. B.

Albert Ernest Carrier-Belleuse
Bust of Woman Wearing a Diadem

Terra-cotta
27¼ × 11¾ in. × 8 in. (69 × 30 × 20 cm)
Gift of the Société des Amis
du Musée d'Orsay, 2012

The prolific output of Carrier-Belleuse is represented in the collection of the Musée d'Orsay by two marble sculptures for the Salon (*Bacchante*, *Hebe Sleeping*), but it was his abundant production of decorative busts in terra-cotta, one of his specialties, that were the bedrock of his sustained success in the 1860s and 1870s. He produced luxury editions designed for the wealthy Second Empire bourgeoisie, with each piece so elaborately reworked that it became unique. These illustrate the pronounced taste of the day for the French Renaissance, a taste inspired both by the sculptures of the Fontainebleau School and the decorative arts. This monumentally extravagant bust lays the references on thick, while highlighting, as Carrier-Belleuse loved to do, the contrast between the smoothness of the skin and the decorative saturation of the hair, jewelry, and clothes. É. P.

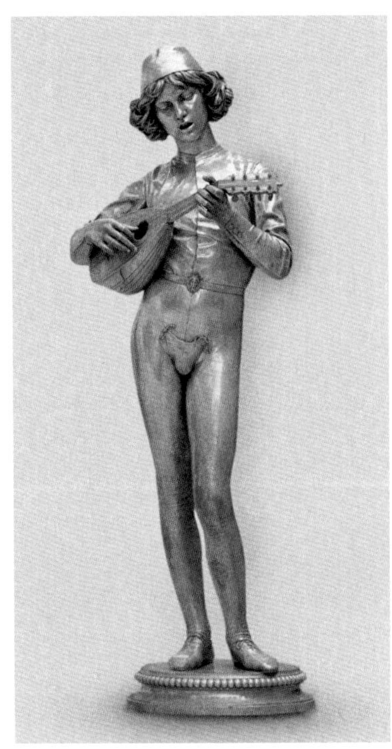

Paul Dubois
The Fifteenth-century Florentine Singer

Silver-plated bronze
5 ft. 1 in. × 1 ft. 10¾ in. × 1 ft. 7¾ in.
(1.55 × 0.58 × 0.50 m)
Acquired in 1866

Influenced by his time spent in Italy, Paul Dubois met with great success from the start with some refined works inspired by the Italian Renaissance. It was in this vein that he carved the *Fifteenth-century Florentine Singer*, and it won him the medal of honor at the Salon of 1865. The sculpture generated a huge buzz and, being one of the most popular of its day, it was brought out in various sizes by the great foundry Barbedienne for nearly a century.

The young boy's slender, elegant silhouette and long, smooth legs contrast with the extraordinarily precise detailing of his garments and accessories—shoe laces, folds of his hose at the knees, cuff links, the strings and pegs on the instrument, and the chiseling of the curly hair. A slightly archaic feeling is combined with the flawlessly delicate execution. The silvering on the bronze gives the work an extra precious quality, which is on the borderline between sculpture and silversmithing.

The first copy was purchased by Princess Mathilde, who hosted one of the most brilliant artistic and literary salons during the Second Empire period. É. P.

Gustave Doré
The Matterhorn Disaster: The Fall

Pen, brown ink, brown and black wash,
watercolor highlights
31¼ × 23½ in. (79.5 × 59.5 cm)
Gift of Louise Lefebvre de Viefville, 1952

Doré is known as the most prolific illustrator of the second half of the nineteenth century, notably for his engravings of major works: Rabelais's complete works (1851), Dante's *Divine Comedy* (1861), Cervantes's *Don Quixote* (1863), the Bible (1866). Doré was a compulsive draftsman. Through his countless drawings, he devised a colossal repertoire of images showing a great gift for storytelling, mixing in realistic details with a fantastic atmosphere. As a seasoned mountaineer, he was particularly affected by the accident that ended the first ever ascent of the Matterhorn on July 13 and 14, 1865. Based on numerous press reports, he gives a realistic yet terrifying account of the fall that occurred on the way back down. Most often watercolors depicting landscapes from life are no more than working instruments. Here the horror of it and the sublime, the loneliness and the drop into the infernal abyss are juxtaposed in this dark monochrome with its intense, sure brushstrokes. I. J.

Gustave Moreau
Orpheus

Oil on wood
5 ft. ½ in. × 3 ft. 3¼ in.
(1.54 × 0.99 m)
Acquired in 1866

Purchased by the French state at the Salon of 1866, this painting belongs in a series of large-format works that gave fresh impetus to Moreau's career and established him as one of the main innovators in the field of history painting. While taking inspiration from mythology and tradition, he invented a personal symbolism that was private and mysterious, far from the edifying, heroic narratives typical of the genre. In his adaptation of the myth of Orpheus, Moreau imagined the episode when the young Thracian woman gathered up the poet's head and lyre. Orpheus, who charmed nature with his music and verse, symbolizes the power of art, but also the solitude of the artist. In many respects, this work is a self-portrait. Proust saw this head of Orpheus inspired by Michelangelo's *Dying Slave* (Musée du Louvre) as embodying "Gustave Moreau's thoughts." The painter also pays homage to another artist and poet, Leonardo da Vinci, in the choice of support (which heightens the smooth, precise finish), in the handling of the landscape with its *sfumato* effects and rocky arch, and in the noble, enigmatic conception of the work. S. Py.

Émile Lévy
The Death of Orpheus

Oil on canvas
6 ft. 9 in. × 4 ft. 4¼ in. (2.06 × 1.33 m)
Acquired in 1866

There was more to ancient Greek culture than Apollo and the Muses. It also had its Dionysian side, as expressed in the uncontrolled life force of the bacchantes, those wild women dedicated to the mysteries of the god Bacchus. Because Orpheus, the first poet of myth, sang only of the memory of Eurydice, his beloved, who had been carried away to the underworld, the bacchantes were maddened with jealousy and killed him, then tore him limb from limb. Lévy, an academic painter, avoided bloodshed; by the same token, he could not resist endowing his figures with nacreous skin tone and luxurious accessories: a brilliant red mane, panther fur, delicate silks on which the youth's tender body rests. Far from canceling it out, however, this preciousness only heightens the violence that is evident in the ecstatic movements. More than a scene of massacre, *The Death of Orpheus* is a combat that pits the clash of cymbals, stridency of flutes, and hissing of snakes, against the song of the lyre, which is the object of the dying Orpheus's last gaze before, like Narcissus, he lets himself slip into the mirror of still water in the foreground. In this tragic work by Émile Lévy, the Dionysian and the Apollonian interpenetrate, foreshadowing the theory of Greek tragedy written by Nietzsche six years later. C. F.

Jean-Baptiste Carpeaux
The Dance

Échaillon stone
13 ft. 9¼ in. × 9 ft. 9¼ in. × 4 ft. 9 in. (4.20 × 2.98 × 1.45 m)
Acquired in 1889

In 1863 Charles Garnier, architect of the new Opéra de Paris, commissioned four sculptural groups from four winners of the Prix de Rome to decorate the building's façade. Carpeaux was given the theme of dance. He spent three years sketching and making models until he came up with this spinning farandole of women surrounding the spirit of dance. The sculptor's great concern here was to convey the sensation of movement, and he succeeded by setting up a twofold, vertical and circular dynamic. The leaping spirit dominates the whole, urging on the teetering circle of bacchantes.

The public was shocked by the realism of the female nudes, which were judged improper. Someone even threw a bottle of ink at the work, and there were calls for it to be removed, but the Franco-Prussian War in 1870, and then Carpeaux's death, put an end to the controversy. L. d M.

Lewis Carroll
Elisabeth "Kate" Terry
as "Andromeda"

Reversal of a collodion wet glass negative
9¾ × 7½ in. (25 × 19.5 cm)
Acquired in 1988

Charles Lutwidge Dodgson, better known by the name of Lewis Carroll, was a man of many passions, among them drama (he wrote, reviewed, and frequently attended the theater) and photography, which he practiced as an amateur for twenty-four years. Having got to know the Terry family through his friend the dramatist Tom Taylor in 1864, he spent three days at their London family home in the summer of 1865. In his diary he marked this stay "with a white stone." While there he made portraits of Benjamin and Sarah Terry and of their daughter Ellen, one of the most brilliant actresses of the Victorian period, as well as of her brothers and sisters. Carroll had first seen the eldest daughter Kate in 1857, acting in Shakespeare, and deem-ed her "exquisitely graceful and beauti-ful." With several dozen plays now behind her, here she plays the mythological figure of Andromeda, the Ethiopian princess who was chained to a rock in punishment for her mother's boastfulness, and only saved from the sea monster by Perseus. Contrary to the literary and pictorial tradition, in which Andromeda appears naked or only slightly veiled, here the young actress appears heavily draped, in keeping with Victorian propriety. However, the staging of this figure (loose hair, eyes lowered, the milky flesh of the forearms covered in bracelets, and the clever arrangement of the bound hands), in which Kate herself had a significant input, adds up to a tableau of incandescent eroticism. M. R.

Claude Monet
The Luncheon on the Grass

Oil on canvas
8 ft. 2 in. × 7 ft. 1¾ in.
(2.48 × 2.18 m)
Acceptance in lieu, 1987

During the 1860s, Monet became interested in placing the human figure in a natural setting. In response to Manet's *Luncheon on the Grass* (p. 81), shown at the Salon des Refusés of 1863, young Monet undertook a sketch for a *Luncheon on the Grass* of his own, painting the canvas in Fontainebleau forest (this is in the Pushkin Museum in Moscow): "I can think only of my painting, and if I had to leave it, I think I'd go crazy." Back in Paris after his preparatory studies, the artist painted the large canvas, which measured around 20 feet (6 m): "I worked … with small studies from life and I composed the whole thing in my studio." He was probably stung by criticisms made by Courbet, whose example may nonetheless have inspired him to produce this "large machine," but Monet abandoned the idea of presenting his youthful masterpiece at the Salon of 1866. The canvas was later damaged by damp, and cut up in the artist's own lifetime: two large fragments, including this central section, hang together in the Musée d'Orsay. The figures are in a sunny forest interior for this almost photographic view of a scene from everyday life. It is clear already that Monet is a master in the art of the landscape, the figure, and the still life. S. P.

Claude Monet
Women in the Garden

Oil on canvas
8 ft. 4½ in. × 6 ft. 8¾ in. (2.55 × 2.05 m)
Acquired in 1921

To convey the freshness of a moment caught in time, Monet began this composition in the open air, in his garden at Sèvres, during the summer of 1866; it continued to preoccupy him during the following winter at Honfleur: "Monet is still here working on some huge canvases, which show some remarkable qualities. … He has one canvas nearly ten feet [3 m] high … smartly dressed women picking flowers in a garden, a canvas he began from life in the open air." We recognize the artist's companion Camille, who sat for three of the figures, and the dresses shown in *The Luncheon on the Grass* again feature here. The figures are animated with a circular movement that gives life to the overall scene. The work was rejected by the judges for the official Salon in 1867, but it was admired for its "modern" subject matter by Émile Zola, who recalled it in 1868: "I have seen some original canvases by Claude Monet. … Last year, he had a painting turned down with figures of women in light-colored summer dresses, picking flowers along a garden path. … Quite the oddest effect. You have to be singularly in love with the times to dare to pull off such a feat, with fabrics sliced down the middle by shadow and sunlight, and neatly dressed ladies in a flower bed." S. P.

Paul Cézanne
Achille Emperaire

Oil on canvas
6 ft. 6¾ in. × 3 ft. 11¼ in. (2.00 × 1.20 m)
Gift of Mme René Lecomte and Mme Louis
de Chaisemartin, 1964

The thick, dark touches of *Achille Emperaire* locate this painting in the period of transition following Cézanne's "ballsy" period, to use the term he chose to designate the style of his early work. The painter liked to accentuate the articulation of the limbs in order to make the architecture of the body more compact, and in his friend, the artist Achille Emperaire, Cézanne found a morphology that was well suited to his very distinctive aesthetic. The head, its nobility worthy of the musketeers of the age of Louis XIII, with its longish hair and Van Dyck goatee, contrasts with the stunted body and the long, unhealthy-looking hands. This disproportion of the deformed man's body echoes the discrepancy between a compositional plan no doubt taken from Ingres's *Napoleon I on His Imperial Throne*, in which the seat back forms a divine aureole, and the subject of a misshapen figure sitting in an ordinary domestic chair. The inscription indeed points to a phonic play on "Emperaire" and *empereur* (emperor), anticipating Marcel Duchamp's dadaist puns of the 1920s. This work, which was rejected from the Salon of 1870, preserves the memory of Cézanne's intellectual and aesthetic closeness to his friend Emperaire, an artist whose talent has not been recognized by posterity, but to whom he remained faithful, as he did to his formative years. X. R.

Édouard Manet
The Fife Player

Oil on canvas
5 ft. 3½ in. × 3 ft. 2¼ in. (1.61 × 0.97 m)
Bequeathed by Comte Isaac de Camondo, 1911

It was the rejection of *The Fife Player* for the Salon of 1866 that first prompted Émile Zola to come to the defense of Manet. As he saw it, the work summed up his friend's talent with its mixture of "precision and simplicity." Manet, he wrote, "powerfully stops his figures … he renders the different objects in their vigor, distinct from each other. His whole being impels him to see in terms of marks, in simple, energetic parts."
The Fife Player effectively belongs to the series of large-format figures that Manet set against a neutral ground, in the manner of Velázquez, whose work he had admired when traveling in Spain: "It is the air that surrounds the man, all dressed in black and alive," wrote the painter at the time. Manet used the uniform of the Imperial Guard to play on the crisp contrast of strong red and yellow with black and white. For some, this simplified, direct treatment of the theme of the uniformed child, generally represented in a more sentimental manner, makes this painting more akin to a "costumier's sign." It was true that, like Courbet before him, and like Cézanne, Manet drew on popular imagery. This masterpiece was nevertheless one of the treasures of the Comte de Camondo's impressionist collection, bequeathed in 1911. S. Py.

Jules Lefebvre
Truth

Oil on canvas
8 ft. 8 in. × 3 ft. 8 in. (2.64 × 1.12 m)
Acquired in 1871

The caricaturist Cham suggested that, "If the truth is sometimes best left unsaid, it is also sometimes best left unpainted," but we can get beyond this wry observation to enjoy Lefebvre's work properly. It is an allegorical nude, which according to the academic tradition is the noblest subject matter for painting, since the visible forms convey an abstract idea, a philosophical concept. But a painting like this also pinpoints the contradictions of the dying Academism. Indeed, despite her attributes (the enlightening mirror, the rope and bucket suggesting the proverb "the truth is at the bottom of a well"), this *Truth* is a highly artificial and anatomically inaccurate construction. Disdaining any direct copying of nature, Lefebvre reverts to the nude manner of Ingres's *The Spring* (p. 54), taking the *contrapposto* and smooth radiance even further to produce a mannerist work. The result is a strange combination: the left side of the body is seen frontally, lengthened to excess and firm, whereas the right half is seen in profile and is all curves and voluptuous roundness—though the philosopher Plato did remind us that truth and reality are two very different things. The triumphant unreality of Lefebvre's nude might therefore give us a more accurate idea of Platonic "truth" than the fleeting shadows that the Impressionists were trying to capture. C. F.

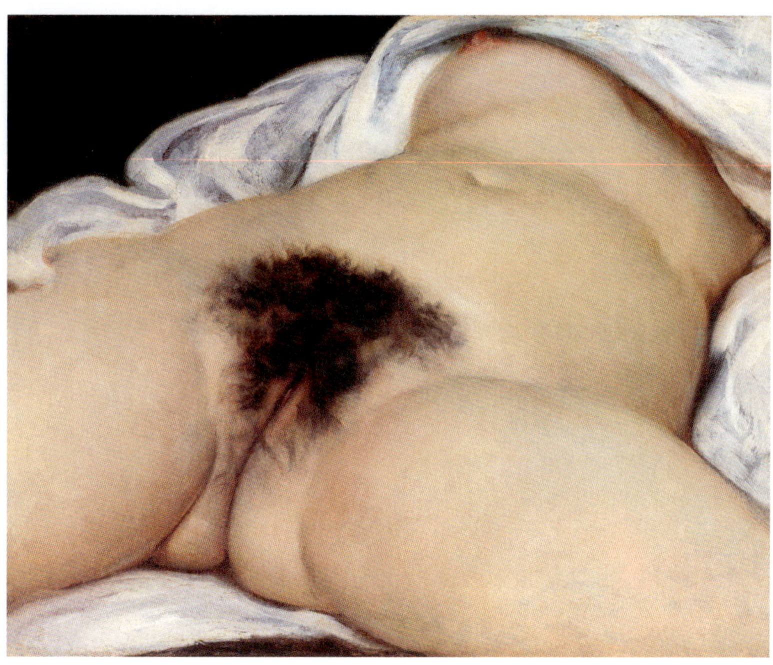

Gustave Courbet
The Origin of the World

Oil on canvas
18 × 21½ in. (46 × 55 cm)
Acceptance in lieu, 1995

The incredible history of this masterpiece—which was virtually unknown to the public up until only a short time before it entered the Musée d'Orsay in 1995 (it was accepted in lieu of payment of death tax by the psychoanalyst Jacques Lacan)—has fuelled the legend that accompanies it. Pushing the boundaries of what it was permissible to depict in paint to their limits, Courbet delivered the painting to its first owner, the Ottoman diplomat Khalil-Bey. But only a few close friends, invited to admire it in his bathroom, were allowed to enjoy the work. As early as 1853, and the exhibition of the *Women Bathing* at the Salon, Courbet had undertaken to look afresh at the nude, the aca-demic genre par excellence, with no qualms about shocking by offering a blunt, warts-and-all view of a posterior with generous, Rube-nesque proportions. Apart from the decidedly rebellious title, the daring of *The Origin of the World* lies in making a starkly truthful pre-sentation of the genitals without showing the model's head. The point of the exercise was to respond to a demand for a female sexual scene while demonstrating his remarkable painterly talent—nothing saucy, just the pursuit of the aesthetic and visual question, despite the reso-nances with the pornographic photography of Auguste Belloc. X. R.

Gustave Guillaumet
The Sahara or The Desert

Oil on canvas
3 ft. 7½ in. × 6 ft. 7 in. (1.11 × 2.01 m)
Gift of the artist's family, 1888

"I saw an Algerian stop in front of *The Sahara* by Monsieur Guillaumet and swear to me that it was a fantasy Sahara," wrote the critic Castagnary after the Salon of 1868, where this impressive work attracted much attention. The poet Théophile Gautier asserted, on the contrary, that "Never has the infinity of the desert been painted in a simpler, grander, or more moving way." Certainly, in this minimalist and sublime evocation of the great arid expanse, Guillaumet managed to move away from Western fantasies fed by anecdotes designed to satisfy the public thirst for exoticism. Original and greatly expressive, the canvas is highly economical, marking a shift away from the kind of lush, flamboyant, romantic colors found in

Delacroix, which Guillaumet was still using in his 1866 *Flute Players in Bivouac*. In 1862 the painter left Rome for North Africa, painting and drawing this exotic land that had aroused so much interest since the French conquest of Algeria, just before the Revolution of 1830. The handling of the light, a key factor when there is nothing to provide perspective, almost suggests the hallucinations induced by extreme thirst. It is easy to imagine the caravan that can just be made out in the distant glow as illusory. In contrast, the animal carcass in the foreground speaks of the grim reality of death awaiting in this monotonous, dusty expanse. Guillaumet reduces the desert to its essence, with precision, but leaves its mystery. X. R.

Edgar Degas
The Parade or Racehorses in Front of the Tribunes

Oil on paper glued on canvas
18 × 24 in. (46 × 61 cm)
Bequeathed by Comte Isaac de Camondo, 1911

Just as the women that Degas depicted at their mirror are the distant heirs of those pictures of Susanna at her bath painted by his predecessors, so his racehorses are contemporary incarnations of the battle horses in the great tradition of history painting. The painter sought modern ways of applying what he had learned from his revered masters, from Uccello to Van Dyck and Géricault, through the prism of the scientific study of equine movement. *The Parade*, one of the first works in a series, features what would be a leitmotiv in Degas's career and no doubt borrowed from his contemporaries Meissonier and Dreux, both of whom reflected the Anglomania of the day. The visible drawing in this work seems to be studying the balance of the trotting mounts before the race begins, although the artist has also represented a galloping jockey in the background, quite at odds with the moment chosen here. In this way Degas is signaling his concern to study the different breeds of horse in different positions, to offer a series rather than capture a given moment. Indeed, the evening light, by which he creates a superb set of chromatic variations, is extremely matt, due to the use of petrol to dilute the oil on the paper, and does not seem to correspond to any very likely moment of the day. This painting preceded the "chronophotographic" studies by Étienne-Jules Marey that broke down movement, and prefigures Degas's last studies of equine anatomy in motion, especially the sculptures. X. R.

Narcisse Diaz de la Peña
The Heights of Le Jean-de-Paris

Oil on canvas
2 ft. 9 in. × 3 ft. 5¾ in. (0.84 × 1.06 m)
Bequeathed by Alfred Chauchard, 1910

Initially known for his painting of romantic scenes and fantasies, Narcisse Diaz made friends with Théodore Rousseau in 1837, and joined him along with other painters and photographers in the village of Barbizon, on the edge of Fontainebleau forest. Nurtured on the example of Constable, these artists revitalized the landscape genre by rejecting the reference to the Italian classical tradition in favor of accurate observation of natural phenomena. The canvases were painted from life; there was no need for nymphs and other goddesses to animate landscapes in which the natural components—trees, ponds, rocks, etc.—had become the actual subject matter.

Here Diaz has painted the "portrait" of a familiar landmark in Fontainebleau forest, Le Jean-de-Paris. Standing out against a leaden sky are some trees whose foliage is magnified by the light in stormy weather. The dark foreground helps to emphasize the dramatic effect, and we can only just make out the silhouette of a woman carrying a bundle of sticks and wending her way through the rocks. This almost theatrical dimension suggests a certain romantic influence, but also the seventeenth-century Dutch painters, most notably Ruysdael, whose paintings, in the Louvre, feature among the Barbizon painters' avowed references. I. P.

Charles Guillaume Diehl, Jean Brandely, Emmanuel Frémiet
Medal cabinet

Cedar, walnut, ebony and ivory marquetry, oak frame, silver-plated bronze and copper
7 ft. 9¾ in. × 4 ft. 11½ in. × 1 ft. 11½ in.
(2.38 × 1.51 × 0.60 m)
Acquired in 1973

A specialist in small furniture and objects, the cabinetmaker Diehl was the man behind this imposing medal cabinet created for the Exposition Universelle of 1867. The drawings for the form, the marquetry, and the bronzes were entrusted to Brandely and the sculpted parts were the work of Frémiet, while Diehl brought his expertise to the cedar-wood and walnut veneer, and to the marquetry. For what was his only collaboration in the field of furniture, Frémiet was invited to work on his pet themes of animals and soldiers.

The central bas-relief represents the triumph of Merovech after the defeat of Attila on the Catalaunian Plains in 451. The framing bronzes amplify the central subject, and in particular the trophy of Frankish arms over the door. Medals evoke the furniture's function.

It is likely that Diehl was hoping to sell this outstanding medal cabinet to Napoleon III, a keen archeologist who had created a Merovingian antiquities section when he founded the Musée des Souverains in 1852. Although the cabinet made quite an impression at the Exposition, Diehl was only awarded a bronze medal, which he refused. Observers struggled to define it, speaking of "Merovingian style," or a "big piece of Gaulish furniture in the Romanesque style." It was highly innovative, but had little influence. Y. B.

Baccarat, Picard frères, Émile Belet
Vase

Opaline, gilt bronze
4 ft. × 1 ft. 5¾ in. (1.22 × 0.45 m)
Mobilier National collection, on
permanent loan to the Musée d'Orsay
since 2009

The Sainte-Anne crystal works was created in 1764 at Baccarat, near Nancy, but it was only in 1823 that the factory received its first commissions from Louis XVIII.

The crystal works exhibited frequently at national industrial shows, regularly winning gold medals. This was the case at the Exposition Universelle of 1867 where, still expanding rapidly but already world famous, the factory exhibited a spectacular fountain 30 feet (7 m) high, two engraved vases by Jean-Baptiste Simon (now at the Musée Baccarat) and a host of lights, objects, and elements for table services that underlined the supremacy of the works. On this occasion the royal furniture repository (Garde-Meuble) acquired two pairs of Baccarat vases. These covered vases are richly mounted on gilt bronze. Each designed with three opaline elements colored on the surface, they were meant to compete with what Sèvres was producing. The virtuoso floral decoration uses the white of opaline, in reserve, to create the tone of the lightest petals. The rarity of these pieces is confirmed by the signature—most unusual for Baccarat—of the flower painter Émile Belet, who also worked for the factory at Sèvres. The model used for the bronze mount, by Picard frères, can be found on other pieces by Baccarat, which indicates that it was made exclusively for the firm. Y. B.

Alfred Stevens
The Bath or Woman Bathing

Oil on canvas
29 × 36½ in. (73.5 × 92.8 cm)
Bequeathed by Léon Lhermitte, 1926

The swan tap, whose subtle gray highlights were admired by Manet as part of the overall harmony of this work, is also found in a print of a woman taking a bath made by Degas some ten years later. While in both works this detail is a sign of changing cultural habits in matters of hygiene in the West, the artistic ambition is quite different in each case. Stevens's *The Bath* seems intent on recording a moment in contemporary life, doing so with a degree of precision and naturalistic style acceptable to a bourgeois public. The Belgian painter does not take the risk of revisiting the ancient genre of the nude by undressing his subject, a contemporary woman, since that might create a scandal. The verisimilitude of the scene, with the book in the foreground bestowing both depth and meaning on the representation, does not prevent the woman's expression from having the poetry of a kind of bourgeois melancholy, something almost neurotic that Stevens seemed to track in his paintings. This languid feel ensures a touch of sensuality, heightened by the visible strap of the undergarment, a clue to the artist's penchant for the intimate boudoir painting of the eighteenth century. It also ensured the success of this work, whose first owner was the collector Ernest Hoschedé, Monet's patron. X. R.

Jean-Léon Gérôme
Jerusalem or Golgotha Consumatum Est: The Crucifixion

Oil on canvas
2 ft. 8¼ in × 4 ft. 9 in. (0.82 × 1.44 m)
Acquired in 1990

"All is accomplished." In front of a vast panorama of Jerusalem, with some sinister storm clouds passing overhead, we see the silhouettes of Roman soldiers withdrawing from Mount Golgotha, leaving the shadows of the three crucified men lengthening across the creviced rock in the foreground. The artist makes use of the "off-camera" technique to remove the image of the historical protagonists, so the landscape alone conveys the power of the event; the topographical authenticity is a result of the artist's recent visit to Palestine. Gérôme's work stands as one of the solutions proposed to overcome the crisis of religious painting in the middle of this positivist, secularized nineteenth century. Four years earlier,

Ernest Renan had published his *Vie de Jésus* (*Life of Jesus*), analyzing the Bible as a historical document and no longer as a sacred text. Likewise, Gérôme no longer wanted to be a director of the transcendental in the manner of baroque painters describing the lamentations of the Virgin Mary and the angels around the Savior on the Cross. As an orientalist painter and a contemporary of Realism, he adopts the standpoint of a reporter arriving on the crime scene after the fact, gathering clues and impressions that are capable of bringing the Gospel story back to life, without venturing into the grandiloquent Crucifixions of a bygone age. C. F.

James Tissot
The Circle of the Rue Royale

Oil on canvas
5 ft. 9 in. × 9 ft. 2½ in. (1.75 × 2.80 m)
Acquired in 2011

This group portrait on the lines of the English conversation piece, commissioned from the artist by the members of the Cercle de la Rue Royale, a Monarchist club, captures the memory of the intellectual, sociable atmosphere during the late Second Empire period. Delighting in the detailed rendering of the sartorial and decorative elements, Tissot seems to have varied the outfits of each of his sitters, ranging from the most casual to the most formal attire, thereby sacrificing any consistency with regard to dress codes. Appearing through the balustrade, the frontal perspective of the colonnade designed by the architect Gabriel for Louis XV's Place Royale, later renamed Place de la Concorde, seems to be seeking to com-pete with photography in its attempt at perfect accuracy. Attitudes, hats, canes, and gloves are all outward signs indicating the status of the members shown. Standing on the right is Charles Haas, a figure of Parisian dandyism from the bourgeois business class, walking into the picture the way he walked into this group of aristocrats, and who inspired Marcel Proust's Swann, a major character in *À la recherche du temps perdu* (*Remembrance of Things Past*). In terms of his ambition to place individuals in their social milieu, Tissot seems to have then been close to his friend Degas. His career in England remained on the fringe of the impressionist avant-gardes, however. X. R.

Luigi Frullini
Chair

Mahogany and velvet
4 ft. 1¼ in. × 2 ft. 2¾ in. × 2 ft. (1.25 × 0.68 × 0.61 m)
Acquired in 2011

Drawing on sources in the Italian Renaissance, the extravagant grotesques and *rinceaux* (garland floral motifs) decorating the backs of these two chairs show them to have been the kind of unique pieces that were popular in the second half of the nineteenth century. The quality of execution of this model is particularly marked in terms of the refinement and exuberance of the sculpted decoration covering the visible parts of the seat. The seat backs and legs were left smooth at the rear, which suggests that the chairs were probably meant for a hallway. The front of each chair back is individual. They feature, respectively, an imaginary bestiary with a bird-woman, a wolf-snail-grasshopper, a winged griffin with a goat's head, and a dragon, in an exuberant teeming of plants and masks. The engraved handwritten signature and date applied at the bottom of each backrest show that this was indeed an ambitious piece of work. The chairs were conceived in the period during which Frullini was at the head of a small wood-sculpture workshop in Via Santa Caterina, Florence, when he was making pieces from his own imagination. Thanks to the success achieved at the Italian Exhibition (Florence, 1861) and World's Fairs (London, 1862; Paris, 1867; Vienna, 1873), Frullini managed to build himself a reputation and a rich international clientele. He enlarged his workshop, delegating construction of the furniture to his best artisans so that he could concentrate on sculpture. Y. B.

Christofle & Cie, Émile Reiber
Inkwell

Bronze, metal, glass, crystal enamel, with velvet morocco leather and silk satin case
3½ × 6 in. (9 × 15 cm), 5 × 7 in. (12.5 × 18 cm) with case
Acquired in 2012

A matchless watercolorist, Émile Reiber made his debut at the Salon in 1859, when he showed twelve drawings in the Renaissance style. This period also saw him start working for the ceramist Théodore Deck, who was established in Paris from 1847. Responsive to the Japanese influences of the day, in 1861 he founded *L'Art pour tous*, a magazine/encyclopedia of industrial and decorative arts published in French, English, and German. In 1865 he became artistic director at Christofle, with the title of "Head of Composition and Drawing Workshops." There he created a line of pieces in gilt bronze with cloisonné enamel, which were very complex to make, among them this inkwell presented with Baccarat crystal and which has kept its meticulously made original holder. The style of the decoration here is more Persian than Japanese. The Christofle archives list only two of these objects, which were also shown at the 1889 Exposition Universelle in Paris. Y. B.

Alexandre Falguière
Tarcisius, a Christian Martyr

Marble
2 ft. 1½ in. × 4 ft. 7 in. × 1 ft. 11½ in.
(0.65 × 1.40 × 0.60 m)
Acquired in 1867

The martyrs of the early Christian era were popular subjects for the artists of the Second Empire. In 1867, still enjoying the kudos from his success at the Salon of 1864, Falguière presented his plaster of *Tarcisius*, a subject taken from the famous novel by Cardinal Wiseman, *Fabiola or the Church of the Catacombs*. Responsible for carrying the consecrated wafer, the young Tarcisius is stopped by pagans who demand that he show them the object he is holding so tightly, but he prefers to die rather than obey. Slight, slender children were in favor with sculptors in the second half of the nineteenth century. Contemporary critics emphasized the formal similarity between the young deacon lying on the ground holding the wafer to his chest, and works by David (a painting) and David d'Angers (a sculpture) representing the death of the young Bara. It is certain, too, that Falguière had admired Stefano Maderno's *St. Cecilia* and the baroque masterpieces of Bernini in Rome. More than a young boy dying tragically under the blows of his killers, Tarcisius is a believer, transfigured by the faith to which he abandons himself, head thrown back and mouth open. For Edmond About, this airy, sentimental vision was "a little masterpiece of sickly grace ... that will advantageously replace the grotesque images given to the young at communion nowadays." O. F.

Auguste Renoir
Boy with Cat

Oil on canvas
4 ft. ½ in. × 2 ft. 2 in. (1.23 × 0.66 m)
Acquired in 1992

Boy with Cat is to this day somewhat mysterious. This male nude is like nothing else in Renoir's work. It is not known who the boy stroking the cat was. Maybe it should be seen as depicting a young professional model taking a short break. The way he glances over his shoulder toward the viewer remains enigmatic. Renoir introduces no narrative element or context. He shuns the recourse to mythology that we find in his female nudes. He seems to be inviting us into the world of the studio, possibly that of his friend Frédéric Bazille. The use of fabrics, and particularly velvet, serves as a foil to the nude and as a way of showing off the characteristic brilliance of the nineteenth-century studio nude. But here Renoir subverts the codes of academic painting to produce a disturbing picture. The unathletic body and rather short legs of the model flaunting his nudity do not meet the canons of Classicism. The painter chooses not to idealize his model. The harsh lighting, the cold, metallic tones used for the skin and the flowery fabric, and also the wan light heightened by the black background, all set this modern figure in the line of Manet's nudes, notably those in *The Luncheon on the Grass* (p. 81) and *Olympia* (p. 83), which had caused such a scandal. S. Py.

Edgar Degas
The Orchestra at the Opera

Oil on canvas
22¼ × 18 in. (56.5 × 46 cm)
Donated by Mlle Dihau, 1923

"I assure you, no art was ever less spontaneous than mine," Degas confided at the end of his life. Certainly, if we consider *The Orchestra at the Opera*, the initial impression of a moment faithfully captured gives way to a sense that there is something strange about the positions of the musicians. The vantage point suggested by the balustrade in the foreground is indeed not credible, particularly regarding the relative positions of the figures. This distortion of space, a device favored by Degas, is paradoxically highly effective, combined with the novel framing inspired by Japanese prints, which decapitates the dancers lit up on the stage in the background. In this bold composition, the foreshortening brings the background abruptly forward. Degas was unusual among the Impressionists in being interested in interiors and the effects of artificial light, which, as a regular there, he first studied at the Opéra. This painting can also be considered as one of the first "situation portraits." Its subject is the bassoonist Désiré Dihau, one of the painter's friends and neighbors, who is shown surrounded by his fellow musicians during a performance—even though, with the exception of the cellist Pillet, many of the faces here are of the painter's non-musician friends, whom he included in this recomposed scene. X. R.

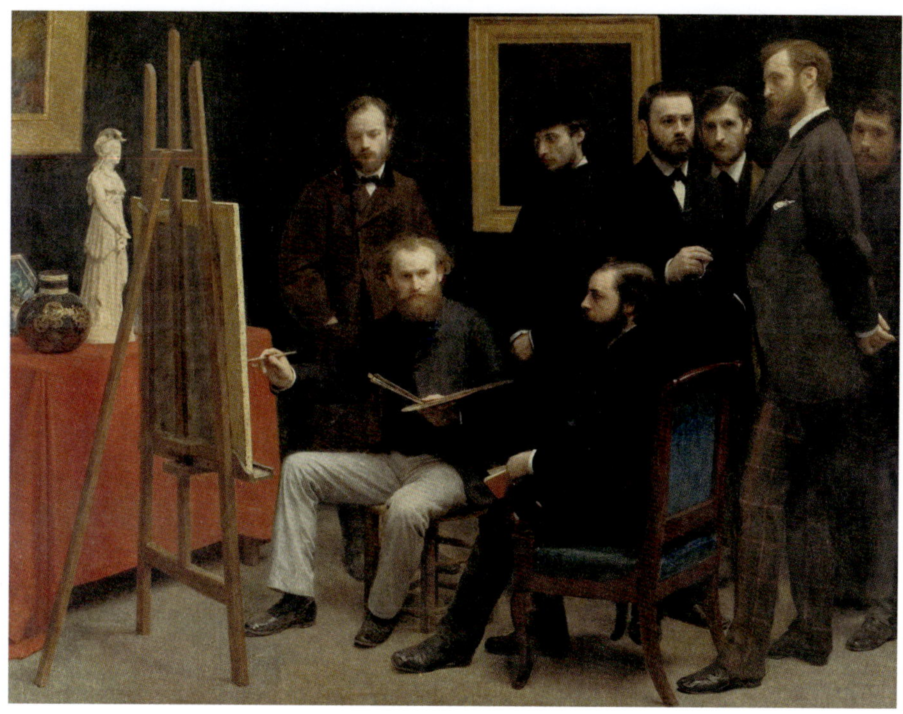

Henri Fantin-Latour
A Studio in the Batignolles Quarter

Oil on canvas
6 ft. 8¼ in. × 8 ft. 11½ in. (2.04 × 2.74 m)
Acquired in 1892

When this imposing collective portrait—worthy of seventeenth-century Dutch painting—was exhibited at the Salon in 1870, the press read it as a manifesto in favor of Fantin-Latour's friend, Manet, a painter with a reputation for scandal. Around him are habitués of the Café Guerbois, a watering hole in the Batignolles quarter of Paris, where the young guard of painters and writers had passionate discussions about the future direction of art. Manet emerged as the leader of this realist tendency, which followed on from that of Courbet in the 1850s. Sitting at an easel in an imaginary studio, Manet is given the central role. Around him, from the left, are Otto Scholderer (a painter from Frankfurt), Auguste Renoir (wearing a hat), the writer and artist Zacharie Astruc (seated), Émile Zola, the musician and collector Edmond Maître, Frédéric Bazille (in profile), and Claude Monet (in the corner). In such a context, the objects are significant as well, the Bouvier vase, for example, recalling the protagonists' interest in Japanese art. Fantin-Latour was already well known to the public for his impeccably painted manifesto-works—pieces such as his 1864 *Homage to Delacroix. A Studio* closes a cycle that the artist would later reopen to celebrate the glory of Wagner, Schumann, and Berlioz, Verlaine and Rimbaud in his 1872 painting, *By the Table* (Musée d'Orsay). S. Py.

Édouard Manet
The Balcony

Oil on canvas
5 ft. 7 in. × 4 ft. 1 in. (1.70 × 1.24 m)
Bequeathed by Gustave Caillebotte, 1894

For this painting, Édouard Manet has brought together three of his artist friends: Berthe Morisot, leaning on the balcony, the landscape artist Antonin Guillemet, and Fanny Claus, a violinist and future wife of the painter and engraver Pierre Prins. In the darkness of the background, we can only just make out Manet's wife's son, Léon Leenhoff. While the characters seem to be representatives of modern Parisian high life, it is hard to tell what social ritual brings them together on this balcony, which is also a reference to Goya. The characters ignore each other. Contrasting with the barely sketched faces of Guillemet and Fanny is the intense gaze of Berthe, then described as a "femme fatale," and later to become one of Manet's favorite sitters. The critics attending the Salon of 1869 were shocked by the strange, enigmatic quality of these motionless protagonists. But the loudest guffaws were no doubt produced by the acid green of the balcony and the shutters framing the composition; it caused Manet to be described as a house painter. Although hopeful of finding a buyer for this ambitious work, the artist never did, and it stayed in his studio until the end of his life. It was purchased in 1884 by the painter and collector Gustave Caillebotte at the auction after Manet's death. S. Py.

Claude Monet
The Magpie

Oil on canvas
2 ft. 11 in. × 4 ft. 3¼ in. (0.89 × 1.30 m)
Acquired in 1984

Following the example of Courbet, who painted several snowscapes, Monet was drawn to this subject very early on, as it allowed him to play on various shades of color and make the ground iridescent with blue reflections instead of painting it a uniform white. It was during the winter of 1868-69 that the artist created this extraordinary "snow effect," as he himself described certain of his paintings. At the time he was living at Étretat, from where he wrote to his friend Bazille in December 1868: "I go into the country which is so lovely here that I perhaps find it even more agreeable in winter than in summer." This symphony of whites seems to have been some sort of challenge, with the painter playing through the range of differently colored whites to express the density of matter and the luminous atmosphere of this wintry landscape, which sparkles in the sunshine. It is highlighted by the black note of the magpie, on the fence, as the sole presence of life in this deserted spot. Shadow and sunlight share the snow-covered ground, made even more dazzling by the reflections of light, while the gate and the tree trunks add some dark lines. This canvas is thought to be one of two Monets rejected by the judges of the 1869 Salon; this supposition may be backed up by the fact that the format adopted is unusually large for a landscape. As a major success prior to 1870 and a demonstration of the artist's precocious talent, *The Magpie* remains one of the most spectacular and best-known snowscapes in the history of painting. S. P.

Henri Regnault
Summary Execution under the Moorish Kings of Grenada

Oil on canvas
9 ft. 11 in. × 4 ft. 9½ in. (3.02 × 1.46 m)
Gift of the artist's heirs, 1872

In 1878 the novelist Huysmans described this repugnant, bloody scene painted by Regnault as a "mess of redcurrant jams or orange jelly," and compared the artist's approach to the obsession with detail that carried Gérôme's work to the point of falsification. This work marked the end of Regnault's period of study: as a winner of the Prix de Rome in 1866 he had obtained permission to range beyond the Villa Medici and look for inspiration in Spain and North Africa, which is where he worked on this painting. Inspired by a legend about the Arab occupation of Andalusia and the Alhambra in Granada, this student of Cabanel stepped boldly beyond the confines of academicism and saturated his evocation with color, with copious blood recalling the heritage of Romanticism, and a grandiose composition full of dramatic angles leaning toward the avant-gardes. This orientalist painting has a majesty and repulsive beauty that recall the contemporary fascination with the beheading theme, a morbid obsession of many artists who depicted the stories of Judith and Holofernes and Salome and St. John the Baptist. Regnault seemed set for a glorious career, but was killed during the Franco-Prussian War in 1871. X. R.

Alexandre Cabanel
The Death of Francesca de Rimini and Paolo Malatesta

Oil on canvas
6 ft. × 8 ft. 4½ in. (1.84 × 2.55 m)
Acquired in 1871

This tragic scene was the piece everyone was waiting for at the Salon of 1870, when Cabanel was at the pinnacle of his career. This time he drew from the romantic repertory, readapting, as Ingres had done before him, Canto V of *Dante's Inferno*: the damned shade of Francesca recounts the moment when she and her brother-in-law Paolo were stabbed to death by the jealous husband Malatesta after confessing their love for each other while reading the courtly adventures of Lancelot and Guinevere. Looking at this work, the viewer has the physical sensation of sitting in the front row at the foot of a theater stage at the moment when, just after the unwatchable violence of the deadly deed, you open your eyes again just in time to spot the murderer escaping into the wings. The melodramatic lighting, the archeological erudition of the scenery, the rich color of the fabrics—this large-budget production has it all. So much so that the critic Castagnary deplored seeing the poem of love and death reduced like this to "a ghastly bunch of fabrics thrown onto a medieval settee." Others, meanwhile, did not fail to notice the disturbing ambiguity of the lovers' pose, midway between convulsive death throes and fainting love pangs, as well as the modernity of the scene, no longer seeking to airbrush out the unsavory reality of props flung forward at the front of the stage, like the overturned stool, the sole of the slipper, or the crotch of the actor wearing tights. C. F.

Hippolyte Marie Pigault
Apartment Building, 109 rue de Turenne and rue des Filles-du-Calvaire

Pencil, India ink, and watercolor
23¼ × 30½ in. (59 × 77.5 cm)
Acquired in 2012

Toward the end of the 1860s, the architect Hippolyte Marie Pigault conceived this large building to occupy a plot of land at the intersection of Rues de Turenne, de Bretagne, and des Filles-du-Calvaire, close to the location where he had just installed his architectural practice. He adopted the broad principles of Haussmannian Paris, which remained in force in the capital at the start of the Third Republic: strict alignment, the use of stone, uniform elevations, horizontal façades underscored by balconies, decoration reduced to structural details (consoles and bays). This drawing shows the monumental effect of perspective that such a mode of construction could create. Made particularly picturesque by the inclusion of human figures, this view is remarkable for the time: architects usually produced more modest representations of Haussmannian rental buildings, a common and controlled form that left little room for initiative. Its architecture almost banal, the Haussmannian rental building is now one of the defining elements of the capital's architectural identity, and a contributor to its very classical urban harmony. A. T.-B.

Eugène Emmanuel Viollet-le-Duc
Steel-framed House with Faience Facing

Graphite, pen, and watercolor
19 × 14½ in. (48 × 37 cm)
Acquired in 2008

This is a legendary plate, a genuine architectural icon from the famous *Discourses on Architecture* (1863–72), admired by Horta, Guimard, Gaudí, and Sullivan, and considered one of the founding texts of modern architecture. In these pages Viollet-le-Duc shows himself to be a visionary, but at the same time concerned with realism in construction. Among other subjects, he expresses his ideas about the use of metal.

In the eighteenth *Discourse*, on private architecture, Viollet-le-Duc considers a load-bearing structure made entirely of metal. This had already been used in 1871–72 at the Menier chocolate mill built by Jules Saulnier at Noisiel, but the daring thing here is that the system is applied to a residential building and that the structure is left visible on the façade both in plan and in its salient features, and given colored cladding, which was strictly forbidden by the Parisian municipal authorities. This discreet polychrome effect enhanced the façade and the squares, playing on the lines of the iron, underscoring the structural lines, the fusion of structure and decoration being one of the architect's key ideas. These elements were to be prefabricated in the factory, with the advantage that their surfaces were easy to wash, without the need for complicated scaffolding. This kind of decoration, which is in faience here, would reach its apogee in the varnished terracotta display at the Expositions Universelles of 1878 and 1889. C. M.

Frédéric Bazille
Bazille's Studio

Oil on canvas
3 ft. 2½ in. × 4 ft. 1½ in. (0.98 × 1.26 m)
Bequeathed by Marc Bazille, 1924

This view of the artist's studio in Rue de la Condamine, Paris, nicely sums up the spirit of the early days of Impressionism, before the group's first exhibition in 1874. Not all the protagonists have been identified, but we can recognize Manet in front of the easel chatting with Bazille—the latter figure painted, as it happens, by the real-life Manet. On the right, the collector and musician Edmond Maître is playing the piano. Like his friends Monet, Renoir, Sisley, and Pissarro, Bazille, who would die in the Franco-Prussian War only a few months after painting this scene, aspired to a clear style that would convey the effects of outdoor light, putting the emphasis on scenes of modern life and bold execution. The works assembled here in the studio, which Bazille was sharing with Renoir, echo these concerns: witness the large framed painting by Renoir to the right of the window and, below, *La Toilette* by Bazille. These canvases also reflect the difficulties faced by this new generation: the Renoir painting was rejected by the Salon in 1866, as was Bazille's in 1870. *Bazille's Studio* was painted the same year as Fantin-Latour's *A Studio in the Batignolles Quarter* (p. 117). Its execution, however, is more spontaneous. Bazille was not trying to make an artistic statement but, in his own words, to enjoy painting a few friends. Still, this work is no less emblematic of the emergence of the "new painting." S. Py.

James Abbott McNeill Whistler
Arrangement in Gray and Black No. 1
or Portrait of the Artist's Mother

Oil on canvas
4 ft. 8¾ in. × 5 ft. 4¼ in. (1.44 × 1.63 m)
Acquired in 1891

Anna Mathilda McNeill Whistler was the sitter for this portrait, painted between 1867 and 1871 in London, where Whistler, an American painter who worked in France and England, was then living with his mother. In addition to the biographical dimension, the artist stated that "the picture should have its own merit" in its arrangement. This indeed is the meaning of the musical and abstract titles he gave to his paintings, here emphasizing the austere modulation of grays and blacks. Whistler takes his search for the soberness that characterizes his portraits to even greater extremes than his friend Fantin-Latour (p. 117), and here it also functions as an echo of the puritanism and rigorism of the particular section of American society to which the model belonged. The artist combines uncompromising realism, especially in the treatment of the face, strictly outlining the profile in the manner of Quattrocento portraits or medals. The stubbornly staring eyes, which some have seen as the mother's disapproval of her son's lifestyle, most of all suggest the old woman lucidly facing the ravages of time and death. Above and beyond the occasional portrait, the painting induces meditation and can be seen as a form of asceticism, favored by the starkness of this masterly *Arrangement*. S. Py.

Julia Margaret Cameron
Mrs. Herbert Duckworth (Julia Jackson)

Carbon print (negative taken in 1872)
15¾ × 10 in. (39.8 × 25.5 cm)
Gift of the Galerie Texbraun, 1986

A highly educated friend of many leading figures of the British intelligentsia, Cameron soon demonstrated her original gift for portraying the famous men of her day, magnified by her very personal aesthetic—including expressive fuzziness, the use of close-up shots and large formats making her faces almost life-size—which earned her both mockery and praise. Tirelessly photographed by Cameron, her niece and goddaughter Julia Duckworth née Jackson is one of the very few women to have had the privilege of being able to remain herself in front of the camera—other female sitters were usually invited to lend their charming features to represent characters from the Bible, mythology, or literature. A tribute to the puritan beauty and to the penetrating intelligence of a woman who posed for many painters, including Watts and Burne-Jones, this is also the portrait of a twenty-six-year-old widow, here pictured a few years before she remarried and gave birth to the writer Virginia Woolf and the painter Vanessa Bell. It is one of the pictures that Cameron chose for reproduction using the carbon print process, supposed to ensure—by its inalterability—the preservation and dissemination of what the photographer considered to be the best of her career. T. G.

Édouard Manet
Berthe Morisot with a Bouquet of Violets

Oil on canvas
21¾ × 16 in. (55.5 × 40.5 cm)
Acquired in 1998

This painting, which joined the Musée d'Orsay collections in 1998, is undoubtedly one of Manet's most admired works. Thus the writer Paul Valéry rates "nothing in Manet's work more highly than a certain portrait of Berthe Morisot," admiring "the overpowering blacks, the cool simplicity of the background, the pale or rosy luminosity of the flesh, the odd silhouette of the hat, which was 'young' and 'the latest fashion,' the confusion of curls, tie strings and ribbon to each side of the face; the face itself with its great eyes whose vague fixity suggests the profoundest abstraction, a sort of *presence in absence*—the total effect adds up to a singular impression of ... *poetry*." His portrait is "poetry," as celebrated by Valéry, owing to the "distinct charm" of Berthe Morisot, and the fascination he had for her, which is perceptible in this portrait when she was thirty-one years of age. A painter and later Manet's sister-in-law, she sat for him more than ten times. This portrait was especially dear to her; Manet, who sold it to the critic Théodore Duret, consoled Berthe with a *Still Life with a Bouquet of Violets and a fan*, both emblems used to characterize the young woman when she is featured in Manet's painting. Berthe snapped up the painting when it came up for sale in 1894, a year before she herself died. S. Py.

Berthe Morisot
The Cradle

Oil on canvas
22 × 18 in. (56 × 46 cm)
Acquired in 1930

The Cradle is the first painting by Berthe Morisot to evoke maternity, and shows the artist's sister Edma with her daughter Blanche, born in 1871. The two sisters had both begun painting and exhibiting in the 1860s, but they were separated when Edma married and gave up her artistic career. Edma told Berthe how she missed the life of the studio and the company of their friends Manet, Degas, and Fantin-Latour. Berthe consoled her with talk of the fulfillment of motherhood. *The Cradle* comes across as a harmonious celebration of a mother watching over her sleeping child—the hint of melancholy in Edma's expression notwithstanding. The artist heightens the impression of intimacy by the veils and curtains that isolate and protect mother and child from the tumult of the outside world. The composition is based on the play of diagonals, and the range of colors is dominated by sober whites and blacks. This painting featured in the first impressionist exhibition of 1874, where Berthe Morisot was the only female participant. She took part in all the group's shows up to 1886, the only exception being 1879, held shortly after she had given birth to Julie, her daughter by Eugène Manet, the brother of the painter, whom she had married in 1874. Julie and Eugène would become the main models for her depictions of modern intimacy. S. Py.

Jean-François Millet
The Bouquet of Daisies

Pastel on beige paper laid on stretched
canvas, 26¾ × 33 in. (68 × 83.5 cm)
Purchase made with the interest accrued from
the Dol-Lair bequest, 1949

In this picture, Millet turns away from pure portraiture, with the smiling yet enigmatic face of his daughter Marguerite fading into the shadows behind a dazzling bunch of flowers. The bouquet, in a blue vase composed from a multitude of contrasting lines, is placed on a window sill that blurs the line between reality and representation, and on which the artist has "engraved" his name. Neither portrait nor still life, *Le Bouquet de marguerites* highlights the multifaceted and ambiguous nature of pastel, standing as it does at the crossroads of drawing and painting and suitable for all subjects and every material effect. Playing on the various meanings of the title, "Marguerite" being both Millet's daughter's forename and the French word for this type of daisy, it is also possible that

the bouquet was meant to evoke the "bloom" of pastel itself—that is to say, the layer of pigment on the surface of the paper, which here seems to shimmer across the juxtaposition of the white of the petals and the bright yellow of the pistils against the soft green of the foliage. In Millet's hands, pastel becomes a fundamentally graphic art: leaving blanks in reserve to build up the volumes of the stone and afford depth to the bouquet, he makes extensive use of black pastel in the form of streaks and hatching. The artist seems to have heeded Camille Flers' warning to his fellow pastel artists not to fall for the idea that "the essence of pastel lies in blurring," as well as his injunction to explore and assert instead "its absolute solidity, which derives from the immutability of each stroke." C. C.-P.

Christofle & Cie, Émile Reiber
Clock from a three-piece fireplace ornament set

Bronze and patinated, gilt, and silver-plated
copper, cloisonné enamel
25¼ × 22½ in. (64.2 × 57.2 cm)
Gift of the Société des Amis du Musée d'Orsay, 1998

The architect and decorator Émile Reiber was taken on by Christofle in 1865 and set about creating a collection of decorative objects. Thanks to the skill of the workers, he could realize his wildest dreams, as he competed in boldness with the creations of the casters, silversmiths, and enamel workers of China, Japan, India, and Persia. This piece is one of the most splendid versions of the clock and matching candelabra set that he worked on for many years from 1869 onward. The words *pendule japonaise* (Japanese clock), inscribed by Reiber on one of his preparatory studies, cannot hide the fact that the form, decoration, and technique here owe as much to China and India as they do to Japan. The clock is an adaptation of a Chinese table screen. The surprising composition of the candlesticks may have been derived from Chinese sources and in particular from prints of the Summer Palace in Beijing. Only the panels on the back of the candelabras are clearly in the Japanese spirit. From a technical point of view, the perfect casting and casing, the red and black patinas, the fine inlays of gold and silver, and the cloisonné enamel are all free and fascinating transcriptions of oriental models. This accumulation of decorative erudition illustrates the tremendous taste for chinoiseries and Japanese objects that inspired French decorators to make some of the most precious masterpieces of the late nineteenth century. Y. B.

Claude Monet
The Railway Bridge at Argenteuil

Oil on canvas
21¼ × 28 in. (54 × 71 cm)
Gift of Étienne Moreau-Nélaton, 1906

"We meet often at the home of Monet, where we recently had a housewarming: he is very well installed and seems to have a keen desire to go up in the world. He has brought back some very fine studies from Holland and I believe that he is destined to be at the fore of our school." This is how Eugène Boudin announces Monet's move to Argenteuil, on the Seine, where the younger artist had come the previous year after sojourns in London and then the Netherlands. Monet's Argenteuil period corresponded with the golden age of Impressionism. On the water there he painted several canvases of the yach-ting regattas, demonstrating perfect mastery of the broken brushstrokes technique. The painter was stimulated by the atmosphere on the banks of the Seine, also evoked by contemporary writers, notably Maupassant in his short stories. Monet made several paintings of the two bridges at Argenteuil: the road bridge and, here, the railway bridge. The passing train underscores the instantaneous nature of the scene. The framing is bold, and much is made of the interplay between light and moving water. S. P.

Claude Monet
Poppies

Oil on canvas
19¾ × 25¾ in. (50 × 65.3 cm)
Gift of Étienne Moreau-Nélaton, 1906

When living in Argenteuil, Monet would on occasion take his easel out into the fields. He was still using mutually invigorating complementary colors, like the reds and greens in this picture of *Poppies* in which two of the figures are thought to be his wife Camille and their older son, Jean. This composition is famous for having featured in what came to be known as the first impressionist exhibition, in 1874: the term was inspired by the title of a Monet seascape in this exhibit organized on the fringe of the official Salon, *Impression, soleil levant* (*Impression, Sunrise*, 1872–73, Musée Marmottan, Paris). "Put *Impression*," he replied when asked for a title that could be printed in the catalogue. Not for a moment did he mean to name a movement. The critic Louis Leroy then seized on the word to create the mocking term "impressionisme." At the second impressionist exhibition, in 1876, Émile Zola wrote: "The painters I'm talking about have been called 'Impressionists,' for the great majority of them seek … to convey the exact impression produced by objects both animate and inanimate, to apprehend and convey it immediately. … Claude Monet is … the leader of the group. His brush stands out for its extraordinary brilliance." S. P.

Paul Cézanne
The Hanged Man's House, Auvers-sur-Oise

Oil on canvas
21¾ × 26 in. (55.5 × 66.3 cm)
Bequeathed by Comte Isaac
de Camondo, 1911

After having several submissions rejected by the Salon, Cézanne moved to Auvers-sur-Oise, where he was helped by Doctor Gachet and worked alongside the artist Camille Pissarro. The latter's advice is certainly evident in *The Hanged Man's House*, which he exhibited in 1874 in what later came to known as the first impressionist exhibition. Pissarro persuaded him to give up the dark, oily style of his earlier works in favor of lighter, broken brushstrokes and working directly from the model, both characteristic of Impressionism. While there is no denying the similarity of composition between the two men's work at this juncture, Cézanne was distinguished by his way of adding successive brushstrokes, working in depth, in line with Courbet's seascapes, and by the relative emphasis of his brushwork compared to the light touch of Monet and Renoir. The transition between planes of representation is also more abrupt, like a visual transposition of the violent literary subjects that had inspired the painter a few years earlier. This picture thus marks a turning point in a career rich in fundamental evolutions. It embodies Cézanne's brief impressionist spell before the structural use of color at the end of the decade. X. R.

Édouard Manet
On the Beach

Oil on canvas
23½ × 28¾ in (59.5 × 73 cm)
Donated by Jean-Édouard Dubrujeaud, 1953

Manet spent the summer of 1873 at Berck in northern France, often painting on the beach. Here he depicts his wife, Suzanne, reading in the company of his brother Eugène Manet. The figures are closely framed, dominating the image (even if Eugène seems rather small compared to Suzanne), whereas the sea and sky are reduced to thin colored bands. The composition is articulated by the diagonal between the two protagonists. The high horizon, rhythmically dotted with boats like notes of music, recalls the composition of the Japanese prints that Manet fervently admired. Although Eugène is leaning on an elbow in a pose similar to the one he has in *The Luncheon on the Grass* (p. 81), painted ten years earlier, these two kinds of modern "conversation pieces" are otherwise very different. The artifices of the studio employed in the first are replaced here by outdoor work. As when Monet painted his wife Camille in Trouville in 1870, Manet captures the effects of light and the movement of the wind near the sea. In this sense, *On the Beach* is certainly one of the most truly impressionist paintings by this artist, who was close to the group but always refused to exhibit with them. However, beyond the depiction of bourgeois leisure, this painting—which belonged to the great couturier and collector Jacques Doucet—can also be seen as the evocation of an impossible dialogue between two people who are unaware of each other. S. Py.

Gustave Caillebotte
The Boating Party

Oil on canvas, 35¼ × 46 in. (0.90 × 1.17 m)
Purchased thanks to the exclusive support of LVMH, one
of the institution's most valuable patrons, 2022

Even before becoming a keen competitor and distinguishing himself at a number of regattas, Gustave Caillebotte had always been fond of boating, a popular pastime among Parisians since the mid-nineteenth century. A whole culture of leisure activities had sprung up in the suburbs, which the Impressionists, in search of modern motifs, quickly seized upon. In 1877-78, Caillebotte, whose family owned a country house in Yerres (Essonne), devoted an entire series of paintings and pastels to boaters on the river that ran alongside the estate. The painter would constantly vary his viewpoint in unexpected ways. Here, he positions himself inside the boat facing the rower, achieving an entirely novel effect of immersion and realism. Unlike Monet and Renoir, who painted landscapes from the riverbank, Caillebotte was concerned above all with the human figure—particularly male—depicting gestures and bodies under tension, and the fascinating outlines created by modern attire. His work exudes a sense of power, confidence, and freedom, combined with mystery and understatement: strangely still sporting a top hat, the figure—of unknown identity—turns his face away to avoid our gaze. The sketchy brushwork and light colors are those of plein air painting, which increasingly appealed to the artist. *The Boating Party* was among the paintings Caillebotte sent to the fourth impressionist exhibition in 1879. At the time, he was thought to be one of the most radical and provocative members of the whole group. P. P.

Félix Bracquemond
Round dish

Fine faience, decoration printed
and painted under glaze
Diam. 13¾ in. (35 cm)
Acquired in 2003

One of the earliest examples of Japanese influence on Western ceramics, the "Rousseau" service was named after the Parisian dealer and producer of pieces in porcelain and crystal, Eugène Rousseau, who in 1866 had commissioned the painter and engraver Félix Bracquemond to produce ornamentation for a faience table service. Bracquemond took his plant and animal motifs from the great Japanese masters of the woodblock print, notably Hokusai and Hiroshige, and etched these in almost haphazard fashion on twenty-four plates from which galvanoplastic reproductions were then made. These were used to make plates for the workers in the Creil and Montereau print works. Their instructions were to print the motifs—which would then be painted under glaze—to a ternary rhythm, combining one main motif and two others smaller in size, but with strictly identical proportions, in a pattern that would give an impression of randomness. The forms of the service were inspired by the eighteenth century, an influence underlined by the use of blue paint on the inner edges of the dishes and plates. Shown at the Paris Exposition Universelle in 1867, the "Rousseau" was soon all the rage. It remained popular until the end of the century, and available until the eve of World War II. Ph. T.

Paul Cézanne
The Bridge at Maincy

Oil on canvas
23 × 28½ in. (58.5 × 72.5 cm)
Acquired in 1955

With the help of a photograph, the spot has been identified as Maincy, near Melun (southwest of Paris). Cézanne executed this brightly colored painting when staying in the area in 1879. At the time he was increasingly asserting his independence from the impressionist movement, then striving for recognition. The use of color clearly partakes of the "constructive" approach that Cézanne developed in the late 1870s and early 1880s, and which remained central to his pictorial experiments through to his last works. Instead of conveying the quality of momentary light, as it did with the Impressionists, the use of distinct, visible brushstrokes—here they are long, thin, and parallel—became a way of structuring perception. Applied systematically, this technique did not create arid forms but, on the contrary, breathed new life into the subject, particularly evident here in the contrast between the foliage and the stability of the bridge and tree trunks. The space is rigorously structured while displaying the artist's freedom of handling. It captures the play of light and exudes real poetry. X. R.

Jean-Paul Laurens
The Excommunication of Robert the Pious

Oil on canvas
4 ft. 3¼ in. × 7 ft. 1¾ in. (1.30 × 2.18 m)
Acquired in 1875

Despite being known as "the Pious," the king of France, Robert II, risked the wrath of Pope Gregory V, who ruled that his love marriage to Bertha of Burgundy, his third cousin, was incestuous. Although they were threatened with excommunication, no pronouncement was actually ever made against them. So the episode painted by Laurens is largely a myth. But it enabled this republican, anticlerical, atheistic artist to paint a scene depicting the ideological battle closest to his heart—denouncing in large frescoes the Church's intolerance and its abuse of power down the centuries, just as the filmmaker D. W. Griffith was to do some forty years later. Laurens foreshadowed the art of the cinema by borrowing from Jean-Léon Gérôme his illusionist technique, the distant shot, and the art of taking advantage of empty space to convey the loneliness and terror of the accursed lovers, the tragic descendants of Titus and Berenice, just after the sentence is passed by the clergy leaving the hall. Facing the implacable candle knocked over and extinguished, signifying the darkness to which their souls are condemned, the frail scepter of temporal power has slipped. As the "painter of Act VI," Laurens is fond of depicting not the dramatic violence per se, but rather its still warm fingerprints, its parting echoes on the empty stage that has become a space in which it resonates. C. F.

Gustave Caillebotte
The Floor Planers

Oil on canvas
3 ft. 4¼ in. × 4 ft. 9¾ in. (1.02 × 1.47 m)
Gift of the artist's heirs, 1894

This was the picture that the painter and patron Gustave Caillebotte showed at his first impressionist exhibition in 1876. The artist chose to illustrate a scene from modern Parisian life. This depiction of workmen at their task is meticulously done, down to the description of the tools. Like Degas with his 1876 *Women Ironing*, Caillebotte dealt with a theme that was rarely broached in French painting but frequently evoked in the naturalist novel. Yet Zola attacked the handling of these *Floor Planers*, describing it as "bourgeois in its exactitude." Certainly, Caillebotte produced large numbers of preparatory studies for this composition so that nothing was left to chance. The torsos of the planers also remind us of the painter's classical training. However, the refusal to idealize the male nude, the play of the golden light, the foreshortened perspective, the low angle, and the almost random framing of the composition all add up to a profoundly innovative work. This painting was donated by the painter's family; it was not included in the extraordinary bequest to the State made by Caillebotte himself in 1894, a bequest that brought works by his friends Monet, Manet, Cézanne, Degas, Pissarro, and Sisley into French national collections. S. Py.

Edgar Degas
The Ballet Class

Oil on canvas
33½ × 29½ in. (85 × 75 cm)
Bequeathed by Comte Isaac de Camondo, 1911

A regular at the Paris opera house, Degas's search for modern subjects led him to start representing the ballet toward the very end of the 1860s. He soon began to focus on dancers exercising. Never satisfied, Degas reworked the composition of *The Ballet Class* between 1873 and 1876, also producing another version (called *The Dance Class*, held at the Metropolitan Museum of Art, New York). While the painting may give the impression of having been painted in the moment, it is in fact more a reconstruction combining various postures that would become leitmotivs throughout Degas's work, and a vector of his stylistic development for the rest of his career. The dancer standing at rest, her hands on her hips, and the dancer scratching her back—they display poses that he would use time and time again as he strove to capture the equilibrium and movement of the body with ever greater precision. The artist dwells on the small details—the watering can used to keep the parquet moist, earrings, ribbons—and uses his translucent paint to set off the highlights on the gauze of the dresses. The lack of concordance in the ensemble may mean that this work was conceived as a portrait of the ballet master Jules Perrot at work, the effect of immediacy being heightened by Degas's fore-shortened perspective. X. R.

Edgar Degas
In a Café or Absinthe

Oil on canvas
3 ft. 1¼ in. × 2 ft. 3 in. (92 × 68.5 cm)
Bequeathed by Comte Isaac de Camondo, 1911

"It is much better to draw what you no longer see except in your memory. You reproduce only what struck you, that is to say, what is necessary." This was how Degas explained his approach to the subject. When he represented two figures sitting at a table in La Nouvelle Athènes, the famous café that he frequented along with fellow artists living around Place Pigalle, he pared down the elements in the scene in order to heighten its impact. The composition places the faces at the edge of the picture—Marcellin Desboutin, the painter and engraver who worked with Degas in his printing experiments, is almost out of the frame—while the foreground is occupied by two geometrical forms, the tables, which seem to be levitating, and which create a sense of depth. As always, the scene was meticulously prepared in the studio (the other sitter was the actress Ellen Andrée). Placed close to the center, the glass of absinthe almost comes across as the main subject, and the likely cause of the drawn features of these two individuals who appear to be strangers to each other in spite of their physical proximity. With his free handling, Degas makes full use of the reflections in the mirrors, a favorite device, using it to disorient perspective although without going so far as to suggest that the two customers are alcoholics to any degree. X. R.

Jean-François Raffaëlli
The Family of Jean-le-Boîteux, Peasants of Plougasnou

Oil on canvas
6 ft. 3 in. × 5 ft. ¾ in. (1.91 × 1.54 m)
Acquired in 1910

The striking depiction of the blood coming to the face of the old peasant woman here epitomizes the naturalist obsession with illusionistic detail. The fixity of the old man's gaze staring out at us from the middle of the composition is almost unsettling. Initially part of a larger composition, this image of a modest if unusually named Breton family revealed a new artistic tendency at the Salon of 1877. It continued the realistic treatment of social themes characteristic of Courbet and Millet, but with an even more blunt, brutal style of representation. Raffaëlli is typical of the painters who achieved success with a freer use of the brush practiced by avant-garde contemporaries of Impressionism. His determination to capture the truth of the world around him suggests a possible comparison with Degas and earned him a place in the impressionist exhibitions of 1880 and 1881. When eventually excluded from the movement, Raffaëlli specialized in more modest paintings evoking the world of small trades. He vested painting with a moral mission and sought to make his art a political manifesto in favor of those left by the wayside. His theoretical writings question the notion of beauty in an industrial civilization. X. R.

Jules Bastien-Lepage
Haymaking

Oil on canvas
2 ft. 7½ in. × 6 ft. 4¾ in. (0.80 × 1.95 m)
Acquired in 1885

The illusion of exactitude in naturalistic painting is inseparable from the literary Naturalism that came to the fore in the 1870s, most famously in the novels of Émile Zola. The triumph of *Haymaking* at the Salon in 1878 made Bastien-Lepage, a former student of the very academic Alexandre Cabanel, the leading proponent of this new aesthetic, which offered a formal synthesis of the grand genre of history painting and the elliptical approach of Impressionism. In what, consequently, is a hybrid visual solution, the painting places realistic figures represented in great detail in a landscape of light colors with a deliberately flattened perspective. However, it was only at the artist's death, in 1884, that this painting was consecrated and the artist celebrated by official institutions, at a time when his style was being copied all over Europe. Photographic objectivity, then the ultimate in pictorial modernity, did not preclude symbolism: the couple seem to be confined in the field, which at once feeds and alienates, being a source both of life and suffering. More than work itself, the painter is interested in the workers' impossible attempts to find rest—note the clenched fist of the man, indicating that his sleep is without dreams. Here, Bastien-Lepage brings a fresh approach to a theme already handled by Millet. X. R.

Auguste Renoir
The Swing

Oil on canvas
3 ft. ¼ in. × 2 ft. 4¾ in. (92 × 73 cm)
Bequeathed by Gustave Caillebotte, 1894

Renoir painted *The Swing* during the summer of 1876. The scene is probably set in the garden of the house he rented in the Rue Cortot in Montmartre, then still a country neighborhood unaffected by the radical urban renovation work undertaken in Paris by Baron Haussmann. In *The Swing*, everything evokes the softness of a fine summer day: the play of sunlight through the trees, shimmering and flickering on the faces and fabrics, filling the composition with a constellation of light patches and blue-mauve shadows. A young woman—the model is a girl from Montmartre called Jeanne—stands motionless and lost in thought on the swing; two men in straw boaters seem to be in conversation while a little girl looks at Jeanne, with a group chatting in the background. Georges Rivière, a journalist friend of Renoir's, wrote enthusiastically of the painting: "What calm, what serenity in this painting! These are definitely people with nothing to do. ... You can feel the lack of any passion; these young folk are enjoying life, the beautiful weather, the morning sun passing through the foliage; they have no care for the rest of humanity! They are happy, these are the last words that come to the mind of anyone seeing this charming picture. None of them gave me more pleasure than this one." *The Swing* did indeed receive a great deal of attention at the third impressionist exhibition of 1877; the painting was shown there alongside the *Dance at Le Moulin de la Galette*. S. Py.

Auguste Renoir
Dance at Le Moulin de la Galette

Oil on canvas
4 ft. 3½ in. × 5 ft. 9 in. (1.31 × 1.75 m)
Bequeathed by Gustave Caillebotte, 1894

Dance at Le Moulin de la Galette depicts a well-known and popular *guinguette*, or café with music and dancing, its name coming from a windmill (*moulin*) on the Butte Montmartre, a short distance from Renoir's studio. The painting's dimensions and complex composition indicate an ambitious project to depict a modern, popular leisure scene, captured in the open air in the format of a history painting. The painting would have been done from life, with a few rapid brushstrokes and enough patches of color to set an object or character, but we know of at least one overall preparatory study. This work is a brilliant and poetic transcription of the animation of dancing, conversations, and exchanges of sometimes flirtatious glances. Renoir depicts a harmonious world, with the joyful atmosphere of the *fête galante* recalling Watteau's *The Embarkation for Cythera*, which Renoir often admired in the Louvre. *Dance at Le Moulin de la Galette* was one of the key works at the third impressionist exhibition of 1877. Twenty years later, it was hailed as a masterpiece when it was hung at the Musée du Luxembourg (the ancestor of the Musée d'Orsay), as part of the legacy of Renoir's friend Gustave Caillebotte. This painter and patron no doubt came into possession of the painting shortly after 1877. S. Py.

Camille Pissarro
Red Roofs, Corner of a Village, Winter

Oil on canvas
21¼ × 25½ in. (54 × 65 cm)
Bequeathed by Gustave Caillebotte, 1894

Between 1866 and 1883, Pissarro painted no fewer than three hundred pictures of Pontoise. He explored various aspects of this country village a few miles outside of Paris. Finding a title for his painting in 1877, the roofs of the houses with whitewashed walls and modern tiles introduce touches of orange-red in various places all over the composition, through the screen of bare trees in the foreground—Pissarro was fond of this procedure. The painter wrote that he wanted to capture a landscape that, with its "skeletal trees," passes from wild gaiety to melancholy. This "winter effect" seeks to render that passage, conveying mobile, changing nature through the seasons and light varia-tions. But instead of a fluid, nimble touch, here Pissarro prefers thick impasto and color (X-ray photography reveals that the landscape has been painted over an earlier composition). He thus obtained surface effects that recall a tapestry but which no doubt owed much to the dialogue he was having with Cézanne, who came to paint the same hillside. Exhibited at the third impressionist exhibition, the painting was largely ignored by the critics, as they saw all Pissarro's landscapes as puzzles. Only Zola hailed these "strikingly true-to-life nature spot[s]," having similar tastes to the painting's then owner, Caillebotte. S. Py.

Alfred Sisley
Snow at Louveciennes

Oil on canvas
24 × 19¾ in (61 × 50 cm)
Bequeathed by Comte Isaac de Camondo, 1911

The countryside in winter was a special favorite of Sisley's, for his quiet loner's temperament was more in tune with its mystery and silence than with the bright, sunny Mediterranean landscapes that Renoir adored. Like Monet, Sisley followed Courbet's lead by painting snowscapes. It was an appealing subject for the Impressionists because it allowed them to study variations in the light, and to play with the different shades on their palette. His fragmented brushstrokes placed tiny touches of color on the canvas, rather than a uniform white, and the ground is iridescent with bluish reflections. The winters Sisley spent in Louveciennes, Mar-ly-le-Roi, or Veneux-Nadon inspired him to paint numerous snow scenes. *Snow at Louveciennes* also illustrates the painter's work on perspective: a snow-covered road tails off into the background, and the one tiny character cuts a lonely figure in the midst of nature. The artist's sensitivity, expressed in these polished, delicate landscapes, where colors play together in discreet harmonies, may be explained by his British background, and the fact that Sisley had seen the works of Bonington, Constable, and Turner. Watercolor, a very popular medium in Britain, had helped to inject a certain freedom into painting. S. P.

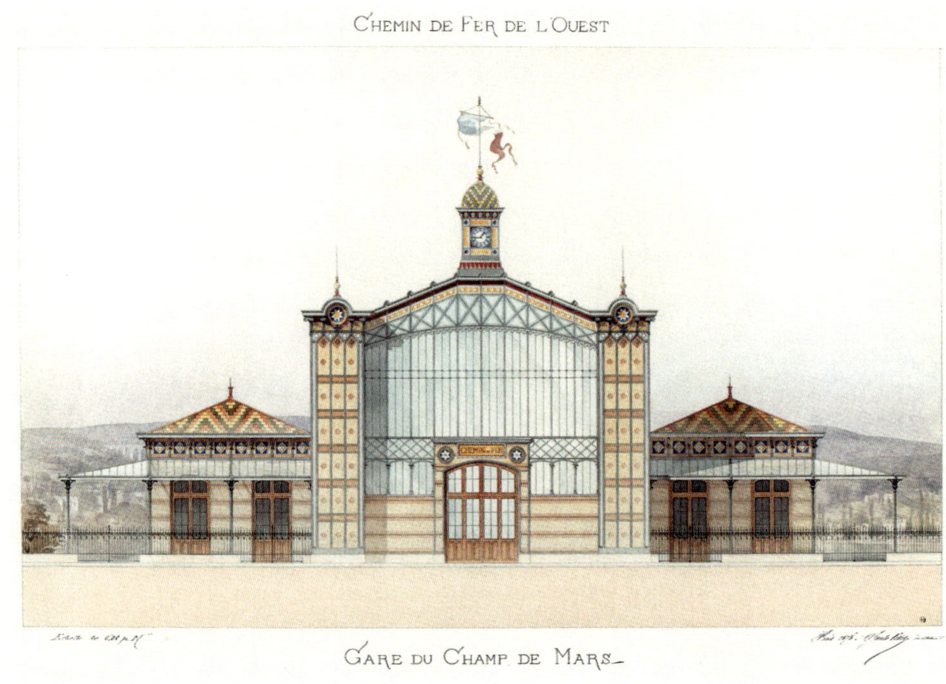

Juste Lisch
Main Façade of the Champ-de-Mars Station
of the Exposition Universelle of 1878

Pen, ink, and watercolor
2 ft. 2 in. × 3 ft. 2¾ in.
(66 × 98.3 cm)
Acquired in 2000

Following the Exposition Universelle of 1855 and the one of 1867, which glorified advances in the modern world, in 1878 Paris hosted this mammoth event for the third time. To cope with the expected influx of visitors, the Compagnie des Chemins de Fer de l'Ouest, which operated the railroad line, decided to build a new station for its terminus in a central location for the exhibition, for which it called upon the company's architect Juste Lisch. As a follower of Henri Labrouste, Lisch took a radical stance, overcoming any temptation to adopt a historicist approach. Ignoring the prestigious architecture of the military academy just southeast of Champ de Mars, he made visible use of modern industrial materials like iron, cast iron, and glass. Brick and glazed ceramics were used as the filler material for this metal structure, producing an attractively multicolored overall effect. Opened in March 1878, the station was in operation for just under twenty years. It was dismantled in 1897 when the line was extended as far as Les Invalides. The company decided to reassemble it for use as a workshop, and later a station. It stands there to this day, in a condition that is now a cause for concern. A. T.-B.

Claude Monet
The Gare Saint-Lazare

Oil on canvas
2 ft. 5½ in. × 3 ft. 5¼ in (0.75 × 1.05 m)
Bequeathed by Gustave Caillebotte, 1894

With the rise of the railroads, the station—a place of transition—characterized the turmoil of modern life, bearing witness to the industrialization of the city, the new glass and metal architecture, and the timely coincidence of the growth of rail links with the birth of plein-air painting. Monet directed his attention to Saint-Lazare railway station—trains ran from here to the Impressionists' favored locations in the Paris area and on the Normandy coast. Sensitive to the light in the open air, to the overhead space under the huge glass canopy, and to the play of billowing smoke blending with the clouds, which he turned into atmospheric effects, the painter composed these "urban landscapes." This "modern" subject matter received praise from Émile Zola as early as 1877, at the third impressionist exhibition, which featured eight views of the station by Monet (including this version, which is constructed with perfect symmetry). Zola described the "superb station interiors. One can hear the rumble of the trains surging forward, see the torrents of smoke winding through vast engine sheds. This is the painting of today: modern settings beautiful in their scope. Our artists must find the poetry of railway stations as their fathers found the poetry of forests and rivers." S. P.

René de Saint-Marceaux
Spirit Guarding the Secret of the Tomb

Marble
5 ft 6¼ in. × 3 ft. 1½ in. × 3 ft. 10¾ in.
(1.68 × 0.95 × 1.19 m)
Acquired in 1879

As proof of Saint-Marceaux's love of Italy, *Spirit Guarding the Secret of the Tomb* was executed following his second stay there, in the early 1870s. The sculptor deeply admired the Florentine Renaissance and Michelangelo. His *Spirit* is thus directly inspired by the male figures in the Sistine Chapel. The body is hunched over, imposing a twist in a way that is reminiscent of the compositions of that great Renaissance master. With remarkable simplicity of line and movement, Saint-Marceaux contrives to arrange the limbs in such a way as to obtain a circular motion. The character is wrapped round a funerary urn, in a defiant pose. Contrasting with the nude, the veil bil-lowing in the wind punctuates the volumes with shaded areas.

Such masterly composition, powerful expression, and broad conception earned the sculptor the medal of honor at the Salon of 1879. The image was popularized in engravings to such an extent that, during the Dreyfus affair, the work was spoofed to denounce the counterfeiter, the anti-Semitic officer behind the captain's wrongful conviction. In a cartoon entitled "Colonel Henry keeping the secret of the General Staff," we see an army man jealously protecting the urn of documents faked by the Army, in a pose similar to that of Saint-Marceaux's *Spirit*. É. P.

Gustave Doré
A Fate and Love

Patinated plaster
90½ × 59 × 59 in. (2.3 × 1.5 × 1.5 m)
Purchased in 2023

Hailed at a very young age as one of the finest draftsmen, caricaturists, and illustrators of the age, Gustave Doré was always set on winning acclaim as a complete artist. Exhibiting his first paintings at the 1851 Salon, he followed these with a significant number of large-sized works. Nothing if not ambitious, twenty years later Doré took up sculpture, and unveiled his *A Fate and Love* at the 1877 Salon.

While the theme of the inextricability of love and death is relatively classic, here the artist renews the relationship between two allegorical characters: the Parca, massive and austere, towers over an Eros shown as a beautiful winged adolescent. Originally, a string ran from one hand to the other, providing the key to the composition: at one end, it bent the bow with which Eros fires love into mortal hearts, before passing between the blades of the (broken) scissors with which the Fates sever the thread of life; it then continued to Eros's left hand and thence to that of Fate, before reaching a distaff on the ground that has also disappeared. Critics were impressed by the scope of this large sculpture and by the artist's ease with the new medium, but more generally, they criticized Doré for his insatiable thirst for fame, as if he could not be satisfied with the laurels he had already earned in the fields of drawing and painting. F. B.

Pierre Puvis de Chavannes
Young Girls by the Seaside

Oil on canvas
6 ft. 8¾ in. × 5 ft. ½ in (2.05 × 1.54 m)
Gift of Robert Gérard, 1970

This painting, praised by the critics at the Salon of 1879, was exhibited by Puvis de Chavannes on a number of occasions. He held it to be one of his best works, selling the canvas for a tidy sum to Boivin, a collector who also wanted to purchase his *Poor Fisherman* (p. 164). *Young Girls by the Seaside* returns to the classical theme of women bathing; there is no element linking the scene to any particular time or place. Gradually, through his intensive preparatory work, Puvis whittled away the accessory, the detail, and the anecdotal, ending up with a monumental work with great rhythm. The artist described it in 1879 as a "decorative panel." Puvis had by then made a name for himself as the leading decor-ator of public monuments in Amiens, Poitiers, and Marseille, and in 1878 had successfully exhi-bited *The Childhood of St. Geneviève* for the Pantheon. *Young Girls* develops the decorative grammar being devised by Puvis since the late 1860s, which was admired by the new gener-ations, from Seurat to Picasso and by Gauguin and the Nabis: legible forms, light colors, and flatness recalling the fresco, stacking of planes so as to respect the flatness of the wall, simplifi-cation and synthesis. The artist thus composed a new, peaceful, and solemn Arcadia, to which, like a figure of melancholy, the girl leaning on her arm on the left adds an elegiac note. S. Py.

Édouard Manet
Portrait of Irma Brunner or Woman in a Black Hat or The Woman from Vienna

Pastel on canvas on stretcher
21 × 17¼ in.
(53.5 × 44.1 cm)
Bequeathed by Comte Isaac de Camondo, 1911

Manet had already ventured into pastel in 1874, drawing a small portrait of his wife reclining on a blue sofa (*Portrait de Madame Édouard Manet sur un canapé bleu*, Musée d'Orsay), but he only took the medium up seriously between 1879 and 1882. The difficulty the artist had in standing for any length of time due to syphilis is often cited as the reason for Manet's turning to the technique, since it allowed him to work more quickly than in slow-drying oil. Manet did not adopt the medium solely for reasons of ease or necessity, however. He wanted above all to follow the trail blazed by Edgar Degas and Eva Gonzalès, who excelled in the art.

Manet chiefly employed pastel in a series of busts of young women from high society or the *demi-monde*, in which he sought less to capture the psychology of the sitter than to stylize woman. The socialite Irma Brunner, although originally from Vienna, here embodies the archetype of the "Parisienne." With a singular economy of means and in a limited range of hues, Manet boldly sketches out her profile in black pastel on a pearl gray ground, bringing out the velvety texture of her snowy complexion enhanced by the bright fleck of red of her lips that matches her pink attire. The peachy feel of pastel here mimics that of face powders, which were often made from similar pigments. Idealizing his model's beauty, Manet transfigures Irma Brunner into the epitome of 1880s elegance.

C. C.-P.

Jean-Jacques Henner
Jesus in the Tomb

Oil on canvas
2 ft. 4 in. × 6 ft. 6 in. (0.71 × 1.98 m)
Acquired in 1879

The tendency to humanize the figure of Christ was not new to the nineteenth century, but in Third Republic France it acquired a particular significance within a general, fundamental questioning of religious beliefs. For a number of republicans who inclined to a secular approach, the Catholic religion was associated with an obscurantism that helped prop up the tyrannical power of the monarchy. They referred to Ernest Renan's *Vie de Jésus* (*Life of Jesus*), published in 1863, which scandalized the clergy by presenting the Son of God as a simple historical figure. This contestation of religious ideas, which on occasion went hand in hand with new forms of mysticism, stimulated a number of artists who were eager to take on the grand genre of history painting—also thrown into crisis by the nineteenth century. For the *Jesus in the Tomb* that he presented at the Salon of 1879, Henner, who enjoyed success as a society portraitist, reprised the formula used by Édouard Manet fifteen years earlier, representing Christ as the flattest, most banally truthful human figure. While there is no denying the references to such illustrious predecessors as Caravaggio (1573–1610), notably in the use of chiaroscuro to convey the mysteries of the faith, the divine body here is reduced to that of a simple mortal. However, the long, horizontal format does endow this Jesus with a certain dignity as well as a pacified humanity, certainly more so than Léon Bonnat's *Job*, produced the following year, which adopted the same extreme realism to depict another biblical figure. X. R.

Édouard Manet
The Spear of Asparagus

Oil on canvas
6½ × 8½ in. (16 × 21 cm)
Gift of Sam Salz, 1959

This spear of asparagus was a complement to the more copious *Bunch of Asparagus*, now held at the Wallraf-Richartz Museum in Cologne. Manet sent this little painting to Charles Ephrussi, the great collector of impressionist paintings, and the critic who inspired a character in Marcel Proust, to thank him for paying handsomely for the *Bunch*. "Your bunch was one short," he wrote in his accompanying note. A similar charm and wit are evident in the painting itself, where, allusive and confident like the "M" serving as his signature, Manet's brush places the asparagus spear in a precarious balance on the marble of the table. In spite of the modesty of the subject and the speed of execution, the painter once again explores the subtle variation of light tones on light tones, as if to echo Proust's "rapture" at the "asparagus tinged with ultramarine and pink which shaded off from their heads, finely stippled in mauve and azure, through a series of imperceptible gradations to their white feet." This is one of a series of late still lifes from the early 1880s, when Manet painted fruit, flowers, and vegetables in isolation or against a neutral ground, combining brio of execution and economy of means, in contrast to the more subtle and complex compositions of the 1860s. With *The Spear of Asparagus*, this spareness attains a degree of simplicity that makes this little picture a minor miracle. S. Py.

Antonin Mercié
David

Bronze
6 ft. ½ in. × 2 ft. 6¼ in. × 2 ft. 8¾ in.
(1.84 × 0.77 × 0.83 m)
Acquired in 1872

After the defeat by Prussia in 1870, French society was overcome with a feeling of humiliation and thirst for revenge. In such a context, this *David* could be taken to indicate the promise that France would one day vanquish the German Goliath, just as the young Israelite shepherd slew the giant with a simple sling. Not surprisingly, the sculpture was a huge success. The plaster cast was made in Rome, while the young artist was still completing his training—he was awarded the Légion d'Honneur, followed by a State commission for the bronze in 1872. The work was placed outside the Musée du Luxembourg, which was dedicated to living artists, in 1874. Its image was much reproduced in the illustrated journals, and was so popular that a small-format edition was produced by the bronze-caster Barbedienne.

Mercié belonged to a young generation of French sculptors working at the turn of the 1870s to bring greater vibrancy to the figures they produced within the classical parameters of academic teaching. For this union of refined composition and lively modeling, he looked to the great sculptures of Renaissance Florence—hence the fine, ample curves of the arm extended by the movement of the sword, the bent leg, and the grace of this David, which encourages viewers to walk around it and appreciate the different planes. Mercié charted an original course between modern Classicism and explicit Realism. C. C.

Auguste Rodin
The Age of Bronze

Bronze
5 ft. 10 in. × 1 ft. 11¼ in. × 2 ft. ¼ in.
(1.78 × 0.59 × 0.61 m)
Acquired in 1880

Rodin, who could not abide academic poses, and who set to work on executing a life-size nude, sent home his professional sitters and had the young soldier, Auguste Neyt, model for it. Served by his fine anatomy, and relying heavily upon the observation of the nudes of antiquity and of Michelangelo, the pose was chosen for its visual qualities rather than after some predefined subject. The relaxed movement of the hips contrasts with the tense upper body, one arm gripping the hair and the other holding what might have been a spear. It was actually untitled when exhibited at the Cercle Artistique in Brussels in 1877. After thinking up the name *Le Vaincu* (The Defeated Man), with reference to the defeat of France in 1870, Rodin finally called it *The Age of Bronze*, depicting "one of the early inhabitants of our world, physically flawless, but in the childhood of understanding, and beginning to awaken to the meaning of the world." In Brussels, then at the Salon of 1887, the critics, thrown by this extremely accurate nude, began to hint that maybe it was a cast from life, i.e. taken directly from a human body. Rodin was hurt by this scandal, which damaged his reputation; however, a letter signed by other artists removed all doubt and enabled the plaster to be purchased by the State in 1880, after which it was cast in bronze. That same year, Rodin received an official commission for *The Gates of Hell* (p. 160), which really launched his career. O. F.

Edward Burne-Jones
The Wheel of Fortune

Oil on canvas
6 ft. 6¾ in. × 3 ft. 3¼ in. (2.00 × 1.00 m)
Acquired in 1980

Illustrating the precariousness of human destinies, a slave, a king, and a poet are dragged along by a wheel, which is turned by a young woman looking down at them. The poet, looking desperate, is the first to sink, against a background of destruction. Burne-Jones wrote of his *Wheel of Fortune*: "We each take our turn on it, and are broken upon it." Of the six versions he did of this subject, a traditional one since the Middle Ages, this was the largest and his favorite. Between 1875 and 1883, he worked on this painting, which shows sure workmanship and numerous references, such as in the male nudes with their debt to Michelangelo, who—for Burne-Jones—was an "immeasurable" master.

From him he borrows the sculptural handling of the figures, while the cold colors and metallic light refer back to Italian mannerism and complete the process of shaking the work free of any reference to reality. With *The Wheel of Fortune*, the Pre-Raphaelites' desire to found an art of the ideal, the imagination, and the symbol, drawing from a reviving, largely mythicized medieval tradition, here finds one of its finest achievements. The painting, summing up Burne-Jones's "art of culture, of reflection, of intellectual luxury," as the novelist Henry James puts it so beautifully, achieved instant fame in 1883, despite the fact that Puvis de Chavannes failed to put it on show in Paris in 1892. S. Py.

Gustave Moreau
Galatea

Oil on wood
33½ × 26 in. (85.5 × 66 cm)
Acquired in 1997 with the help of M. Philippe Meyer and
Japanese sponsorship coordinated by the *Nikkei* daily
newspaper and the collaboration of the Fonds du Patrimoine

"I am burning … and it leaves you cold, inhuman Galatea," cried Polyphemus in the story from Ovid's *Metamorphoses* that inspired this painting. Moreau's painting shows the Cyclops, a rejected suitor, contemplating the unmoved nymph shortly before he kills Acis out of jealousy. Galatea basks in the glory of her nudity, offering it to the gaze while refusing herself to Polyphemus. Moreau brings out the whiteness of her skin, the Leonardo-like harmony of her curves, and the sensual flow of her blonde hair. The grotto and its extraordinary vegetation—the artist made careful studies at the Muséum d'Histoire Naturelle—form a rich setting for Galatea's stunning beauty. This is the first painting by Moreau to feature this nymph, a new addition to the *femmes fatales*—Salome, Delilah, Messalina—who already haunted his work. In this masterpiece, which was acclaimed at the Salon of 1880, Moreau once again demonstrated his principle of "necessary richness." The play on varied textures, heightened by the smooth surface of the wood, and the extravagant accumulation of plants both terrestrial and marine (some, simple accumulations of color, others chiseled like jewels) add to the mystery and emotional power of this refined but implacable vision of a suffering lover spurned by inaccessible beauty. S. Py.

Auguste Rodin
The Gates of Hell

Plaster
20 ft. 10 in. × 13 ft. 1½ in. × 3 ft. 1 in.
(6.35 × 4.00 × 0.94 m)
Acquired in 1880

Before the construction of the Gare d'Orsay (today's Musée d'Orsay) in 1900, the site was occupied by the Cour des Comptes (the State audit body). When this burned down in 1871, plans were made to replace it with a museum of decorative arts, and in 1880 the State commissioned Rodin to create a monumental doorway representing Dante's *Divine Comedy*. By the time the artist had come up with a first version that satisfied him, which was not until three years later, the museum project had been shelved. For Rodin, this doorway without a destination turned into a kind of creative storehouse whose groups and figures began to acquire independent existences (*The Thinker*, *The Kiss*, etc.). *The Gates of Hell* became emblematic—for some, of Rodin's untrammeled creative genius; for others, of his inability to complete a project. An eminently symbolist work, this high-relief piece gives free rein to the vehemence and expressive power of the human body within an indeterminate space whose contours are broken up by the strong play of shadow and light. At the top, the group of three *Shades* are in fact the same figure with one arm amputated, repeated three times—an extremely modern device. On the pier, *The Thinker* (Dante himself) perches over the abyss. On the right-hand door we recognize *Ugolino*; on the left-hand door, *Paolo and Francesca*. The convulsive postures convey despair, grief, and accursedness, while the proliferation of forms over the structure is such that they sometimes seem to replace the architectural elements. C. C.

Mihály Munkácsy
Christ before Pilate

Oil on canvas
2 ft. 11¼ in. × 3 ft. 9¾ in. (0.89 × 1.16 m)
Acquired in 1979

Christ before Pilate by the Hungarian Munkácsy caused a sensation in Paris in 1881. In *Bel Ami* (1885), we may recall, Guy de Maupassant's narrator speaks of critics acclaiming it as "the most amazing masterpiece of the century." Over 19 feet (6 m) wide, the work was truly spectacular, a real *machine*. The version held at the Musée d'Orsay is one of the preparatory studies, and differs in a number of ways from the finished painting. Here, the painter shows Christ, his hands tied (behind, and not in front of him as they are in the definitive work), being brought before the governor Pontius Pilate. Both are dressed in white, and stand out against the Sanhedrin assembly and the crowd, where the painter runs through a great range of human passions, from accusatory vehemence to com-passion for the man about to be crucified. Following the trend established by Ernest Renan in his 1863 book, *Vie de Jésus* (*Life of Jesus*), Munkácsy emphasizes Christ's humanity—indeed, Renan actually thanked the artist for capturing his description in paint. More generally, Munkácsy's work was part of a movement aiming to reinvigorate religious painting by focusing on historical or ethnographic truth and dramatizing feelings. He also anticipates the cinema of the early twentieth century, right down to the exhibition of the large version, which went on a world tour and was shown in darkened rooms. Visitors thus had the impression that this tragedy of a man's condemnation by the crowd was taking place before their own eyes. S. Py.

Edgar Degas
The Little Fourteen-Year-Old Dancer

Patinated bronze, tulle skirt, satin ribbon,
and wooden base
3 ft. 2½ in. × 1ft. 2 in. × 9½ in. (98 × 35 × 24 cm)
Acquired through the generosity of the artist's
heirs and the Hébrards in 1931

On Degas's death in 1917, his studio was found to contain a hundred and fifty wax or clay sculptures. During the artist's lifetime, these figures had remained virtually unknown to the general public, with the exception of *The Fourteen-Year-Old Dancer*, which Degas put on show at the 1881 impressionist exhibition. In lifelike colors, with real hair, wearing a ballet skirt and real slippers, she is an example of hyperrealism and verism taken to extremes. Presented in a display case like some museum specimen, the statue reveals Degas almost as an anthropologist or a Naturalist. The critics had no doubt, and the work was violently accused of depicting the little girl in a bestial way; she was compared to a monkey or an Aztec; she was found to have a face "in which all the vices leave the imprint of their detestable promises, the mark of a particularly depraved character."

Thus, with this warts-and-all, almost scientific depiction of the society of his day, Degas took Realism, which was otherwise so fashionable, to its logical conclusion. The bronze version that was made after his death, of which the Musée d'Orsay statuette is a copy, sought as far as possible to preserve the characteristics of the wax one. The glass cage is the one element that Degas himself wanted, asserting the *Dancer*'s status as an artwork. É. P.

Camille Pissarro
The Shepherdess or Young Peasant Girl with a Stick

Oil on canvas
32 × 25½ in. (81 × 64.8 cm)
Bequeathed by Comte Isaac de Camondo, 1911

The Shepherdess marks a turning point in Pissarro's career, which had hitherto been dominated by landscape. In the early 1880s he started making paintings of rural figures. Eight of his works at the 1882 impressionist exhibition showed men and women at work or, like this young shepherdess playing with a stick, resting. At the time, the artist was living at L'Hermitage, in the countryside near Pontoise, and got the local peasant girls to pose for him. However, for all the strength of his political opinions, he did not try to describe—let alone denounce—a specific social and geographical situation. He took what was a favorite natu-

ralist subject, but without a hint of realism, narrative, or social pathos. Ignoring the rules of perspective and anatomy, Pissarro aimed for simplification and the synthesis of forms, rather like Millet, although he criticized the latter's biblical overtones. Ultimately, Pissarro's dreaming shepherdess does not seem to belong to the real world so much as to a harmonious society where the harshness of working life does not exist—a place that perhaps resembles the utopias of the anarchists, with whom the painter sympathized. This monumental and gracious *Shepherdess* is one of the artist's most sensitive attempts at figure painting. S. Py.

Pierre Puvis de Chavannes
The Poor Fisherman

Oil on canvas
5 ft. 1¼ in. × 6 ft. 3¾ in. (1.56 × 1.93 m)
Acquired in 1887

The Poor Fisherman has the power of an artistic manifesto, and marks a turning point. Exhibited at the Salon in 1881, it met with a mixed reaction. It offers a response to the then fashionable Naturalism by taking up one of that movement's favorite themes: poverty. Puvis had been struck by the wretched condition of the people he observed at Saint-Valéry-sur-Somme, which is no doubt where he began work on this painting in 1879. The artist depicts a fisherman and his two children (the elder daughter has to look after the infant, the mother having died), dressed in torn, earthy rags. The context, however, remains vague. Puvis rejected the realism of the day: "More and more nowadays the atmosphere is hostile to imaginative conceptions. Photography and sewing machines are the true expression of our times. This is not far from a total eclipse of all personal and poetic aspiration," he wrote. The "vision of poverty" he had painted was, he claimed, "taken only from myself." Not that this excludes a debt to Millet. The colors, composition, and rhythm are carefully designed to serve the expression. This work's economy of means and synthetic qualities make it a masterpiece, and an extremely influential one—we need only think of Signac, Seurat, the Nabis and the young Picasso. This was also the first painting by Puvis to be acquired by the State. S. Py.

Léon Lhermitte
Paying the Harvesters

Oil on canvas
7 ft. ½ in. × 8 ft. 11 in. (2.15 × 2.72 m)
Acquired in 1882

Lhermitte hailed from a farming area north of Paris, and was a worthy representative of artists from humble backgrounds who gradually climbed the ladder to fame on the basis of their talent. His attraction to peasant scenes is deeply rooted in his attachment to a region that he only left at the age of twenty, to go to Paris. As Courbet did, he used some farm laborers from his home village to pose for *Paying the Harvesters*. The picture was purchased by the State for the Musée du Luxembourg at the Salon of 1882, and numbered among those contemporary icons that met with great popular success—so much so that, as with Millet's *Angelus* (p. 69), many reproductions were made of it. In the wake of Bastien-Lepage's *Haymaking*

(p. 143), Lhermitte returns to the subject of resting from work in a naturalist vein. The more complex composition, following the model of history painting, does touch on other themes, though; the ages of man are embodied symbolically by a babe at the breast and the large scythe in the foreground, its glinting blade producing a photographic effect. The truth of everyday life is also evoked in the background, with the paying of the harvesters as described in the picture's title. So the militant thrust of this staged scene was not obvious at a time when the new republican regime was celebrating the honesty of its people—here duly rewarded for their toils. X. R.

Christofle & Cie, Émile Reiber
Teapot

Silver-plated metal, ivory
5 × 9¾ in. (12.8 × 24.8 cm)
Acquired in 1985

This zoomorphic teapot was designed by Émile Reiber after a Japanese bronze in the collection of Henri Cernuschi, a rich Italian banker who had settled in Paris and built up a huge collection of art from the Far East. It shows how ready designers were toward the end of the century to take on surprising Japanese subjects, and how humorously they could do so. Reiber discovered Japanese art in the 1860s and was fascinated by the Cernuschi collection of Japanese bronzes, which he drew and published in *Le Premier Volume des albums de Reiber* (The First Volume of Reiber's Albums) in 1877.

As head of the composition and design workshop at Christofle, he particularly remembered the smooth, ovoid forms of the perfume burners, observing that "*Familiar subjects* taken directly from Nature … seem destined, in the future, to contribute mainly to the ornamentation and gaiety of the home. This will be the way of a true 'popular art' whose main characteristics would be *simplicity*, *naivety*, and *freedom* of execution." The teapot here is at some remove from this ideal vision. It is a luxury object and a very rare model in Christofle's output. Y. B.

François Gauzi
Lili Grenier dressed in Japanese costume

Albumen print
7 × 5 in. (18 × 12.9 cm)
Pre-emptive purchase at auction, 2022

Aged just sixteen, Noémi Amélie Sans, known as Lili Grenier, sat as a model for the princess and artist, Mathilde Bonaparte. By twenty-two, she was posing for Fernand Cormon, a painter whose free private studio in Montmartre catered to Vincent van Gogh, Émile Bernard, Louis Anquetin, and Henri de Toulouse-Lautrec. Edgar Degas asked her to model for one of his women in the bathtub, while sculptor Jules Desbois created busts and medallions of her. At the age of thirty, she began working for the painter and lithographer Albert de Belleroche, and became his lover.

A professional model and muse of bohemian Paris, Lili Grenier was the toast of high society, charming contemporaries with her imagination, her outspokenness, and her unconventional love life. With a later partner, the painter Albert Grenier, she organized fancy-dress parties and *tableaux vivants* for friends and acquaintances. A fellow student in Toulouse of Grenier and Lautrec, the painter François Gauzi took photographs of her wearing a kimono, which Lautrec used to create his portrait of her.

For as long as she lived, Lili Grenier collected photographs—studio portraits, snapshots of her get-togethers, and studies in art studios. She arranged the pictures in albums whose sole subject is herself. Recording memorable encounters and preserving memories of happy days, perhaps they were also meant to leave some durable trace of her fleeting existence. With these photographs, Lili Grenier composed the story of a life lived in the first person feminine singular. M. R.

Fanny Brate
Konstvänner [Art Friends]

Oil on canvas
45 × 67¾ in. (1.15 × 1.72 m)
Purchased with a donation from the Meyer Louis-Dreyfus Fund
for the development of the foreign artists' collections, 2022

Deep in the Swedish countryside, some women and children watch a young female painter seated at her easel; a parasol protects her from the bright sunlight bathing the summer landscape she is busy sketching on the canvas. Barefooted, wearing worn-out clothes, the little villagers surrounding her seem intrigued by the sight of this elegant woman focused on her work.

Fanny Brate, then aged 24 (and not yet married: the painting is signed with her maiden name, Fanny Ekbom), depicts a scene she witnessed during one of the summer camps organized around Stockholm by the Royal Swedish Academy of Fine Arts, where she was a student.

There, she and her fellow female artists not only had the opportunity to acquire a solid artistic education —in the Academy's "women's department", accessible to them—, but were also permitted to practice plein air painting during excursions together. Carefully composed (all eyes are focused on the painter—or her paint box—as are the diagonals formed by the path, the clouds, and the low stone wall), this large painting was actually executed in the studio. Nonetheless, it skillfully captures the effects of light and open air the artist would have studied on those outings, rendered here in a style that is both naturalistic and descriptive.

Painted with affection and humor, "Art Friends" would launch the artist's career. In May 1885, the painting won first prize at the exhibition of the Royal Swedish Academy of Fine Arts, as well as—a supreme accolade—a King's Medal; it also earned the fledgling painter the epithet, "best of all." A. R.

Paul Cézanne
The Flowerpots

Watercolor over graphite
9¼ × 12 in. (23.5 × 30.7 cm)
Bequeathed by Comte Isaac de Camondo, 1911

Cézanne spent several winters in the 1880s at Le Jas de Bouffan, the family property in Aix-en-Provence. There he converted one of the greenhouses in the grounds into a studio where he worked when it was cold outside. This watercolor was the result of direct observation of this environment: ten pots of geraniums had been put inside on a tray to protect these decorative Mediterranean plants during the cold season. Their appearance, with fairly tall stems and few leaves, indicates that Cézanne painted them toward the end of winter. The light coming from the left is balanced by pale touches of blue wash evoking shadows, which grow more and more dense toward the right of the drawing, further from the light source. This is a discreet but effective way of capturing the qualities of Provençal light on a winter afternoon. The arrangement of the interior is very much under control. The flowerpots are seen frontally, and a sense of depth results from their staggered arrangement. The leaves and flowers intertwine in a way that is both lyrical and natural. This mature work gives an idea of the role played by the support, and of the fluid color of the palette he used, showing Cézanne's union of formal and expressive ideas. I. J.

Georges Seurat
The Veil

Conté pencil on laid paper
12¼ × 9¾ in. (31.1 × 24.5 cm)
Acceptance in lieu, 1982

Seurat attended the École des Beaux-Arts in Paris from 1878 to 1879 and then, after a year of military service in Brest, returned to the capital in 1880. The years leading up to *A Sunday Afternoon on La Grande Jatte* (1884, Art Institute of Chicago) are best known for his black-and-white drawings in Conté pencil on laid paper, which he often had specially made. These works represent social types and forms rather than distinct individuals. The rendering of the subject is outstanding in terms of both technique and economy. Form is simplified in the extreme, and the composition organized by the variations in density of gray and black.

The modernity and abstraction of the subject (encouraging the beholder's imagination), the hieratic quality of the figure, and the deep, velvety black, all create a mysterious atmosphere which brings to mind Odilon Redon's style. The drawing evokes the figure of a young woman sitting in a coach with the hood down, as indicated by the black mass around her bust—one of the many *flâneurs* to be found making their way in leisurely fashion along the city's new boulevards. The veil suggests a desire for anonymity and gives the beholder the sensation of a chance meeting with a stranger. I. J.

Pierre Puvis de Chavannes
Woman at Her Toilet or La Toilette

Oil on canvas
29½ × 24¾ in. (75 × 63 cm)
Gift of the Société des Amis du Louvre, 1932

With this painting, Puvis de Chavannes joins a rich artistic tradition in which goddesses, nymphs, and heroines like Venus, Diana, or Esther afford us a look at the female nude, like an indiscreet peek at some intimate ritual, or preparations before meeting a lover. But, unlike Millet or Corot, Puvis does not quote some fable, nor does he transcribe a scene from modern life the way Degas does. The young woman and her maid are here placed in a timeless interior, even though the matt finish and the detail of the basket of pears—still lifes are extremely rare in Puvis's work—evoke ancient mural painting. The artist has carefully arranged the choreography of the bodies along the diagonals of the compo-sition, deliberately going off the edge of the pic-ture. As a wall painter, Puvis is suggesting here a deployment of the motif beyond the limits of the easel painting. In the manner of Ingres, of whom we are reminded through the treat-ment of the seated woman's neck and bust, the artist subjects the anatomy of his boneless bo-dies and the movement of the hair to the play of line. Thus, in this silent scene in which, absorb-ed in their daydreams, the protagonists seem each to be in a world of their own, the domi-nant rhythm is calm and serene, ending in this radical simplification and monumentality that we later find, for example, in the large nudes of Picasso, who was a keen admirer of Puvis. S. Py.

Oil on canvas
5 ft 10¾ in. × 2 ft. 11½ in. (1.80 × 0.90 m)
Acquired in 1979
Oil on canvas
5 ft 10¾ in. × 2 ft. 11½ in. (1.80 × 0.90 m)
Acceptance in lieu, 1978

Auguste Renoir
Country Dance
City Dance

In the same year, 1883, Renoir painted three dances: *Dance at Bougival* (Museum of Fine Arts, Boston), and the two owned by the Musée d'Orsay. The journalist Paul Lhote dances first on the arm of Renoir's companion, Aline Charigot, and then with Suzanne Valadon, who wears an elegant white silk evening gown. The theme of the contrast between the city and the country (or rather the suburbs, as Renoir gave *Country Dance* the title *Dancers (Bougival)* in 1883), between a smart salon and the popular dance hall, between an interior and an open-air scene, also comes with an opposition between cool colors and warm tones, restraint and high spirits, artifice and nature, and even winter and summer (titles sometimes used for the paintings on show). So, as their format suggests, these two *Dances* function as a decorative pair. During the artist's lifetime, except in 1912, they were always exhibited together, and they hung in the Paris apartment of the Impressionists' art dealer, Paul Durand-Ruel. While this is Renoir's last look at a subject that had inspired him to paint *Dance at Le Moulin de la Galette* (p. 145), here he gives it a novel treatment, placing the emphasis on line and drawing, and looking for the grandeur and simplicity that so struck him in the early 1880s, having seen the painting of Raphael and ancient art in Italy. S. Py.

Claude Monet
Studies of a Figure Outdoors:
Woman with a Parasol, Facing Right
Woman with a Parasol, Facing Left

Oil on canvas
4 ft. 3¼ in. × 2 ft. 11¼ in. (1.30 × 0.89 m)
Oil on canvas
4 ft. 3½ in. × 2 ft. 11 in. (1.31 × 0.88 m)
Gifts of Michel Monet, 1927

Monet gradually abandoned the portrait to focus all his attention on nature. Suddenly, in 1886, and for practically the last time, he returned to inserting a human figure in the landscape in two matching canvases. Treating the subject matter as a landscape artist and Impressionist, the artist transposes the instant character of the scene that comes into his view on some raised ground at Giverny. Suzanne, the third daughter of Alice Hoschedé, and his future stepdaughter, inspired him to paint two versions of the *Woman with a Parasol*, which (significantly) he subtitled *Study of a Figure Outdoors*. The girl is moving forward, stand-ing out in the light in the open air, against the open sky. The painter has barely sketched in the model's features, going as far as to depersonalize the model depicted, focusing instead on painting the play of light and shade obtained with the parasol and the sheath of light around the figure—the flapping scarf, the swirl of the dress, and the partly flattened grasses indicate the blowing wind, while the silhouette moves and the clouds respond. "I am working … on some new attempts, figures in the open air as I understand them, done like landscapes. It is an old dream that still bothers me." S. P.

Paul Signac
Rue Vercingétorix

Conté pencil on paper
8½ × 12¼ in. (21.7 × 31 cm)
Gift of Mme Françoise Cachin in memory
of Ginette Signac (her mother), 1996

Signac, an enthusiastic member of the neo-impressionist group and friend of Seurat, whom he first met in 1884, was renowned as a fine colorist. Like Seurat, he produced some early drawings in black and white. The annotation at the bottom of the sheet, "Drawing for *Les Sœurs Vatard* by J. K. H.," references the connection between the scene shown here and the novel published by J. K. Huysmans in 1879. Rue Vercingétorix was a location in one of the new arrondissements of Paris, the fourteenth, where countryside and new industry met. The street is not named in the novel, but many of its scenes take place in nearby Rue Vandamme. Huysmans describes the embankment of the Western railway, "the large drag of black buildings," and "the lamentable distress of the old suburbs." The angular, empty perspective expresses the sadness of these landscapes on the edge of the city. A puff of smoke suggests the din of a passing train, while a solitary individual makes off into the distance. Signac uses a Conté pencil, drier than the type chosen by Seurat, to express the desolate scene with great effectiveness. I. J.

Edgar Degas
Women Ironing

Oil on canvas
30 × 32 in. (76 × 81.5 cm)
Bequeathed by Comte Isaac de Camondo, 1911

The theme of women ironing first appeared in Degas's work in the early 1870s and, like most of his themes, he repeated it—so much so that Zola would recognize his debt to the painter for his 1876 novel *L'Assommoir*, which describes an ironing workshop and its unhealthy atmosphere. It would appear that these were the first working women to interest the artist, who went on to depict prostitutes and singers at café-concerts, striving to capture their physical type in line with the Darwinist ideas then underlying social thought. *Women Ironing* at the Musée d'Orsay is emblematic of the artist's technique in the mid-1880s, notably as regards the equilibrium of the composition and the decorative,

almost square format which adds grandeur to this otherwise banal scene of modern life. While the artist catches the figure on the left yawning as she leans on a bottle, in what is a particularly vulgar pose, he also renders the women's complexions with great meticulousness and conveys the pressure exerted on the linen by the woman on the right, who sums up the harsh working conditions endured by the two ironing women. Although never militant, Degas aimed to inscribe an unvarnished genre scene painted on crude canvas within the great pictorial tradition, simply by dint of novel formal solutions. X. R.

Jean-Baptiste Baujault
Young Gaul
or "Au gui l'an neuf"

Marble
7 ft. 11¼ in. × 1 ft. 8¾ in × 1 ft. 9½ in.
(2.42 × 0.53 × 0.55 m)
Acquired in 1875

The fashion for Gaulish themes took off under the Second Empire, encouraged by Napoleon III himself. The emperor ordered excavation at the purported site of the battle of Alesia, wrote a *History of Julius Caesar* and founded the Musée des Antiquités Nationales. This taste continued after 1870 both in sculpture and in painting. Among the many books from which artists could take inspiration were *The Gallic Wars* by Julius Caesar and the *Histoire de France* (History of France) by Henri Martin.

Baujault, who had already produced a sculpture of a *Gaul*, combined the popular custom of young children crying out at the doors of houses, "Au gui l'an neuf" (in reference to the New Year custom of kissing under the mistletoe—*gui* in French), with the druidic practice of picking mistletoe from oaks on the winter solstice. The brochure for the Salon of 1875 explained this unusual iconography: "The first person to announce the new mistletoe was considered by the Druids to be favored by the gods. He thereby won the right to join their order."

Baujault was not trying to represent a historically authentic figure, however. This Gaul with thick, tousled hair is not represented in his costume, but naked. His idealized anatomy and academic pose betray the artist's training at the École des Beaux-Arts, as does the face, recalling expressive heads. A vigorous figure, holding a pruning knife and (before it was lost) a branch of mistletoe in the other, his bright eyes and open mouth express spontaneous joy. O. F.

Auguste Bartholdi
Liberty

Bronze
9 ft. 5 in. × 3 ft. 5¼ in. × 2 ft. 5½ in.
(2.87 × 1.05 × 0.75 m)
Acquired in 1900

A gift from the young French Third Republic to the United States for the centenary, in 1876, of its Declaration of Independence, the Statue of Liberty has become one of the iconic figures of nineteenth-century French sculpture. This republican monument, celebrating Franco-American friendship, was created thanks to the commitment of a deputy at the French national assembly, Édouard Lefebvre de Laboulaye, and Bartholdi, the ambitious and talented "official sculptor" originally from Colmar in Alsace. When the Suez Canal was being opened up, Bartholdi proposed to the khedive of Egypt that he should build a colossal statue of a woman to function as a lighthouse. The project went no further, but it did inspire his ideas for the Statue of Liberty. The sculptor chose a classical image, drawing on Greco-Roman antiquity and European neoclassicism. The simple, austere, and compact form of the sculpture, dictated by the constraints of its huge dimensions, was set off by eloquent attributes: the torch bringing light, the tablets of the law, and the broken chains of servitude. The crown was inspired by the figure of *Faith*, conceived by Canova for the tomb of Pope Clement XIII. Bartholdi thus offered a powerful, serene image of the values shared by the two Republics in a world that at the time was mostly monarchic. The colossus, with its metal structure designed by Gustave Eiffel, was inaugurated in 1886. This scaled-down version was acquired by the French state in 1900. É. P.

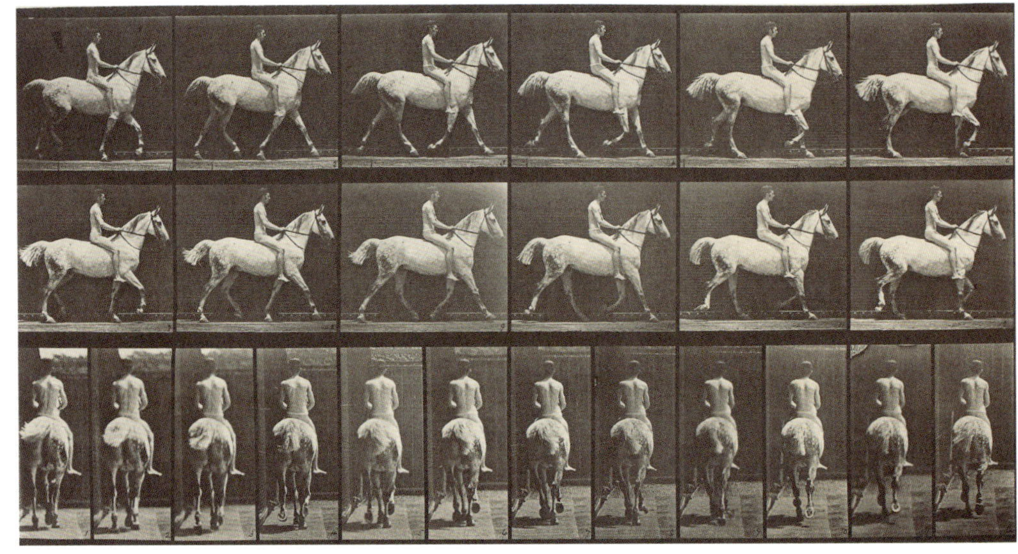

Eadweard Muybridge
White Horse Walking

Photomechanical print
7¾ × 14¾ in. (19.5 × 37.5 cm)
Gift of the Kodak-Pathé Foundation, 1983

In 1887 the British photographer Eadweard Muybridge published *Animal Locomotion*, eleven volumes of photographs in which each plate showed a view of successive phases of a given movement. Over five hundred of these plates featured human beings, while a hundred presented horses at different speeds, and some one hundred and twenty other animals such as deer, elephants, cats, parrots, etc.

Muybridge had become the first photographer to analyze the locomotion of living creatures some ten years earlier, at the instigation of the railroad magnate and former governor of California Leland Stanford. Stanford was a great horse lover, and wanted Muybridge to take photographs confirming the results found by Étienne-Jules Marey in his study of galloping horses, which were hotly debated at the time. The plates in *Animal Locomotion* were made for the University of Philadelphia, where Muybridge was invited to work by the painter Thomas Eakins, who was also interested in the representation of movement.

Made possible by a series of cameras with automatic release mechanisms, these images caused a real stir in Europe and the United States. Scientists were greatly influenced by the pictures, as were artists—not only Eakins, but also Ernest Meissonier, and Edgar Degas, whose various versions of *Rearing Horse* repeated the positions captured by Muybridge. J. B.

Ernest Meissonier
The Traveler

Wax, fabric, and leather
18¾ × 23½ × 15½ in. (47.8 × 60 × 39.5 cm)
Gift of M. Pasquier, 1984

Bent forward over his horse's neck, facing a headwind in the pouring rain, *The Traveler* is probably the most remarkable of all the statuettes produced by the painter Meissonier, and the most romantic in its expression. It gains extra intensity through the animal's powerful frame, the straightening of the horse's legs and the rider's upper body. But the model is also impressive in its concern for verism: witness the use of real material for the coat and the miniature leather reins. It was not until after Meissonier's death that the public discovered his work as a sculptor. Apparently he started modeling preparatory pieces for his paintings in around 1840, and sculpture for him would always remain linked to his painting. However, it is not always clear which the artist thought up first, the statuette or the painting, as Meissonier did several paintings of this traveler between 1879 and 1885. Meissonier himself said that he took great pleasure in modeling. He worked almost invariably in wax: "You get this instant creative rush … You have no idea how appealing and exciting it is to work on a model." Although he liked wax for its malleability, he went to great pains to prepare his models, building up the horses over tiny skeletons that he bought from art supplies stores. É. P.

Vincent van Gogh
The Italian Woman

Oil on canvas
32 × 23¾ in. (81.5 × 60.5 cm)
Gift of Baroness Eva Gebhard-Gourgaud, 1965

Agostina Segatori was probably the sitter for this portrait. She had modeled for Corot, Gérôme, and Manet, and was now the owner of a café in Paris called Le Tambourin. During his time in Paris (1886-88), Van Gogh made friends with her. He mounted an exhibition at Le Tambourin with Toulouse-Lautrec, Bernard, and Anquetin, and regularly decorated the walls with his paintings. We see Agostina face-on, against a yellow ground. She is wearing a *ciociaro* folk costume, a favorite motif for painters since the start of the nineteenth century, and a reference both to her roots and to the life of the café, where the barmaids wore Italian dress. The assertive frontal pose, the simplicity of the layout, the occasionally angular outlines, the thick impasto of bright colors, and the asymmetrical edging all give a primitive flavor to this painting, rather like the Japanese prints that Van Gogh greatly admired—he had hung his collection on the walls of Le Tambourin. The uncompromising treatment of the face, streaked with acid green, and even Segatori's absent or sad look contribute toward the profound humanity of this painting, making us feel all the compassion and empathy with which Van Gogh painted his portraits. S. Py.

Georges Seurat
Model, Front View

Oil on canvas
9¾ × 6¼ in. (25 × 15.8 cm)
Acquired in 1947

This nude is a study for *The Models* (Merion, Barnes Foundation), undertaken during the winter of 1886-87, and the third of the great figure paintings that punctuated Seurat's short career. *The Models* depicts three models in the studio in which we see a *mise en abyme* of *An Afternoon at La Grande Jatte*, which caused a furor in 1886 and suddenly made Seurat the leading exponent of Neo-Impressionism. The composition of *The Models* occupied the artist for a whole year. Seurat, who only very occasionally painted female nudes from life, here outlines the figures very precisely, highlighting the awkwardness of the juvenile body associated with an out-of-proportion adult head. For the

first time, he applies the pointillist division of color to that touchstone of the classical tradition, the nude. In both the preparation and the execution, everything in this sketch is masterfully measured, so much so that the preparatory study attains the status of an independent work of art. Thus *Model, Front View* was framed, signed, and reworked for exhibition in 1889 in place of the large canvas, which was then still unfinished. Above everything, there is a feeling of intimacy and dreaminess, a subtle, disturbing poetry in this panel of "miraculous art," as Félix Fénéon described it; he held onto it up until his death. S. Py.

Auguste Renoir
Julie Manet,
or Child with Cat

Oil on canvas
25½ × 21¼ in. (65 × 54 cm)
Acceptance in lieu, 1999

In 1887, Berthe Morisot and her husband Eugène Manet, a brother of the painter Édouard Manet, asked their friend Renoir to do a portrait of their only daughter, Julie Manet then aged nine. Renoir replied: "You cannot do a portrait. … Once a painter becomes involved, there is nothing left, no more likeness." He accepted the commission, though, which is a moving testimony to the friendship and artistic complicity between Renoir and Morisot. After Berthe died, the painter took care of Julie.

This portrait represents a watershed in Renoir's work, as he aimed for more solid forms and clearer drawing. Berthe Morisot, who had seen drawings in Renoir's studio that she thought were worthy of Ingres, admired this new style, which at the time disconcerted some art lovers and friends. For this composition, Renoir made some preparatory drawings and painted the picture in fragments. In fluid caresses, his brush thins and stretches the forms, like the young model's hands or the cat's curled-up body. *Julie Manet* or *Child with Cat* is one of the masterpieces of Renoir's so-called "Ingresque" period; while the painting was exhibited immediately in 1888 and became famous, it nevertheless remained in Julie's possession until her death, as she had no doubt grown fond of this delicate evocation of a moment of youthful reverie.
S. Py.

Anna Boch
Gathering

Oil on canvas
29 × 42 in. (0.74 × 1.07 m)
Acquired with the support of the Meyer Louis-Dreyfus
Fund through the SAMO, 2024

A luminous painting left unvarnished to preserve the freshness of the pigments, *Gathering* marks a watershed in the oeuvre of Anna Boch, who henceforth adopted a light palette for landscapes and rustic scenes often painted en plein air. Before a sun-drenched greenhouse partially covered with straw to keep out the heat, a little girl picks flowers, fruits, and berries. In the foreground, in a layered composition that reveals the influence of Japonisme, a vegetable garden full of dappled cabbages with marigolds to deter pests is rendered in splashes of red and bluish green.

Like the Impressionists, Boch challenges the traditional distinction between figure and ground, and seeks new methods to construct depth. Handling the brush freely, she seeks to capture the sincere expression of emotion. Rigorously constructed, this neo-impressionist canvas centers on complementary colors and optical mixing.

Exhibited for the first time in 1891 in Brussels at Les XX, a circle of the artistic avant-garde set up by Anna Boch's cousin, art critic Octave Maus, and at the Salon des Indépendants that same year, *Gathering* was described by the Press as "a painting [...] of a breadth of execution rare for a woman." (*L'Impartial Bruxellois*, February 15, 1891). This review betrays the sexism faced at that time by female painters, including Anna Boch, who was the only woman to participate in Les XX and La Libre Esthétique (which succeeded Les XX in 1893). Nevertheless, going toe to toe with her male colleagues, she left her mark on Neo-Impressionism.

At once painter, ceramist, collector, traveler, and music lover, Anna Boch was a liberated and forceful woman. Born into a family of renowned faience manufacturers, her background proved of some assistance, and she met little resistance in choosing to become an artist. A patron of the arts, she acquired works by her contemporaries, including James Ensor, Georges Seurat, and Vincent van Gogh, who painted a portrait of her brother, Eugène Boch (1888, Musée d'Orsay).
L. J.

Émile Bernard
Madeleine in the Bois d'Amour

Oil on canvas
4 ft. 6 in. × 5 ft. 4¼ in. (1.37 × 1.63 m)
Acquired in 1977

This girl daydreaming, lying down in a wood, is the artist's sister Madeleine. She had entranced Gauguin, who had come to paint with Bernard at Pont-Aven in the summer of 1888, and who even had thoughts of eloping with her. Bernard's portrait is set in the Bois d'Amour, on the banks of the River Aven (in the background)—a spot often painted by artists, who had been regular visitors to the Breton village since the 1860s. The Bois d'Amour also inspired Sérusier and Bernard to paint some of their most innovative pictures. This one, with its monumental dimensions, stood as a manifesto, at a time when Gauguin and Bernard were inventing their symbolist painting of synthesis and color.

Bernard later described this portrait as a "caricature." The outlines are defined and simplified, the trees rhythmically lined up, the "mistakes" (such as the overlarge hands) claimed to be deliberately primitive features that do not exclude the elegance of line praised by Van Gogh. All the visual elements, up to and including the colors, are aimed at characterizing rather than describing. Thus the dominant atmosphere is one of strange melancholy. The young woman is depicted in a stiff, sculptural pose like a recumbent figure on a gravestone, apparently dreaming and accessing the mysteries of this sacred grove, suggesting something beyond the reality of the five senses and of representation. S. Py.

Vincent van Gogh
Self-portrait

Oil on canvas
25½ × 21¼ in. (65 × 54.2 cm)
Gift of Paul and Marguerite Gachet, 1949

"It is hard to know yourself. But it is not easy to paint yourself, either," wrote Van Gogh to his brother Theo. This self-portrait was painted in August–September 1889, several months after the onset of the mental disturbances for which he had entered the asylum at Saint-Rémy-de-Provence in May. After the inactivity forced upon him by his fits, Van Gogh was overcome with a "pent-up appetite for work," and wanted to show that he had regained his calm and self-mastery by using a "fine blue of the South," as he called it, a light color associated with calm. This dominates what is an almost monochrome composition. The artist was satisfied with his painting and encouraged his brother, the dealer Theo van Gogh, to "take some time to look at it … [the] expression [has] calmed down a great deal, although the gaze is lost." This gaze, which Van Gogh also described as "veiled," seems to offer the only stable point in a composition made up of brushstrokes that spiral like the cypresses, fields, and skies of Provence that he was also painting at this time. In May 1890 he took this *Self-portrait* to Auvers-sur-Oise. It inspired the enthusiasm of Doctor Gachet, who went on to have himself painted by the artist (p. 208).
S. Py.

Henri Rivière

The Eiffel Tower: assemblage of beams with the Île aux Cygnes in the background

Silver print from a glass negative
3½ × 4½ in. (9 × 12 cm)
Gift of Mme Bernard Granet and her
children, and Mlle Solange Granet, 1981

A master engraver, Henri Rivière was also an amateur photographer, like many of his contemporaries, painters and writers, who took up the medium in the late nineteenth century when the focusing technique became simpler, and cameras became lighter and easier to operate, and as a hypersensitive emulsion came onto the market that brought the exposure time down to mere fractions of seconds. Armed with his wooden bellows camera and his glass plates, shortly before the building work on the Eiffel Tower was completed, he climbed it along with several friends from the Chat Noir cabaret. He captured his comrades' brief pranks, the workmen's poses as they balanced in midair, and he tackled the monumentality and the modernity of this steel architecture with a great freedom in terms of the layout. Rivière showed remarkable boldness in his framing and composition; he was an adept of the close-up, playing with perspective, backlit effects, and a dynamic viewpoint, namely the high-angle shot. In 1902, Rivière brought out an album of color lithographs, *Thirty-six Views of the Eiffel Tower*, influenced by the series of Japanese prints that were the current fashion, most notably Hokusai's *Thirty-six Views of Mount Fuji*. This tangle of steel girders is turned directly into the matrix for plate 25 of the album. M. R.

Édouard Detaille
The Dream

Oil on canvas
9 ft. 10 in. × 13 ft. 1½ in. (3 × 4 m)
Acquired in 1888

Édouard Detaille specialized in military paintings commemorating the events of the Franco-Prussian War in 1870-71, which brought down Napoleon III's Second Empire. Appropriating the dramatic and illusionistic effects of 1880s Naturalism, the painter engineered one final flowering of history painting by taking a modern subject. With his fellow artist Alphonse de Neuville, Detaille depicted the battle of Champigny in a monumental panorama that, by virtue of its veristic details and theatrical presentation, seems to foreshadow the birth of cinema. At the Salon of 1888, *The Dream*, with its celebration of France's brave soldiers, evoked General Boulanger's exhortation to revenge, uniting those who were disillusioned with the republican regime, which at the time was struggling to avoid another conflict with France's powerful neighbor. The dream of the sleeping soldiers comprises a chrestomathy of military feats that constituted the modern French nation, from the victories of the soldiers of Year II (1791) to the heroic resistance put up against the Prussians, the campaigns of Napoleon and of Algeria. Like an exorcism, this work confronts defeat and seeks to galvanize republican patriotism. In doing so, it also helped to create the cultural atmosphere for World War I. X. R.

Paul Sérusier
The Talisman or The Aven River at the Bois d'Amour

Oil on wood
10½ × 8½ in. (27 × 21 cm)
Acquired in 1985 with the generous support of M. Philippe Meyer, through the Fondation Lutèce

In the summer of 1888, Sérusier traveled to Pont-Aven in Brittany to meet Gauguin, who invited him to join an outdoor painting session in the Bois d'Amour. This wooded hill along the Aven river was a favorite with walkers and painters. Maurice Denis reported this conversation between the younger painter and the master: "How do you see these trees? They are yellow. So, put in yellow; this shadow, rather blue, paint it with pure ultramarine; these red leaves? Put in vermilion." The elements of the landscape (trees, bank, house, reflections on the water) are thus rendered by simplified marks of pure color in which the reduction of the drawing and forms led to a synthesis which would be decisive in the formation of the Nabi group: on returning to Paris in fall 1888, Sérusier showed this painting to young fellow students at the Académie Julian—Bonnard, Ranson, Ibels, and Denis, and then Vuillard, Roussel, and Piot. The panel made a strong impression and was baptized "talisman," a term consecrating its seminal value. The artists took turns to keep the work. When Sérusier died in 1927, it went to Maurice Denis, who kept it for the rest of his life. S. Py.

Paul Gauguin
Les Alyscamps

Oil on canvas
3 ft. × 2 ft. 4½ in. (91.5 × 72.5 cm)
Gift of Countess Vitali, 1923

On October 23, 1888, Gauguin arrived in Arles and joined up with Vincent van Gogh to set up the "Studio of the South" where they were to live and work together. *Les Alyscamps* is among the first examples of this collaboration: the famous path lined with sarcophagi and cypresses was painted by both artists. Ignoring the train to the left, apart from the smoke, and passing over the sarcophagi, Gauguin chose a motif familiar to tourists: Arlésiennes out for a walk. The regional costume reflects his search for primitivism, combined with the feeling, common to anyone traveling to Arles, of treading on ancient ground. With its bright, arbitrary colors, its partitioned forms set side by side with no perspective construction, *Les Alyscamps* carries on the experimentation of the years 1886–88 in Brittany, recalling *The Talisman* painted by Sérusier under his guidance. This controlled, melancholy view contrasts with the more naturalistic and tumultuous depiction of the site by Van Gogh, foreshadowing the failure of their artistic fraternizing: "Vincent and I on the whole rarely see eye to eye, especially about painting … he is a romantic, while I am more of a primitive," Gauguin wrote. Their time together ended on December 23, when Vincent cut off his own ear. S. Py.

Georges Seurat
Harbor at Port-en-Bessin at High Tide

Oil on canvas
26¼ × 32¼ in. (67 × 82 cm)
Purchased in 1952 with funds from an
anonymous Canadian donation

Seurat visited Port-en-Bessin in the summer of 1888. He brought back six seascapes on canvas, which he worked on from life but probably finished in his Paris studio. The artist confided in 1887: "In summer, [I] wash my eye clean from the days spent in the studio and catch the bright light more accurately, with all its shades. An existence divided in two by art itself."

Port-en-Bessin was then a fishing village and not yet a tourist attraction. Seurat is interested in the harbor's many different aspects, which he explores by circling around his motif. Here he has taken up a position on a bluff overlooking the harbor and offering a view across the gulf of Calvados as far as Trouville and Le Havre, recommended in the tourist guides. Yet the spectacular effect provided by the view did not stop the painter indulging his taste for rigor-ous construction. The geometric ordering is softened, however, by sinuous lines—a frequent device in Seurat's work. The wild grasses in the foreground introduce, not without humor, an untidy note in this still, controlled landscape. Despite the impression of abandonment conveyed by a harbor and boats devoid of any human figures, *Port-en-Bessin* offers a calm, harmonious picture of nature, rendered by the subtle dust haze of touches of color. S. Py.

Vincent van Gogh
Starry Night

Oil on canvas
2 ft. 4¾ in. × 3 ft. ¼ in (73 × 92 cm)
Gift of M. and Mme Robert Kahn-Sriber, in memory of
M. and Mme Fernand Moch, 1975

In 1889 Paul Signac was in Arles admir-ing *Starry Night*. Van Gogh had just put the fini-shing touches to a painting that had obsessed him since February the year before: "I often think that the night is more alive and richly colored than the day," he wrote. Painted after nature, the work illustrates his reflections on color: "At last, the starry sky painted at night, by gaslight. The sky is blue-green, water is royal blue, the land is mauve. The town is blue and purple. The gas is yellow and its reflections are reddish-gold going all the way to bronze-green. On the blue-green field of the sky, the Great Bear has a green and pink shimmer whose dis-creet pallor contrasts with the brutal gold of the gas." In the foreground, "two colored figures of lovers" add a romantic note to the scene and remind us that in Van Gogh's work night has a particular poetic, religious, and philosophical resonance. "The sight of the stars always makes me dream … we take death to go to a star," he wrote. In 1889, when the landscape was exhi-bited in Paris, the press failed to notice the experimentation with color or its cosmic, medi-tative dimension. A friend of Signac's and sup-porter of the Neo-Impressionists, the art critic Félix Fénéon, for example, attacked its "extra-vagances," the colors squeezed straight from the tube and the "baroquely gloomy creatures." S. Py.

Vincent van Gogh
The Dance Hall in Arles

Oil on canvas
25½ × 33½ in. (65 × 85.5 cm)
Gift of M. and Mme André Meyer, 1975

On December 11, 1888, Van Gogh wrote to his brother, "(Gauguin) is very strong, very creative." Both artists had been working together in Arles since that September, and this *Dance Hall*, painted sometime around mid-December, is definitely the painting in which Van Gogh comes closest to Gauguin. This begins with his choosing to paint a gathering in which the protagonists are seen from behind, closing off the foreground. But instead of Breton pardons or sermons, Van Gogh is certainly recalling here the dance of December 1, a rousing success in Arles, which was no doubt attended by Gauguin and himself. Like Gauguin and Bernard, Van Gogh insists on the regional component of the costumes (the coiffes in the foreground),

and he partitions off his forms with thick, dark outlines. Responding to Gauguin's criticism of his painting too hastily and with too much impasto, Van Gogh here applies a thinner, more even layer of color inside his outlines, which recall the lead in a stained-glass window. Such control does not prevent him from expressing his frenzy, with this packed crowd (among whom we recognize a friend and model of the painter, Mme Roulin), which seems to spill out of the picture frame. Van Gogh also gives a personal interpretation of a favorite theme in modern painting, following in the footsteps of Renoir in the *Dance at Le Moulin de la Galette* (p. 145) and Toulouse-Lautrec, whose dance scenes he would admire in 1889 and 1890. S. Py.

Émile Bernard
The Pardon

Oil on canvas
28¾ × 36¼ in. (73 × 92 cm)
Acquired through the exclusive patronage
of the AXA Group, 2019

Émile Bernard was only twenty years old when he painted *The Pardon*, yet he already harbored ambitions to revolutionize painting. Seeking to radically simplify form and the use of color, he rejected the illusions of perspective and shading. Inspired by enamel work, medieval art and Japanese prints, and fueled by his meeting with Louis Anquetin and Vincent van Gogh, he became the spearhead of a new, uncompromising aesthetic. His aim was not to present a dutiful image of reality; it was rather to endow the artwork with a kind of primeval, popular, childlike, mystical power. Bernard's encounter with Paul Gauguin in Pont-Aven in the summer of 1888 proved decisive. Both artists shared the quest for an art which, as Gauguin wrote, would hark back "to the infancy of humanity."

Several figures appear to be taking a break from a religious festival on a lawn. The vast expanse of acid green is punctuated by the black patches of dresses and the white, blue-tinged swirls of the Breton women's headdresses, together with a few hints of orange and red. There is no horizon, no cast shadows, few features, and little expression on the faces: the canvas is structured by color, compounding its strength and its strangeness.

Gauguin was so stunned by the picture that he took it with him when he went to stay with Van Gogh in Arles in October 1888. Finding it "magnificent," the Dutch artist made a copy in watercolor. *The Pardon* also inspired the young Nabis, notably Maurice Denis, and became a pioneering and seminal work of Synthetism. J.-R. T.

Giovanni Boldini
Celebration at the Moulin-Rouge

Oil on canvas
3 ft. 2 in. × 3 ft. 5 in. (0.96 × 1.04 m)
Acceptance in lieu, 2010

An Italian living in Paris since 1871, Boldini was a portraitist of Parisian high society but also a chronicler of the times. His friend and occasional model, Robert de Montesquiou (p. 257), summed up Boldini's art in the words, "Parisianism, modernity." Fascinated by nightlife, Boldini painted scenes at the Folies-Bergère and, as seems most likely here, the Moulin-Rouge, an establishment that opened in 1889 and combined the functions of café, dance hall, and cabaret. Boldini's protagonists are standing a little way from the dance floor, which was often taken over by the *quadrille naturaliste* (aka the French cancan) for which it became famous. The painter does not moralize about the somewhat seedy crowd mixing in with the crowned heads and Parisian celebrities, who earned these establishments their reputation for debauchery. Nevertheless, seduction seems to determine the relations between the figures, one of whom, the man with the glass of champagne, may be the artist himself. The brio of the execution and the vivacity of the colors add to the festive feel of the scene. As can be seen from the sketchy areas, the artist left this painting unfinished. Like the works of Manet and Degas, to whom Boldini was close, and also those of Toulouse-Lautrec, this sybaritic scene illustrates artists' fascination with these nighttime entertainments that were emblematic of the new Paris. S. Py.

Louis Anquetin
Henri Samary

Oil on canvas
28 × 23¼ in. (71 × 59.3 cm)
Acquired in 2010

The young Anquetin probably met the actor Henri Samary through his friend Toulouse-Lautrec, who painted his portrait as well (also at the Musée d'Orsay). The two painters met in Léon Bonnat's studio in 1882 and became firm friends, together making regular visits to the cabarets of Montmartre. Samary came from a family of actors: his grandmother, his aunt, Madeleine Brohan, who was painted by Paul Baudry (Musée d'Orsay), and his two sisters all trod the boards. His sister, Jeanne, who posed for Renoir, was particularly famous. A *pensionnaire* of the Comédie-Française, Henri Samary acted in the plays of Molière but also in contemporary works by dramatists such as Octave Feuillet, Victorien Sardou, and Jean Richepin. This portrait is typical of Anquetin's work at the end of the 1880s when, like his friends Van Gogh and Bernard, he looked to give his forms vigorous outlines. Here, though, the line is like an arabesque—loose, light, and purified. It wittily encloses zones of cold color, put down without shadows or modeling in the manner of Japanese prints, but also reminiscent of Holbein and Ingres. The vivacity of the brushwork results in an expressive portrait of Samary, which verges on caricature in its treatment of this ostentatiously elegant and thespian character. S. Py.

Vincent van Gogh
Van Gogh's Bedroom in Arles

Oil on canvas
22½ × 29¼ in. (57.3 × 73.5 cm)
Entered the Louvre in accordance
of the peace treaty with Japan in 1959

Having settled in Arles, and while waiting for the arrival of Gauguin, with whom he was going to found a "new school of colorists," Van Gogh took the time to paint his bedroom. He produced three versions of what, in reference to the lack of human presence, he called this "interior with nothing in it." For the artist, this ordinary-looking room was in fact a refuge, a salutary and consoling haven. In producing this soothing image, he believed that "a look at the picture ought to rest the mind, or rather the imagination." Color was to play a key role: "by simplifying it I am lending it more style, cre-ating an overall impression of rest or sleep." This "more masculine" simplification also meant dispensing with cast shadows and the application of "bright flat tints like the Japanese prints." However, the energy of the brushstrokes, the foreshortening of perspective, and the vivacity of the colors somewhat undermine this feeling of "undisturbed rest" and make this version of *Van Gogh's Bedroom in Arles*, executed during a moment of mental disturbance at the hospital in Saint-Rémy-de-Provence in 1889, a poignant self-portrait. S. Py.

Henri de Toulouse-Lautrec
Red-haired Woman or La Toilette

Oil on cardboard
26¼ × 21¼ in. (67 × 54 cm)
Bequeathed by Pierre Goujon, 1914

The downward, sideways view of the model's back is no doubt reminiscent of the charcoals of Degas, the master most revered by Toulouse-Lautrec. The suggestive stockings, probably indicating that the subject is a prostitute, also hark back to the older artist's depictions of brothels, although Lautrec may not have seen these. Shown in the avant-garde exhibition by Les XX in Brussels in 1890, *Red-haired Woman* is emblematic of the juxtaposition of fine brushstrokes—like the fine pastel lines used by Degas in the 1880s—that afforded a supreme and very realistic modern rendering of female skin.

The clothes strewn over the chair and wrapped round the woman's body confirm what we already knew: that this undressed woman is portrayed in the middle of a very banal, every-day activity, and not as an ideal artistic nude. Without refusing the sensuality of such a view, from behind, her legs unambiguously apart, Toulouse-Lautrec nevertheless offers a relatively modest pose, and the skinny body itself is hardly voluptuous. Even so, by inscribing the figure in a harmonious form, he manages to take the ordinariness of his model onto a higher level. X. R.

Jean Carriès
Vase in the shape of a gourd with a double bulge

Enameled stoneware and gold streaks
H. 8 in. (20.5 cm)
Acquired in 1991

At a time when his reputation as a sculptor was well established, Jean Carriès, devoured by the demon of fire which actually brought about his early demise in 1894, moved away from Paris in 1888 to Saint-Amand-en-Puisaye in central France, the centuries-old center for traditional pottery. In 1891 he had his own kiln built at the manor at Monriveau, notably to handle the execution of a monumental door commissioned by Winaretta Singer; the following year at the Salon de la Société Nationale des Beaux-Arts, he presented a set of stoneware that turned him into the star of the event and earned him a knight's cross in the Légion d'Honneur. Although what had made him want to become a potter was discovering Japanese ceramics at the Paris Exposition Universelle of 1878, it was never Carriès's intention to produce more Japanese stoneware. He found the enamel was overglazed, too shiny, and preferred matt, less shiny polished finishes, as he showed with the skillful patinas he was already applying to his bronzes and plasters. Devoid of decoration, his ceramic pieces offer layer upon layer of glazes and runs that are as thin as possible, and a completely non-brilliant satin finish. The enamel is applied onto matt, fine, close-grained clay, with a blend of russets, fawns, and ochers showing through in places. The gold, also matt, produces an extremely refined contrast with the rustic quality of the clay. Ph. T.

Paul Gauguin
La Belle Angèle

Oil on canvas
3 ft. ¼ in. × 2 ft. 4¾ in. (92 × 73.2 cm)
Gift of Ambroise Vollard

Marie-Angélique Satre, whose parents ran a bistro at Pont-Aven, sat for Gauguin in July 1889; in around 1920, she recalled that her reaction to the portrait had been, "How horrible!" The painter "was very sad and he said, crestfallen, that he had never painted such a good portrait as that one." Having gone to Brittany because the cost of living there was lower than in Paris, Gauguin was also looking for "the wild, the primitive. When my clogs resound on the granite ground, I hear the powerful, dull, flat sound that I am looking for in painting," he wrote. *La Belle Angèle* rejects the picturesque Brittany then in vogue at the Salon. While the girl is wearing the traditional festive costume of Pont-Aven,

the headdress and embroidery work add most of all to the composition's simplified decorative form. Slightly out of proportion, the model is set face-on in an inset, which is in the style of certain Japanese prints, but also of shop signs and sales material. The artist does not place Angèle in a unified space: the flowery background has no depth to it, the ceramic—of Peruvian inspiration—and the inscription all make this portrait a composite, complex, "wild" picture. The work was a milestone in Gauguin's development; while it unsettled its subject, who rejected it, *La Belle Angèle* delighted Degas, who bought it in 1891 and kept it until his death. S. Py.

Edgar Degas
Blue Dancers

Oil on canvas
3 ft. 4¼ in. × 3 ft. 1 in. (1.02 × 0.94 m)
Donated by Dr. Albert Charpentier, 1951

"They call me the painter of dancers. They don't understand that for me the dancer has been a pretext for painting pretty fabrics and for rendering movement." When Degas made this demurral he had already attained considerable fame. Certainly, for several decades, the dance motif accompanied an interest in equilibrium and movement aroused by the discoveries enabled by the chronophotography of Étienne-Jules Marey and Eadweard Muybridge. In the 1880s Degas abandoned his naturalist style in favor of a more nervous style of drawing, and also began to concentrate on the articulation of bodies. While this work maintains his characte-ristic use of a strip of color down the right side of the composition, suggesting a curtain or a wall and creating the beholder's desire to take a peep at what is going on behind the scenes, this work is less about the illusion of immediacy than about the sequence of a choreography. The three main ballerinas, with little to tell them apart, seem to represent different phases in a single movement, an effect heightened by the black line that floats, distinct from the colors. These are applied with great freedom, especially in the background, where it is clear that Degas used his fingers, anticipating pictorial practices that developed after World War II. X. R.

Paul Cézanne
Bathers

Oil on canvas
23½ × 32¼ in. (60 × 82 cm)
Gift of Baroness Eva Gebhard-Gourgaud, 1965

Two works in the Musée d'Orsay collection, *Idyll* and *A Modern Olympia*, show the young Cézanne taking on the time-honored challenge of placing the nude in a natural setting, just as Manet had before him. Beginning with mythological and religious themes, he then began producing studies of bathers, male or female, in a light-colored outdoor setting. This theme became something of an obsession, as can be seen from the many variants accompanying the artist's stylistic developments, all the way up to his last great masterpiece, *The Large Bathers* (Philadelphia Museum of Art). Cézanne said he wanted to "paint like Poussin, but from nature," and did indeed measure his art against the Old Masters he knew so well. He gave new life to his theme by working toward the perfect fusion of bodies, which he handled increasingly schematically over the years, and landscape, also treated in an even, modern way. Without dwelling on skin tones, in these *Bathers* Cézanne established a series of echoes, such as the one between the vertical pose of the central model, possibly taken from Signorelli, and the upward thrust of the trees. The figures at the sides lean inward, in a pose that Cézanne would reprise on many later occasions, thereby closing the composition in an ogival form, in which the bodies tend toward abstraction at the forefront of modernity. X. R.

Stephan Sinding
Bench

Oak, partially stained, modern upholstery
6 ft. 5½ in. × 6 ft. 1½ in. × 2 ft. 4¼ in.
(1.97 × 1.87 × 0.72 m)
Acquired in 2010

Stephan Sinding was one of the best-known Scandinavian sculptors of his day: Carl Jacobsen gave him pride of place in the museum he founded in Copenhagen in 1888, the Ny Carlsberg Glyptotek, and he was also commissioned to make many major commemorative monuments for the cities of Bergen and Christiania (present-day Oslo).

Having studied variously in Christiania, Berlin, Paris, and Rome, Sinding developed a syncretic style, combining naturalism with national-romantic subject matter.

The sculptor made incursions into the field of the decorative arts by supplying bas-relief models for the Bing & Grondhal porcelain factory in Copenhagen, and chryselephantine statuettes marketed by the Berlin firm of Keller & Reiner, and most of all by creating several items of furniture for his personal use, including this imposing bench.

Although it owes a typological debt to the models extolled by Viollet-le-Duc and William Morris's arts and crafts movement, its decorative work links it to the symbolist movement tinged with Wagnerism: the bas-relief decorating the high back might be seen as an allusion to Parsifal assailed by Klingsor's flower maidens, or to Siegfried hearing the plaintive Rhinemaidens. Ph. T.

Maurice Denis
Sunlight on the Terrace

Oil on cardboard
9½ x 8 in. (24 × 20.5 cm)
Acquired in 1986

A little girl with a hat stands on the terrace at Saint-Germain-en-Laye, where the silhouettes of people walking can be made out, and, to the right, a row of trees, their dark fronds cutting away a portion of green sky. In this painting Denis boldly transfigures a familiar place in the Saint-Germain area in Paris, somewhere he lived all his life. As in Sérusier's *Talisman* (p. 188), which quite shocked Denis, *Sunlight* is "a formless landscape, by dint of being synthetically formulated … in pure colors," as the artist put it. Denis takes hold of a favorite subject of the Impressionists, contemporary figures in the open air, and gives it new life by breaking free of any need to imitate, following the example of Cézanne, who later told him: "I was pleased with myself when I discovered that the sun could not be *reproduced*, but that it had to be *represented* by something else … by color." Denis celebrates the flat patches of bright colors, reversing the tonal relationship between shadow (light orange) and full sunlight (deep red). Under the influence of Gauguin and the Japanese print, the simplification of forms, outlined with snaking arabesques, is taken to extremes. This painting was apparently never exhibited during the artist's lifetime, but it is surely one of those small-format pictures that the Nabis (a word meaning "prophet" in Hebrew and Arabic) Vuillard, Bonnard, Ranson, Sérusier, and Roussel would have shown each other at their meetings in the early 1890s, as they experimented with the new aesthetics. S. Py.

Winslow Homer
Summer Night

Oil on canvas
2 ft. 6 in. × 3 ft. 4¼ in. (0.77 × 1.02 m)
Acquired in 1900

The sea was a fertile source of inspiration for the American artist Winslow Homer, who was fond of painting its pleasures and dangers in his spectacular depictions of gales and rescues, and its economic activities, with many fishing and sailing paintings. This *Summer Night* is different because it replaces the seamen, fishermen, bathers, and strollers with two women waltzing in the dark on the terrace of a verandah facing the ocean. The artist has captured and recomposed the scene in the village of Prouts Neck, in Maine, north of Boston, where he moved in 1884. In addition to the light coming from the house is the tremendous effect of moonlight, gleaming on the water and giving this *Night* an atmosphere of joyful, poetic strangeness that is heightened by the dark mass of onlookers to the right. While underscoring the vital energy of the dance, the sharp contrasts of light and shade bring gentleness and melancholy to the realism of Homer's invariably clear-cut and vigorous execution. To the artist's great disappointment, for ten years *Summer Night* found no takers, until in 1900 the work earned him one of the most coveted awards of the day. At the Exposition Universelle in Paris, the picture won a medal and was purchased by the French state for the Musée du Luxembourg, where it was admired by Monet. Homer thus achieved international recognition with what is to this day his most important work outside of the United States. S. Py.

Paul Cézanne
Montagne Sainte-Victoire

Oil on canvas
2 ft. ½ in. × 3 ft. ¼ in. (65 × 92 cm)
Donated by the granddaughter
of Auguste Pellerin, 1969

As Courbet did for his native region of Doubs, Cézanne had a lifelong fondness for the landscapes around Aix-en-Provence. They provided him with leitmotivs for his formal experiments, especially his handling of the Mediterranean light and the way it flattens relief, reducing three-dimensional entities to mere "silhouettes." The composition of this *Montagne Sainte-Victoire*, in short, orderly brushstrokes, creates an impression of evanescence. While the rhythms were more pronounced and the colors more intense when Cézanne returned to this motif at the end of his life, this version, dating from around 1890, already evinces a tendency toward geometrical schematization of the rocks and stones by a simplification of perspective, with the different levels, and especially the low wall at the front, somehow coming together in the picture plane. This gradual abandonment of depth is also manifest in the stylization of the trees, whose foliage is rendered in the fine, oblique lines Cézanne began using ten years earlier. The object of the representation gradually but serenely disappears into a fusion of technique and pictorial elements, leading to an autonomy of the painting while endowing this grandiose landscape with real sublimity. X. R.

Odilon Redon
Closed Eyes

Oil on canvas
17¼ × 14¼ in. (44 × 36 cm)
Acquired in 1904

This picture marks a turning point in Redon's work, as he shifted the themes previously explored in his *Noirs* ("black works": charcoals and lithographs) into a new register using paint and color. It was also the first piece of his to enter the Musée du Luxembourg, in 1904: recognition came late in the artist's career, but was still appreciated. This mysterious face is probably that of his wife, Camille Falte, but the work clearly refers to *The Dying Slave* by Michelangelo (Louvre) just as Moreau's *Orpheus* (1865, p. 94) had done. "Behind the closed eyes of his slave, how lofty is the action of the mind!" wrote Redon. "He sleeps, and the worried dream that crosses the brow of this marble lifts our dreams into a pensive and moving world. The sleep of the slave awakens our dignity." As in Moreau's painting, the closed eyes of this slave concentrating intently on his rich inner world are like a manifesto calling for an art of suggestion and indeterminacy. Because of its association with dream, sleep was one of the favorite themes of the Symbolists. But this should not be confused with the open-eyed creative meditation wherein the artist shapes forms "in accordance with my dreams," as Redon put it: "I have created an art after my own heart. I have created it with my eyes open to the wonders of the visible world and, whatever may have been said, sought constantly to obey the laws of nature and life." S. Py.

Vincent van Gogh
The Church in Auvers-sur-Oise: View of the East End

Oil on canvas
3 ft. 1 in. × 2 ft. 5¾ in. (94 × 74 cm)
Acquired in 1951 with the help of Paul Gachet and the contribution of an anonymous Canadian donor

In May 1890, after his stay in Arles and then in the psychiatric hospital in Saint-Rémy-de-Provence, Van Gogh headed north for Auvers-sur-Oise, where, at the urging of his brother Theo, he joined Doctor Gachet. *The Church in Auvers-sur-Oise* is one of the most ambitious of the seventy-something canvases he painted during these last two months of his life. In Van Gogh's view of the apse, the Gothic church becomes a shifting, imposing monument whose forms seem to be raised up by some tellurian force, pushing against the inky-blue sky. Bold, out-lined patches of color taken from the "synthetic" vocabulary combine with the spiraling brushstrokes in the background to heighten the painting's expressivity. Regarding the intensity of the color, in a letter to his sister Wil, Van Gogh wrote: "I've done a larger picture of the village church—with an effect in which the building appears purplish-blue against a sky of deep and simple blue, pure cobalt. The stained-glass windows appear as patches of ultramarine, the roof is purple and partly orange. In the foreground, a little greenery in bloom and some pink sunlit sand." This painting, originally owned by Doctor Gachet, entered the French national collections thanks to his son Paul Gachet and an anonymous Canadian donation made in 1951. C. B.

Vincent van Gogh
Portrait of docteur Gachet

Oil on canvas
27 × 22 ½ in. (68.2 × 57 cm)
Gift of Paul and Marguerite Gachet, 1949

"The thing I am most passionate about … more than anything else in my craft, is the portrait, the modern portrait. I look for it through color," Van Gogh wrote at the time when he had Paul Gachet sit for him twice. Gachet was a "bizarre" fellow, Van Gogh said—a physician, and also an artist when the fancy took him, and a collector associated with the Impressionists who settled at Auvers-sur-Oise. It was Pissarro who recommended him to Theo van Gogh, who was casting around for somewhere reasonably near Paris for his brother to stay; Vincent had been in hospital at Saint-Rémy-de-Provence after several fits of dementia. Between the time he arrived in May of 1890, and his suicide in July of that same year, the painter found an enthusiastic supporter in Gachet, and wanted to paint his portrait straightaway. He has shown him in the traditional melancholic pose (melancholia was the subject of Gachet's thesis), "the sorry expression of our day and age," as Van Gogh wrote to Gauguin. To portray this modern character, Van Gogh eschews the "photographic likeness," instead exalting the expressive power of color, heightened by the straightforward composition and the fairly cursory treatment of certain elements such as the foxgloves. This innovative portrait, which Van Gogh said his contemporaries would not understand, was much admired by the sitter, who held onto it all his life. S. Py.

Paul Gauguin
Portrait of the Artist with the Yellow Christ

Oil on canvas
15 × 18 in. (38 × 46 cm)
Acquired in 1994 with the help of M. Philippe Meyer
and Japanese sponsorship coordinated by the
Nikkei daily newspaper

The *Portrait of the Artist with the Yellow Christ* brings together three self-portraits. Gauguin depicts himself in the center, between two of his works, a device that stands the test of time and tradition in artists' portraits. The expression is serious and the gaze focused on the reflection in the mirror. On the right, an anthropomorphic tobacco jar, sculpted in 1889 (and in the Musée d'Orsay collection), repeats the movement of the face and the direction of Gauguin's gaze. This earthenware vessel, "calcined" in the "hell" of the great fire, is as much a tragic, grotesque self-portrait as an image of the artist's solitude, a "poor devil all doubled up to endure his pain," the artist wrote. The pot also symbolizes matter, contrasting with *The Yellow Christ* (Albright-Knox Art Gallery, Buffalo) painted in Brittany in 1889, a painting within the painting, reversed in this mirror image. Inspired by the crucifix in the chapel at Trémalo near Pont-Aven, this *Yellow Christ*, whose popular rustic and primitive quality Gauguin had found attractive, symbolizes the spirit and the ideal, and sums up the artist's sacrificial dimension as a prophet misunderstood by the society of his day. This painting once belonged to Maurice Denis, who kept it until he died. He admired it for its "brightness, a sign of intelligence," making Gauguin in his eyes a classical master on a par with Cézanne. S. Py.

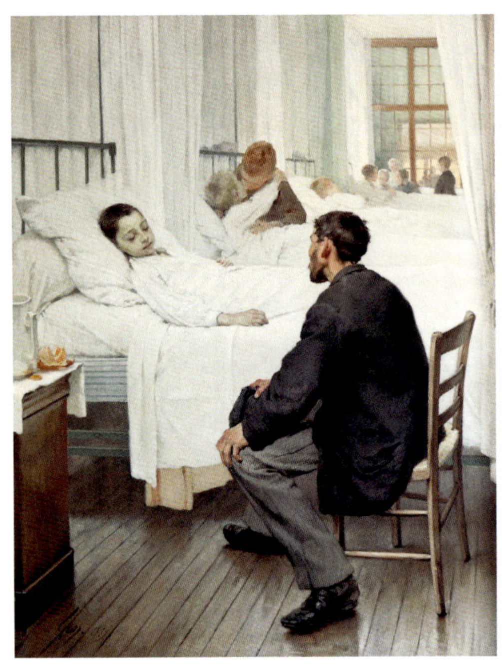

Henri Geoffroy
Visiting Day at the Hospital

Oil on canvas
3 ft. 11¼ in. × 3 ft. 1½ in. (1.20 × 0.95 m)
Acquired in 1889

Nicknamed Geo, "the painter of children and the humble," Geoffroy epitomized the kind of popular favorite artist whose pictures are passed from hand to hand like holy images. His scenes with docile schoolchildren spread the secular values of the Republic, whose roots were sinking deeper thanks to Jules Ferry's laws instituting obligatory education for children. Surely Geoffroy's greatest hit, *Visiting Day at the Hospital* plays on the sentimental register by depicting the touching reunion of a father of modest condition and the son who has had to be taken away from the family because of his illness. In the background, children from an-other family hug and embrace. Geoffroy pulls out all the emotional stops here: the child's touching face still bearing the scars of its recent suffering, the father's conspicuously threadbare clothes, the sense of health conveyed by the white sheets and the mandarin—an extremely rare fruit at the time—on the bedside table to cheer up the young patient. While mustering all the dramatic effectiveness of the kind of genre scene with children produced during the Dutch Golden Age, this edifying picture is also a positivist paean to public welfare provision that made progress in hygiene and medicine available to all. X. R.

Édouard Vuillard
In Bed

Oil on canvas
28¾ × 36½ in. (73 × 92.5 cm)
Bequeathed by Édouard Vuillard, 1941

Vuillard turns what seems an ordinary, every-day subject into something both bold and mysterious. The identity of this model sleeping deeply before us here is unknown, as is her location. This painting from the early 1890s remained in Vuillard's possession up to his death in 1940, and was only found at the moment of effecting the bequest. Here, the artist places himself within a rich tradition and takes up a theme favored by symbolist painters before the dissemination of Freudian thought, namely the association of sleep and dream, with the latter an integral part of human experience and identity. Vuillard may not hint at the dreams welling up from the deep sleep of his subject, but he does suggest the state of dream and withdrawal from the world by his use of muted colors and attempt to achieve a pure, serene rhythm. Like his contemporaries Puvis de Chavannes, Seurat, and Signac, he uses horizontal lines and successive waves to convey calm and peace (not forgetting the humorous note of the legs tucked under the blanket). The clear, outlined figures are formed by swaths of color in a pared-down depiction where the only thing disrupting the chromatic unity of the wall is a cross. Possibly echoing the religious conviction of this artist raised by Marian friars, both the space and the signature are divided by a lighter band of color which brings an enigmatic quality to the composition that can come across as surprisingly radical even today. S. Py.

Émile Bernard
Symbolic Self-portrait

Oil on canvas
32 × 23¾ in. (81 × 60.5 cm)
Acquired in 2008

Bernard painted self-portraits at every stage of his career. The artist depicts himself here at the age of twenty-three, at a key moment after sharing five years of artistic companionship with Toulouse-Lautrec, Van Gogh and, above all, Gauguin, with whom he painted in Brittany in 1888 (p. 184). Here Bernard is in three-quarter profile. The portrait purports to be a likeness and the framing places the sitter in the same space as the viewer, whereas the status of the background is more ambiguous. Bernard has painted two self-portraits against a ground of female nudes, the bathers in homage to Cézanne that decorated his studio at Asnières. Here the bodies, seemingly reddened in Hell, and foreshadowing Derain's fauvist bathers of 1905–06, resemble some painful apparition, possibly echoing the painter's difficult love life during this period. In response to the controlled expression on Bernard's face is the face of Christ crowned with thorns, appearing here as a possible remedy for the torments and visions assailing the painter. The juxtaposition of these two different registers, contrasting dream and reality, the resulting strangeness and the expressive use of color make this self-portrait, above and beyond the autobiographical presentation and the artistic manifesto, the more universal mirror of a crisis—that of a man at a crossroads attempting to take charge of his destiny. S. Py.

Édouard Vuillard
Profile of a Woman in a Green Hat

Oil on cardboard
8¼ × 6¼ in. (21 × 16 cm)
Acceptance in lieu, 1990

Never shown in the artist's lifetime, *Profile of a Woman* is doubtless an "icon," the name the Nabi artists gave to those little experimental compositions that were crucial to formulating their aesthetic in the early 1890s. At the time, Vuillard was one of these "prophets" of the new art, alongside Denis, Bonnard, Sérusier, Ranson, and Roussel. Against a rapidly brushed pink ground, the artist has painted this spirited silhouette of a smartly dressed young woman. The hat, with its exuberant touches of bright green, held in check by being cut off by the edge of the picture, shows Vuillard's taste, as a seamstress's son, for contemporary sartorial matters. Like Bonnard, the painter applies the grammar of synthetism to the subject matter of modern life: cloisonné forms with blue outlines and patches of flat tints, with no relief or modeling. The face, suggested with just a few brushstrokes, looks away, as often with the artist during this period. In shy avoidance, the elegant woman bends forward, the nape of her neck somewhat out of line with her back, also recalling a posture often seen in the Japanese prints that the Nabis so admired, whereby the head leaning forward gives the body an unnatural curve. This strange face, like a playing card, seems to contain other profiles in reverse and remains indecipherable, somewhere between a cartoon and a feeling of anxious flight. S. Py.

Louis Comfort Tiffany
Armchair

Carved oak, straight back with uprights carved with braided patterns and upholstered with punched leather stamped with knot patterns, row of three arcs and two halves under the back and seat
3 ft. 9¼ in. × 2 ft. 2¾ in. × 32¼ in. (1.15 × 0.68 × 0.82 m)
Acquired in 2010

Louis Comfort Tiffany went up to the National Academy of Design in 1866, and in 1881 filed patent applications relating to the production of glassware. As early as 1885, he set up in business and invented the new method of making opalescent glass that made him famous. In 1892, he completed the decoration of Henry and Louise Havemeyer's New York home that housed their magnificent collection, in collaboration with Samuel Colman. Several sources of influence are noticeable in his furniture, with his preference for oak and ready use of carving on these soberly constructed and generous forms. This definite taste for decorative work

unquestionably links Louis Comfort Tiffany's furniture to the American aesthetic movement. The armchair shown here is a variant on the pair from the Havemeyer home, split between the Metropolitan Museum of Art in New York and the Louis Comfort Tiffany Garden Museum in Japan. It is slightly different, however, with less protuberant knobs on the armrests. This chair has the special feature of having kept its studded, embossed leather backrest decorated with interlacing of Celtic inspiration, showing how harmoniously the carving on the wood matched the original upholstery. Y. B.

Paul Gauguin
Tahitian Women or On the Beach

Oil on canvas
27¼ in. × 36 in. (69 × 91 cm)
Gift of Vicomte Guy de Cholet, 1923

From 1891 to 1893, Gauguin had a first spell in Tahiti, keen on making a break with "that European struggle for money. There in … Tahiti, I shall be able to listen to the sweet murmuring music of my heart's beating, in amorous harmony with the mysterious beings of my environment," and work toward the "great renaissance of art … that will have the Tropics for its homeland," he declared. *Tahitian Women* expresses both this mythical, ideal vision, overriding the artist's material hardships and disillusionment, while also reflecting the Maori acculturation under the effect of Western colonization that had so disappointed Gauguin. The same model likely posed twice over, on the left wearing a *pareu*, and on the right weaving palm fibers and wearing a strict Western mission dress. Gauguin captures "the people who can stay for hours, for days, sitting without saying a word and gazing mournfully at the sky," and whom he observed in fascination. The firm, vigorous outline draws full, massive forms. Gauguin monumentalizes the bodies still further with his close-up view, reducing the landscape to strips of color in alternation. He thus attains that "simple" and "mysterious art" on the agenda for his "Studio of the Tropics." S. Py.

Georges Seurat
Circus

Oil on canvas
6 ft. 1 in. × 5 ft. (1.85 × 1.52 m)
Bequeathed by John Quinn, 1927

Circus is the last picture Georges Seurat painted. Begun in the summer of 1890, it was shown at the Salon des Indépendants, which opened on March 20, 1891, nine days before the artist's death. After *Circus Parade* and *Cancan*, Seurat here continues his grating evocation of urban entertainments. The subject matter belongs to the repertoire of naturalist literature. Here Seurat is depicting the Medrano Circus, which also inspired Degas and Toulouse-Lautrec. In the foreground, a clown is pulling back a curtain and dramatically revealing the ring to us; Monsieur Loyal is performing his act as are a stable-girl and two clowns, seemingly weightless to the sound of violins. The sparse, hieratic audience are seated according to their social status. Seurat did an overall preparatory sketch for his canvas (which is also at the Musée d'Orsay). Seurat fully subscribed to Charles Henry's theory of the psychological charge linked to the direction of lines, using ascending lines and colors such as would convey a "demonic rhythm" and gaiety, according to the critic Lecomte. The lines also serve a constructive and decorative purpose, in the tamer's whip, for example, its curves foreshadowing the vocabulary of Art Nouveau. Conversely, the angular outlines and schematic figures are the final touch in turning this simultaneously frenzied and frozen scene into a world of artifice. Disturbing and loaded with theory, the painting was given a lukewarm reception in 1891. S. Py.

Paul Sérusier
Breton Wrestling

Oil on canvas
3 ft. 1¼ in. × 2 ft. 4¾ in. (92 × 73 cm)
Bequeathed by Mlle Henriette Boutaric, 1984

In the late 1880s, after Gauguin's lengthy stay there, Brittany became the laboratory for a new kind of painting based on simplification and synthesis. In this quest for an art that was authentic, primitive, and free of academic convention, the region seemed particularly attractive, because artists and writers saw it as a land of legends and a place where ancestral society had been spared the effects of the Industrial Revolution. Here, like Gauguin before him, Sérusier shows the *gouren*, traditional Breton wrestling. *Gouren* was a very popular sport in the countryside, and tournaments were organized between villages. The wrestlers occupy the frontal plane, where the ground is a solid, yellowish, bright green. The spectators wear the traditional costume of Pont-Aven. As in Japanese prints, the forms are defined by vigorous outlines and filled in with solid color. "If the drawing is simple and beautiful, if the color is harmonious and expressive, is this not ... the whole of Art?" wrote Sérusier. The lines are emphatic and caricatured and, like the somewhat ridiculous gendarme, remind us that Sérusier was interested in all popular forms and, with his Nabi friends, liked to depict puppet shows. S. Py.

Pascal Dagnan-Bouveret
In the Forest
(drawing related to)

Watercolor wash, charcoal, pastel, red chalk, oil paint, pen strokes, and black ink on very fine pasted vellum paper
18¾ × 15½ in. (47.6 × 39.1 cm)
Gift of Worth to the Musées Nationaux, 1914

Dagnan-Bouveret was a leading figure in the naturalist movement that spread through Europe in the 1870s and 1880s, describing men and situations in an objective, unaffected spirit, and representing subjects from everyday life in a format that heralded cinema. In around 1890 he became an active member of the Société Nationale des Beaux-Arts, which is where he exhibited *In the Forest* in 1893. This remarkably large sheet is not a study for the painted composition, but probably a stage in the making of the final design for the well-known etching. The quality of the paper (extremely fine vellum) and

the size, close to that of a print, both suggest as much. At this stage in his career, a deep moral crisis led the painter to abandon naturalism in favor of transcendentally mystical subjects painted with an impressive lyrical and poetic intensity. These workers shown resting in the forest are sitting in a circle, communing as they listen intently to the music. They exude a spirituality akin to that of figures in Millet and Puvis de Chavannes. The calm, simplicity, and concentration of the participants are heigh-tened by the muted brown colors. I. J.

Claude Monet
Haystacks, Late Summer

Oil on canvas
1 ft. 11¾ in. × 3 ft. 3½ in. (0.60 × 1.00 m)
Purchased with funds from an anonymous Canadian
donation by the Musées Nationaux in 1975

In 1890, Monet's art took a step in a decisive new direction, which had been on the cards for a long while before. From now on, the artist only rarely painted single compositions, preferring to treat a motif through the "series" process. This method was finalized at Giverny, at a time when Monet expressed his attachment to the country by deciding to purchase the property where he had been living since 1883: "I'm hard at it, working stubbornly on a series of different effects (grain stacks), but at this time of the year the sun sets so fast it's impossible to keep up with it … the further I get, the more I see that a lot of work has to be done in order to render what I'm looking for: 'instantaneity', the 'envelope' above all, the same light spread over everything," he wrote to Geffroy. Monet painted a score of canvases of haystacks (his first proper "series"), through different seasons, from the end of summer up until winter, and at various times of day, from dawn to dusk. The artist's sole concern in focusing on this particular motif was to study forms in the light and capture transient effects. The various versions of the *Haystacks* reflect the position of the sun at the given "instant," as indicated by the shadows on the ground. Comparing these canvases with each other is what the artist wanted, and in 1891 he presented fifteen different versions at the Durand-Ruel gallery. In the catalogue they were announced by a title probably chosen by Monet himself: "Série de Meules 1890–1891". S. P.

Henri Edmond Cross
The Golden Isles

Oil on canvas
23½ × 21¼ in. (59.5 × 54 cm)
Acquired in 1947

In 1891 Cross made a permanent move to the South of France. In this painting *The Golden Isles*, or islands of Hyères—"so beautiful that they are called the Golden Isles," wrote the poet Émile Verhaeren—are observed from the beach at Cabasson, where the painter was renting a house. In this painting, executed under the spell of the Midi, Cross applied the neo-impressionist precepts he had recently absorbed from Georges Seurat and Paul Signac to a landscape reduced to a succession of horizontals, to which the sinuous line of the reliefs adds a subtle variation. In the style of Japanese prints, the high horizon leaves a strip of sky as narrow as the one formed by the sand, in what is a fine effect of symmetry. The format heightens this geometrical order and the decorativeness of the composition. The reflections of the sun occupy the main part of the painting: far from trying to capture the changing and transitory character of this light, the painter expresses "the immutable stillness" of this "white glow," as Stéphane Mallarmé put it. With Cross, the division of brushstrokes into a sprinkling of regular points and the use of calm horizontals combine the dream of an art as science with a musical, rhythmic interpretation of the landscape, in which the colored stippling of the shimmering, magical shore verges on abstraction, while inspiring irresistible thoughts of travel. S. Py.

Albert Bartholomé
Mask of Tadamasa Hayashi

Bronze with red patina
10 × 7½ × 6 in. (25.5 × 19 × 15.5 cm)
Gift of the Société des Amis du Musée d'Orsay, 1990

Tadamasa Hayashi was one of the first ambassadors of Japanese culture in France. He came to Paris in 1878 as interpreter to the dealer and curator Kenzaburô Wakaï at the Exposition Universelle. In 1883 he opened a shop selling *Japonaiseries*, which attracted numerous enthusiasts. This activity brought him into contact with artistic and literary circles.

Albert Bartholomé most likely met Hayashi in Degas's entourage. Fascinated by his face, which he found exotic, the sculptor began work on a portrait in 1892. He took inspiration for his representation from the masks worn in Noh theater, considered in those days as one of the highest forms of Japanese culture. However, thanks to the realistic modeling, the portrait is remarkably close to life.

A bronze version of this work was presented in 1894 at the Salon de la Société Nationale des Beaux-Arts, but it is not known if it was the copy now held at the Musée d'Orsay, which is remarkable for the quality of its casting and its warm red patina. Degas himself owned a plaster cast of this mask. É. P.

Paul Gauguin
Idol with Shell

Ironwood, *meleagris margaritifera* egg,
and parrot fish pharyngeal tooth
13½ × 5¾ × 7¼ x in. (34.4 × 14.8 × 18.5 cm)
Gift of Mme Huc de Monfreid, 1951

Gauguin took his sculptor's chisels with him when he went to Tahiti. There, disappointed at the lack of authentic art objects, he started working on utensils in guava wood and then, as here, ironwood. In 1900 he entrusted these misunderstood and unsellable "savage trinkets" to the painter Daniel de Monfreid, his correspondent in France. The chest containing Gauguin's sculptures reached France in 1901. Matisse saw them in 1903. Exhibited at the 1906 Salon d'Automne, they projected their energy to artists hungry for novelty. Was Gauguin trying to restore a mythology to those who had lost it? His Maori sculptures were his own invention, since no original monumental works were left on the island. The *Idol with Shell* is a god figure, its mouth filled with cannibal teeth (in fact the pharyngeal tooth of a parrot fish), and its legs tattooed. The pectoral and belt are in mother-of-pearl. On each side, a figure is represented twice over. The arms end in flattened, rake-like fingers, while the half-flexed legs suggest the sexual movements of the tamure dance. The ears are Maori decorative elements. Heads of *tikis* (second-order divinities that mark the boundaries of sacred places) adorn the base of the shield. In this sculpture, using a technique that was new to him, Gauguin went even further in exploring his "savage-in-spite-of-myself" than in his painting. A. P.

Akseli Gallen-Kallela
The Great Black Woodpecker

Oil on canvas mounted on cardboard
57½ × 35¾ in. (1.46 × 0.91 m)
Purchased with support from the family of
Akseli Gallen-Kallela, 2020

A native of western Finland, Akseli Gallen-Kallela developed a deep affinity for his country's natural environment, characterized by woodland, islands, and lakes. During his formative years in Paris, and in the decades that followed, the artist regularly returned to these remote regions to capture their vast spaces and majestic beauty. In the summer of 1892, the artist settled in the northeast of the country, on the shores of Lake Paanajärvi (now in Russia). Exploring his surroundings, here he adopts a high vantage point, gazing down over the vast forest.

Impressed by this striking view, Gallen-Kallela depicted it twice: first in a large gouache, with which he was deeply unhappy, and tore up. Two years later, however, in the painting here, he reproduced the exact same composition. In both versions, the artist accentuates the verticality of the landscape by way of a slender tree trunk cutting across the picture. Standing before this site, the artist felt, in his own words, "at one with nature." In the foreground, on the stump of a dead tree, a large black woodpecker characteristic of the region hammers away at a hollow branch with its pointed beak; its loud yaffle perturbs the silence of the forest.

While Finland, then a grand duchy of the Russian Empire, was struggling for autonomy—through a nationalist movement in which Gallen-Kallela was actively involved—this dry branch, proudly erect, and the bird's piercing shrieks not only attest to the artist's deep feeling for his homeland, they also personify Finland's quest for independence. A. R.

Henri de Toulouse-Lautrec
Jane Avril Dancing

Oil on cardboard
33½ × 17¾ in. (85.5 × 45 cm)
Bequeathed by Antonin Personnaz, 1937

Along with La Goulue, Jane Avril was one of the most famous dancers to promote the cancan, the very outré dance created in the mid-nineteenth century and synonymous with the pleasures of Montmartre in the Belle Époque. Toulouse-Lautrec gets straight to the point and shows her performing the famous leg-waggling action loved as a transgression of the general social prudishness that many found tiresome. Inspired by the layout of Japanese prints, the painter uses a vertical format with a somewhat upward viewpoint which heightens the sense of movement and contrasts with the dancer's absent, melancholy gaze. Behind her, we recog-nize Warrener who later served as a model for Toulouse-Lautrec. The following year, the painter took the quintessence of this composition and stylized the leg movements to make the poster *Jane Avril at the Jardin de Paris*, expressing the elegance of the model's action even more effectively. Toulouse-Lautrec and Jane Avril were artistic allies, each in a sense contributing to the other's fame: the artist's representations of Jane Avril were among his most famous works. X. R.

Henri de Toulouse-Lautrec
The Bed

Oil on cardboard mounted on parquet
21 × 27½ in. (53.5 × 70 cm)
Bequeathed by Antonin Personnaz, 1937

Like Degas some twenty years earlier, Toulouse-Lautrec found the world of Parisian prostitution an excellent vehicle for evoking the mores of the day. But whereas his much-admired elder was a discreet and distant chronicler whose monotypes were kept out of public view, Toulouse-Lautrec ran the risk of shocking critics by exhibiting the everyday life of these women who were like a second family to him in the bohemian, lowlife Paris of the Belle Époque. Refusing to reduce these inmates of the brothels to social types, or set them up for righteous opprobrium, he responded sympathetically to the lives of these women and avoided any form of moral judgment.

When dealing with female homosexuality, a great masculine obsession of the nineteenth century, he rejected all the scabrous or erotic innuendo peddled by earlier art and literature. Less explicit than his *Kiss*, in which two women passionately embrace, *The Bed* conveys the intimacy of love through the subtle exchange of gazes after the lovemaking itself. Dominated by the contrasting red of the counterpane and white of the sheets, the composition daringly gives us the singular presence of the two androgynous heads on the pillows, which seem almost drowned by the bedding, without renouncing a certain voyeurism. X. R.

Pierre Bonnard
Twilight or The Game of Croquet

Oil on canvas
4 ft. 3¼ in. × 5 ft. 3¾ in. (1.30 × 1.62 m)
Gift of Daniel Wildenstein through the Société des
Amis du Musée d'Orsay, 1985

When he first presented this ambitious painting in 1892, Bonnard gave it the title *Twilight*, making a sideshow of the game being played by the protagonists. Croquet, a fashionable game since the 1850s, is here being played at the family property, Le Clos au Grand-Lemps, in Isère, southeastern France, by the artist's father, his brother-in-law (the composer Antoine Terrasse, married to his sister Andrée, who was his favorite model at the time), and probably some cousin. The family scene actually inspired Bonnard to paint many pictures in the early 1890s, but this croquet game has none of the biting irony of *The Bourgeois Afternoon* of 1899 (Musée d'Orsay). Rejecting any descriptive purpose or psychology, the artist cuts out, juxtaposes, and interlinks these linear figures and the elements of scenery in the manner of a patchwork, with no obvious hierarchy. As in Japanese prints, the patterns on the fabrics play a crucial role in a composition dominated by Andrée. Full of sinuous curves and arabesques, everything about her contributes to the decorative refinement of the paradoxically enclosed open-air scene, artificial and silent despite the gaps through to the orange sky, or the lively round dance with its unreal dancers. Thus Bonnard's decorative ambition cannot be reduced to surface processes, but it reveals and engages a shrewd, subtle, ambiguous eye, showing the disquiet beneath the delicacy and the harmony. S. Py.

Paul Gauguin
Arearea or Joyousness

Oil on canvas
2 ft. 5¼ in. × 3 ft. ¾ in (74.5 × 93.5 cm)
Bequeathed by M. and Mme Lung, 1961

Produced in December 1892, just a few months before his return to France in June 1893, Gauguin counted *Arearea* among the three best paintings he made during this first stay in Tahiti, going as far as buying it back in 1895. His trip to Tahiti was an attempt to place his art back in contact with "virgin nature" and "savages," as he put it; he sought to penetrate the Maori culture, and to put it into pictures. Thus, the background of *Arearea* features a monumental idol, Hina, the goddess of the moon and of regeneration, dear to Gauguin. In fact, this impressive statue is an imaginary creation, inspired by the Marquesan *tikis* and by the idea Gauguin had of the monumental sculptures on Easter Island. *Arearea* does not capture the reality of Tahiti, which had fallen short of the artist's expectations, but invites us to a new Arcadia, the mysteries and harmony of which are celebrated by the sound of the flute (the *vivo*) and ritual dancing on a fine tropical evening. Hence, instead of learned decoding of possible local symbols such as the red dog, which became the target of the Paris critics in 1893, Gauguin uses his own metaphors and, most of all, the invention of pictorial equivalents: "Everything in my work is calculated, premeditated. It is music ... I obtain by an arrangement of lines and colors ... symphonies, harmonies which represent nothing absolutely real," but which provoke thoughts "simply through the mysterious relationships." S. Py.

Claude Monet
Rouen Cathedral, the Portal, Morning Sun
or Harmony in Blue
Rouen Cathedral, the Portal, Gray Weather
or Harmony in Gray

Oil on canvas
35¾ × 24¾ in. (92.2 × 63 cm)
Oil on canvas
3 ft. 3½ in. × 2 ft. 1¾ in. (1.02 × 0.65 m)
Bequeathed by Comte Isaac de Camondo, 1911

The "series" approach became systematic and highly meaningful for Monet when he started paying close attention to the play of light and shadow on the west front of Rouen Cathedral. Dated 1894, the cathedrals were painted on the spot in two campaigns, in 1892 and 1893 (the viewing angle hardly changes from one canvas to another), then finished in his studio at Giverny. This was the biggest "series" in number (some thirty versions), and it offers a spectacular demonstration of Monet's deep-felt desire to capture "instantaneity." The multiple studies correspond to the painter's increasingly acute sensitivity to changes in the light and atmospheric variations at different times of day and in different weather conditions. The Gothic architecture is not the object of study per se, but rather acts as a medium for Monet's pictorial research as he sought to render perceptible how its forms changed under the influence of the ever-changing light. Even a motif of a kind as solid and permanent as a monument is subject to such transformations: "Everything changes, even stone."

To suggest the material of the subject being treated, the painter resorts to an unusual, rugged technique that catches the light and restores the vibrations in the sunlight. For the exhi-

Claude Monet
Rouen Cathedral, the Portal and the Tour Saint-Romain, Morning Effect or Harmony in White
Rouen Cathedral, the Portal and the Tour Saint-Romain, Bright Sun or Harmony in Blue and Gold

Oil on canvas
3 ft. 6 in. × 2 ft. 4¾ in. (1.06 × 0.73 m)
Oil on canvas
3 ft. 6 in. × 2 ft. 5 in. (1.07 × 0.73 m)
Bequeathed by Comte Isaac de
Camondo, 1911

bition of twenty versions at Durand-Ruel's in 1895, Clemenceau wrote a rave review titled "Révolution de Cathédrales". "With twenty pictures, diverse effects aptly chosen, Monet has given us the feeling that he could have, that he would have made fifty, one hundred, one thousand, as many as the seconds in his life. Analyzing this exceptional "series," Clemenceau emphasized the "lesson" to be drawn from the set while regretting, as Pissarro later did, the dispersal of the paintings that would surely follow. Hanging on the walls of the Musée d'Orsay are five versions of the *Cathedrals* in different harmonies (one, the *Harmony in Brown*, snapped up by the State directly from the artist in 1907, and four others bequeathed to French museums by Comte Isaac de Camondo in 1911), which regain their original meaning by featuring in relation to each other in line with Monet's wishes. The painter was fond of spending hours of his time gazing at them while working on the various different versions through a comparative approach: "I could not dispose of a painting before I … had looked over it on more than one occasion back in Giverny." S. P.

Auguste Delaherche
Vase

Enameled stoneware
H. 20¼ in. (51.2 cm)
Acquired in 1992

The ceramics section at the 1889 Exposition Universelle in Paris was notably innovative, with many new creations demonstrating the possibility of going beyond the simple imitation of past productions. Ernest Chaplet freed himself of the notion of decorativeness and began experiments that would occupy him for the rest of his life, creating stippling effects on porcelain obtained simply by the combination of firings. As for Auguste Delaherche, active in the Pays de Bray area of Picardy, he stood out for his stunning mastery of enamel and stoneware firing, in which effects that appeared to be due to the simple process were in fact carefully planned. As this unique piece shows, by his mastery of the firing process the artist achieved an ideal union in which form and decoration (the latter due simply to the effects of the material) set each other off. This vase also attests to the rather chaotic experimentation with the famous Chinese reds that had begun in the 1840s, notably at the Manufacture de Sèvres. The efforts both of this major national institution and of independent ceramists did not begin to bear satisfactory fruit until the late 1870s. Ph. T

József Rippl-Rónai
Park at Night

Pastel on paper, mounted on canvas
15 × 18 in. (38.4 × 46.2 cm)
Gift of the Société des Amis du Musée d'Orsay, 1994

Throughout the nineteenth century, artists from all over Europe came to study in Paris. The capital of the arts and of fashion attracted the young and inquisitive who had dreams of discovering the latest trends. Artists coming from the East often stopped off in Germany for a while on their way to confronting Parisian innovation; one who did this was Rippl-Rónai, born south of Budapest in 1861, whose first stopping point was Munich. In 1886 he moved on to Paris and the studio of his fellow-countryman, the painter Mihály Munkácsy. In the summer of 1889, his first brief stay at Pont-Aven was a chance to meet Gauguin, whose new expressive manner fascinated him. In 1893, he exhibited with the Nabis. He was then nicknamed "the Hungarian Nabi." This pastel by Rippl-Rónai dates from his time in Paris, called his "black period," and depicts a nameless nocturnal landscape devoid of any human presence. The streetlamp in the center of the composition and the patches of light on the sheet evoke the presence of man and the growth of the modern city. The ghostly tree trunks give rhythm to the page and give off an uncertain, bewitching, and disturbing feeling. I. J.

Jean Carriès
Faun

Bronze
14 × 13½ × 9¼ in. (35.3 × 34 × 23.8 cm)
Acquired in 1984

Born in Lyon in 1855 into a humble family, and dying in Paris in 1894, Jean Carriès was an untypical sculptor who was greatly admired in the late nineteenth century. He was noticed at the Salon of 1881 for his subtly patinated busts of Déshérités (The Disinherited), combining Naturalism and Symbolism. Carriès was extremely demanding in terms of the quality of his bronzes, and in October 1883 he met the caster Pierre Bingen, who specialized in lost-wax casting; given the excellence of his product, his reputation soared. Lost-wax casting has the aura of prestige of the Renaissance and offers a faithful rendition of the plaster model. Through this crucial collaboration between the two men, who were described as working as a team in a "frenzy to get things right," the sculptor was able to design his own patinas for his bronzes. The *Faun*, which Carriès also produced in various colors of earthenware as well as in patinated plaster, is one of the most evocative works in this introspective vein, in which the hybridization of man and beast takes on a melancholy, dreamlike tone. É. P.

Henri Edmond Cross
The Evening Air

Oil on canvas
3 ft. 9¾ in. × 5 ft. 5¼ in. (1.16 × 1.66 m)
Gift of Mme Ginette Signac, 1976

"Why, since we both love and know this sunny land, should we not try to raise up a decorative monument to it?" wrote Signac to his friend Cross in 1893, bewitched by the charm of Provence. *The Evening Air* is Cross's response to this idea, which in Signac's case bore fruit in the vast *In the Time of Pleasure* (in the city hall of Montreuil, northeast Paris). In what is also one of his biggest works, Cross, as he put it, evokes "happiness, happy beings who will have become true men in a few centuries from now, when pure anarchy will have been achieved." Inspired by the "great magical or decorative aspects" of the Mediterranean coastline, this golden age painting owes a great deal to the spare compositions of Puvis de Chavannes. Like him, but also like Maurice Denis in *The Muses*

(p. 236), Cross uses the same model (his wife) repeatedly for different figures, which adds to the unreality and abstraction of the scene. Like Signac's, Cross's work demonstrates the validity and fecundity of neo-impressionist thought in the area of decoration, which was a key issue for the avant-gardes after 1890. It offered the expressive and rhythmic power of line and color, which here are dominated by the complementary oranges and mauves of the sunset, divided into mosaic-like slabs. In 1905 this painting was acquired by Signac, who hung it up in his villa at Saint-Tropez, alongside Matisse's *Luxury, Calm, and Pleasure*. The Matisse painting reflects his admiration for *The Evening Air*, which he saw in the summer of 1904. S. Py

Edward Burne-Jones, designer
George Titcomb, master stained-glass maker
Morris & Co., manufacturer
Enoch

Stained-glass panel
50½ × 19¾ in. (1.29 × 0.50 m)
Donated by the Société des Amis
du Musée d'Orsay, 2020

Morris & Co. was established in 1861 by William Morris, founder of the Arts & Crafts movement in England and a close friend of the Pre-Raphaelite painters, including Edward Burne-Jones. The company regularly produced furnishings and furniture for churches, such as the chapel at Cheadle Royal Hospital in Manchester, which was decorated between 1906 and 1915. The stained-glass windows were based on drawings Burne-Jones had made between 1874 and 1876.

Enoch is a biblical patriarch who, in the Book of Genesis, was taken up to heaven by God to sit at his right hand. A rare theme in iconography, Morris & Co. turned to it again for the cathedral in Calcutta and at Holy Trinity Sloane Square in London. Burne-Jones's composition throws into relief the imposing figure of the patriarch just as he is being called aloft by God. The hands of the patriarch and the Almighty are seen clasped in the upper right corner. This gesture testifies both to Enoch's closeness to the Lord in his earthly life and to God's desire to raise the patriarch up from the secular world and bring him to His bosom. Enoch's features and morphology betray Burne-Jones' love of the figures of the Italian Renaissance.

The stained glass is an example of the quest for a tonal depth comparable with that attained by medieval glass makers, as well as of the more contemporary idea of allowing daylight to flood into a building by using lighter grounds. É. D.

Paul Signac
Woman with a Parasol

Oil on canvas
32 × 25½ in. (81 × 65 cm)
Gift of Dr. Charles Cachin, 1989

The model for this portrait was Berthe Roblès, a milliner who became Signac's companion in the early 1880s and his wife in 1892. She had sat for the painter before, but always with her face hidden. Here her face is shown for the first time, standing out against the parasol, and clearly visible in spite of the shade. *Woman with a Parasol* satisfies the criteria of resemblance while importing the neo-impressionist aesthetic, which Signac rarely used as he considered it had lost its vigor. This extremely simplified portrait is based on the organization of clear-cut forms and the alternation of straight and curved lines, which even form sinuous arabesques on the mutton sleeves, then the height of fashion. The rigor of the presentation does not exclude a few highly stylized details, such as the tassel and the columbine at bottom left. In spite of the rich, vibrant scattering of colored dots, the artist gives us the impression of a limited number of colors dominated by the contrasts between red and green, yellow, and purple. Dismissing psychology, Signac here offers a carefully thought-out portrait whose deliberately hieratic look and apparent simplicity bring to mind Georges Seurat, but also the Italian primitives, whom he greatly admired. S. Py.

Maurice Denis
The Muses

Oil on canvas
5 ft. 7½ in. × 4 ft. 6¼ in. (1.71 × 1.37 m)
Acquired in 1932

Shortly after exhibiting *The Muses*, Denis married Marthe Meurier, in June 1893. This painting is a hymn to the love he felt for her. The three dreamy, meditative muses in the foreground and their sisters are indeed all portraits or evocations of Marthe, who is shown in multiple forms. The figures tread on a carpet of stylized horse chestnut leaves in a "sacred grove" that owes a great deal to Puvis de Chavannes. Denis gives his own very personal take on a classical theme; he deprives the muses of their attributes and replaces their ancient drapes with modern dress. Most of all, he adds a tenth muse. In the background and in full sunlight, like the communicant in *Landscape with Green Trees*, she is the chosen one, Marthe, the one who inspires him and enables him to reconcile art and life, the mind and the flesh, idea and form. This painting stands as a manifesto for a new Symbolism, in which ideas are expressed by purely visual means and not through descriptive or narrative processes. By exhibiting *The Muses* as a "decorative panel" in 1893, Denis stresses the ambition of this large format, based on the colorful, rhythmical simplification of the landscape and the figures: in Denis's eyes, "art is a sanctification of nature." S. Py.

Maurice Denis
Landscape with Green Trees
or Beech Trees in Kerduel

Oil on canvas
18 × 17 in. (46 × 43 cm)
Acceptance in lieu, 2001

In 1889, Denis asserted that "a picture, before being a battle horse, a nude woman, or any anecdote, is essentially a plane surface covered with colors assembled in a certain order." *Landscape with Green Trees* reflects the aesthetic principles of the Nabis. The vertical lines of the tree trunks set the rhythm of the composition and heighten the flatness of the painted surface. Simplified outlines surround the patches in brightly colored flat tints, released from any descriptive calling. Denis is nonetheless depicting a particular place, a forest near Kerduel Castle, King Arthur's forest evoking the Breton legends dear to him. *Landscape with Green Trees* is not just a radical painting; it is also a symbolic meditation on life and art. The communicant girls in Catholic processions here also represent what the artist called "soul figures," walking through the forest of life or of the mind. As in *The Muses*, one of them is detached from the group and is about to pass over the pure blue wall, having been called by a winged angel. She also represents the chosen one, who has found the right path; she symbolizes accomplishment in art, religion, and love. S. Py.

Georges Rochegrosse
The Knight of the Flowers

Oil on canvas
7 ft. 8½ in. × 12 ft. 4 in. (2.35 × 3.76 m)
Acquired in 1894

If there were a pantheon of kitsch at the Musée d'Orsay, this work would have to be the altarpiece. Many art historians take the view that this painting wins, as American critic Robert Rosenblum put it, "first prize for the silliest, most extravagant, and pretentious Wagner illustration ever." But the work needs to be seen in context. Rochegrosse, one of the last of the great history painters, has not produced a literal illustration of the episode in Richard Wagner's opera *Parsifal* when the hero, predestined to find the Holy Grail, passes through the magician Klingsor's enchanted garden, deaf to the flower maidens seeking to seduce him. Rising above the tale itself, Rochegrosse sought to produce an effigy of the "being smitten with the ideal," creating a truly symbolist work. In this way the artist reverses the iconographical tradition of the Temptations of St. Anthony—for, while the saint had convulsions, being attacked by lecherous, bestial monsters in the darkness, the chaste knight, gazing up to heaven, serenely ignores the joyful riot of colors, bodies, and flowers, solely through the reflective powers of his polished suit of armor, the image of his soul tempered in the steel of faith. He borrows the atmosphere of romance and its acid colors from the English Pre-Raphaelites, whose success spread to France in the 1890s. But these female bodies are so undevilish that this academic work comes uncannily close to Renoir's hedonistic open-air nudes, and to the cultural movement of naturism that was coming into being around the same time in Germany. C. F.

Henri Rousseau, known as le Douanier Rousseau
War or The Ride

Oil on canvas
3 ft. 9 in. × 6 ft. 4¾ in. (1.14 × 1.95 m)
Acquired in 1946

In a short biography written in 1895, Henri Rousseau observed about himself: "He has increasingly perfected the original genre that he has adopted, and is in the process of becoming one of our ablest realist painters." When, a year earlier, the artist presented his great allegory of *War* at the Salon des Indépendants, the work did not go unnoticed. At the time, however, its "realist" qualities were less eye-catching than its absolute originality. Above and beyond the sarcastic remarks that inevitably accompanied his presentation, it was "his brave attempt in the direction of the symbol," his innovative "strangeness" that Louis Roy, then a critic with *Mercure de France*, singled out for praise.

Rousseau attained the symbol through his keen sense of synthesis. War, an ageless, grimacing woman, holding a sword and smoking torch, is riding a flying horse side-saddle. She floats above a desolate landscape and a heap of corpses. With no anecdotal or narrative elements, the composition is more like an icon; indeed it is a composition that Rousseau is thought to have borrowed from a press engraving presenting a serial titled *The Czar*. The stylization of forms, the absence of any realistic perspective, and the flat patches of color are those of popular imagery.

Having fallen into oblivion after the exhibition, the work was rediscovered after the Liberation, rolled up in a farmer's barn. It was one of the key exhibits at the retrospective held in Paris in December 1944 for the centenary of the painter's birth, and was later purchased by the Louvre. C. B.

Édouard Vuillard
Public Gardens: Little Girl Playing, The Question

Oil on canvas
7 ft. ½ in. × 2 ft. 10½ in. (2.14 × 0.88 m);
7 ft. ½ in. × 3 ft. ½ in. (2.14 × 0.92 m)
Bequeathed in 1978 by Mme Alexandre Radot

According to the often quoted testimony of the painter Verkade, "Early in 1890, the war cry went out from studio to studio: 'Walls, walls to decorate! … There are no easel paintings, just decorations!'" Rejecting the traditional hierarchy and boundary between fine art and applied art, the Nabis held the view that "decorative art" and wall painting were also areas to be exploited and revived. With few public commissions forthcoming, Nabi decorative work mostly blossomed thanks to private art lovers, with the Natanson brothers leading the way—the editors of *La Revue Blanche*, an avant-garde journal to which the Nabis were regular contributors. More than just a journal, it was an intellectual home, a whole mindset. The Nabis held exhibitions at the review's offices.

The Natansons provided support, buying and commissioning works. Between 1892 and 1899, Vuillard painted no less than four decorative cycles for them.

In 1894, the elder brother, Alexandre, asked Vuillard to do the first Nabi set of large-scale works, *Public Gardens*; the Musée d'Orsay owns five of the nine panels, which were originally set in the woodwork of the dining room at their private mansion on the Avenue Hoch, and which went their separate ways in 1929. Vuillard proposed a monumental rendering of subjects taken from modern life (here the Bois de Boulogne, just round the corner). "Humble subject matter," as the artist put it, in the spirit of the Cluny tapestries he then admired, rather than edifying heroic tales for a complex set for

Édouard Vuillard
Public Gardens: Nannies, Conversation, The Red Parasol

Tempera on canvas
6 ft. 11¾ in × 2 ft. 4¾ in. (2.13 × 0.73 m);
6 ft. 11¾ in × 5 ft. ½ in. (2.13 × 1.54 m);
7 ft. ¼ in. × 2 ft. 8 in. (2.14 × 0.81 m)
Acquired in 1929

which Vuillard was given free rein. Seeking, he wrote, the "expression of a private feeling on a large surface," he brings into play a mostly female world, of smartly dressed mothers, children playing or running around, and nannies gossiping. The gestures and poses are occasionally exaggerated and some of the faces are caricatures. The layout is spacious, its rhythm provided by the play of arabesques and the bold, skillful alternation of full and empty areas, in the manner of the Japanese screens that the artist admired. The high, curved horizon and stacked planes form a kind of panoramic space but with no depth, and the shadowless figures seem to have been added onto it. For decorative work, as Vuillard noted at the time in his diary, the imagination needs to genera-

lize without the description being objectively accurate. Thus everything, down to the fresh, bright colors of the fresco-like matt distemper, conspires to create an animated, sparklingly cheerful atmosphere (despite the woman in mourning with a parasol, sitting on her own), and a definitely happy, carefree feeling that we do not often see in Vuillard's art. S. Py.

Georges Lacombe
Existence

Walnut
27 × 16¼ × 2¼ in. (68.5 × 41.5 × 6 cm)
Acquired in 1956

At the request of his future mother-in-law Gabrielle Wenger, Georges Lacombe made for his Versailles studio a bed in which his two daughters were born. The "Nabi sculptor" carved the wood panels directly, in a primitivist style akin to Gauguin's own work around this time. The life cycle is portrayed in four reliefs, *Conception*, *Birth*, *Death*, and *Existence*. This last panel, steeped in occultism, links the others and explains them in kabbalistic language. Having steeped himself in his reading of the works of Papus, the *Absolute Key to Occult Science* (1888), and *The Tarot of the Bohemians* (1889), in *Existence* Paul Sérusier's pro-tégé expounds his mystical take on the enigma of the world. A large serpent biting its own tail symbolizes the endless new beginning and the energy governing the universe. The coils of its body draw at once the eyes of two faces in profile kissing, and those of one face seen frontally, and a formal syncretism influenced by so-called "primitive" art. The large mouth thus formed refers to the second Tarot card, featuring woman in her relationship to man. Their union is also evoked through the double pentagram symbolizing man, the filaments undulating like spermatozoa, and the large lance-shaped leaf resembling female genitals. O. F.

Joaquín Sorolla
Return from Fishing

Oil on canvas
8 ft. 8¼ in. × 13 ft. 3 in. (2.65 × 4.04 m)
Acquired in 1895

Exhibited by Sorolla at the Salon in 1894, this painting on a grand scale was immediately purchased by the State for the Musée du Luxembourg. At a time when the representation of everyday labor was a dominant theme in the French naturalism that was spreading through Europe, the Spanish painter managed to achieve a personal aesthetic solution by his depiction of these sailors bringing their boat onto the beach with the help of an ox. In this scene, set on the seashore of his home city, Valencia, Sorolla was certainly offering a variation on the familiar theme of the alliance between man and beast, but he was also applying a broad, bright brushstroke that was close to the luminist work of Scandinavian painters, reflecting with marvelous precision the sparkling of the Mediterranean light on the surface of the water. There is no sign here of decrying the social condition of fishermen or lamenting man's tragic struggle with nature. Here, Sorolla appears to abandon the militancy of *And They Say Fish Is Expensive* (Casón del Buen Retiro Museum, Madrid) for a celebration of the concentration that the sailors bring to a calm, everyday activity. In this canvas, which fully exploits the developments of outdoor painting, we can begin to observe the freedom with which, in around 1900, Sorolla would describe a new relation to nature in his paintings of naked boys lying on the beach. X. R.

Pierre Fix-Masseau
The Secret

Polychrome plaster
30 × 7 × 7 in. (76 × 17.5 × 18 cm)
Gift of Christiane Hillemand, 2003

In the late nineteenth century, Fix-Masseau, who was director of the École des Arts Décoratifs in Limoges up until 1935, was among the artists engaged in modern decorative art. He created objects combining dream and fantasy with an evocation of nature. Certain features, like hair, or here the drapery, take on a strange importance. Fix-Masseau included the most varied materials in his works, thereby heightening their decorative appearance. The sculptor explored the expressive properties of ivory and ceramics, and researched special patinas for bronze, producing a range of inkwells, candelabras, vases, and so on. His marked taste for the female figure combined with floral motifs, his fascination for the unusual, and his interest in household items make him an exponent of Art Nouveau and of Symbolism as well.

The Secret is a perfect illustration of this: a huge veil reveals more than it covers of the nakedness of a priestess or magician figure, her face half concealed under the striking drape effect. The ivory box is the initial focus of attention and the precious material is matched by the beautiful, wood-like finish. It was with figures like this that the artist came to the notice of people like the caster Siot-Decauville, who brought out *The Secret* in bronze. É. P.

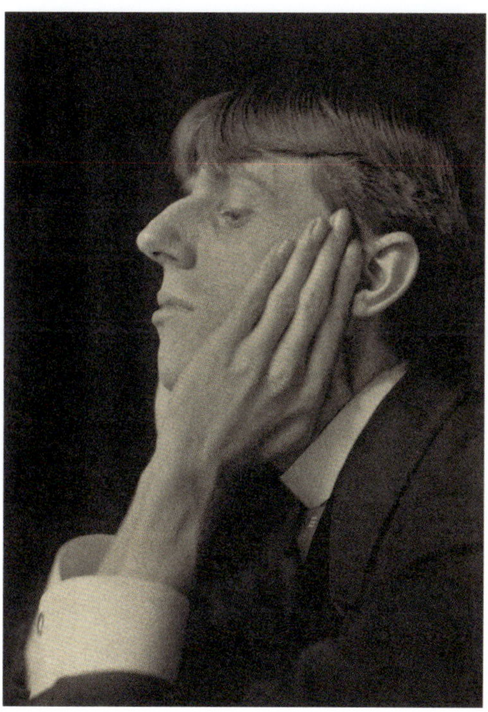

Frederick Evans
The Illustrator Aubrey Beardsley

Platinum print
6 × 4 in. (15 × 10 cm)
Acquired in 1985

What we see in this portrait of the English artist Aubrey Beardsley by the London photographer and bookseller Frederick Evans is not meta-physical questioning but inspired boredom. It is known that the sitting went on forever, and yet here we are charmed by the disarming natu-ralness of the dandy's pose. It could well be that Evans—a master of architectural photography, and particularly medieval architecture—took his final inspiration from the famous chimera on Notre-Dame de Paris, known as the Stryge. In this possible nod to the grotesque spirit and to the decorative line, typical of the young illustrator, the photographer opted for a bold close-up, taken from a slightly low angle, which, while conferring a sculptural monumentality on the model, draws our attention to the long, nervous hands, the draftsman's tools, which so fascinated him. Beardsley was so pleased with the result that he decided to include this por-trait in his edition of Thomas Malory's *Morte d'Arthur*, the illustration of which had been his first major commission the previous year, at the age of seventeen, obtained through Evans. T. G.

Théodore Rivière
Salammbo and Matho,
I Love You! I Love You!

Bronze, ivory, gold, and turquoise
15¾ × 8½ × 7½ in. (40 × 21.4 × 19 cm)
Bequeathed by Paul Cosson, 1926

There was something of a craze for polychrome sculpture in the nineteenth century, as can be seen with this *Salammbo* made of ivory, gold, bronze, and turquoise. When gold and ivory are combined, as in this instance, it is known as "chryselephantine" sculpture.

Théodore Rivière was a leading orientalist sculptor. He drew on literary texts and traveled extensively in North Africa, the Far East, and South America.

The subject of this work is taken from Gustave Flaubert's novel, *Salammbô*, published in 1862. The action takes place between 241 and 238 BCE, during the war between Carthage and her rebellious mercenaries. The chief of the barbarian soldiers, the Libyan Matho, is in love with Salammbo, the daughter of his Carthaginian enemy Hamilcar Barca. Rivière has chosen the moment when Matho is lynched by the people and dies at the feet of his beloved, crying: "I love you! I love you!" Many other symbolist artists were also inspired by Salammbo, the "femme fatale".

The statuette created a sensation at the Salon of 1895. Many copies were made in bronze, and in biscuit, which is unglazed white porcelain. É. P.

Aristide Maillol
Woman with a Parasol

Oil on canvas
6 ft. 2¾ in. × 4 ft. 10¾ in. (1.90 × 1.49 m)
Acquired in 1955

Maillol began his career in the fields of painting and the decorative arts. His tapestry work, in particular, was admired by Gauguin. He joined the Nabis, whose stimulating companionship can be felt in this ambitious full-length portrait. Struggling against the wind like the figure in Monet's painting on the same theme (p. 173), this *Woman with a Parasol* was probably modeled on the Mediterranean shore by one of the nieces of his sculptor friend, Faraill, whose family originally owned the painting. The picture echoes the seaside scenes favored by the impressionists and by artists like Jacques-Émile Blanche. A reformulation of Puvis de Chavannes's earlier *Young Girls by the Seaside* (p. 152), the image is deliberately simplified. Like

Georges Seurat, Maillol plays on the tension between an attentive evocation of the modern world, seen in the details of the clothing and realism of the face, and archaic inflections, such as the strict profile and eschewal of psychology, the geometrical posture and the reduction of the background to four horizontal bands of color, which bring this elegant figure closer to the painted and sculpted friezes of Egypt, but also the protagonists of Quattrocento frescoes, whose color spectrum Maillol adopts here. His portrait-cum-tableau contributed to the redefinition of the relations between painting and decoration, a crucial artistic issue in the early 1890s. S. Py.

Henri de Toulouse-Lautrec
Lady Clown Cha-U-Kao

Oil on cardboard
22¾ × 17 in. (58 × 43 cm)
Bequeathed by Comte Isaac de Camondo, 1911

Toulouse-Lautrec conceals nothing of the buxom acrobat's bosom, a motif he returns to in one of the plates in the album of eleven lithographs *Elles* (They)—a succession of scenes of feminine intimacy—which he brought out in 1896. The presence in this set of Cha-U-Kao, with her legs apart, sounds a discordant note, and shows the artist's attachment to this clown he met either at the Moulin-Rouge or at the new circus on the Rue Saint-Honoré. This stage name, no doubt a jokey pun derived from "chahut-chaos" (*chahut* being her cancan-like dance and *chaos* the uproar that greeted her), accounts for the trademark odd outfit and pointed hairstyle worn by this celebrity of late-night entertainment. The yellow ruff is another distinguishing feature, as well as an excuse for a splash of bright yellow amid the play of subtly transparent tones, with the black of the costume and the red mass of the sofa. Although he uses a close-up angle reminiscent of Manet and Degas, artists he admired, Toulouse-Lautrec devises a whole staging in this dressing room, with the presence of a man revealed in the mirror in the corner of the composition. It allows us to see the—generally seedy—flip side of the destiny of these entertainers, who offer society a distraction from decent morals, going as far as to embody an unconscious already revealed by Baudelaire in his poems. X. R.

Paul Signac
The Red Buoy

Oil on canvas
32 × 25½ in. (81 × 65 cm)
Donated by Dr. Pierre Hébert, 1957

It was a tranquil late afternoon, and the *tartanes* (fishing ships) had returned to harbor at Saint-Tropez, a village that Signac was captivated by in 1892: "I have material here to work on for the rest of my life. What I have just discovered is happiness." He made many long stays and painted several views of Saint-Tropez harbor. *The Red Buoy*, whose title indicates the primacy of color, came at a moment of transition. Acclaimed from 1890 as the "young glory of Neo-Impressionism" by his friend, the critic Félix Fénéon, Signac had successfully experimented with the divisionist touch, distributing color in slight, regular dots. Here, Signac applies the color in stratified brushstrokes, modulated in accordance with the zones of the painting, focusing attention on his study of the reflections in the handsome light of the South. What he called "diluting the finish" enabled him to go back to the initial objective of Neo-Impressionism, a term to which Signac long preferred the formulation "chromo-luminarism": "maximum light, color, and harmony." This combined liberation of touch and color would be decisive for the emergence of Fauvism in 1904-05: during the summer of 1904, Matisse painted in Saint-Tropez in the company of Signac, Henri Edmond Cross, Maximilien Luce, and Fénéon. S. Py.

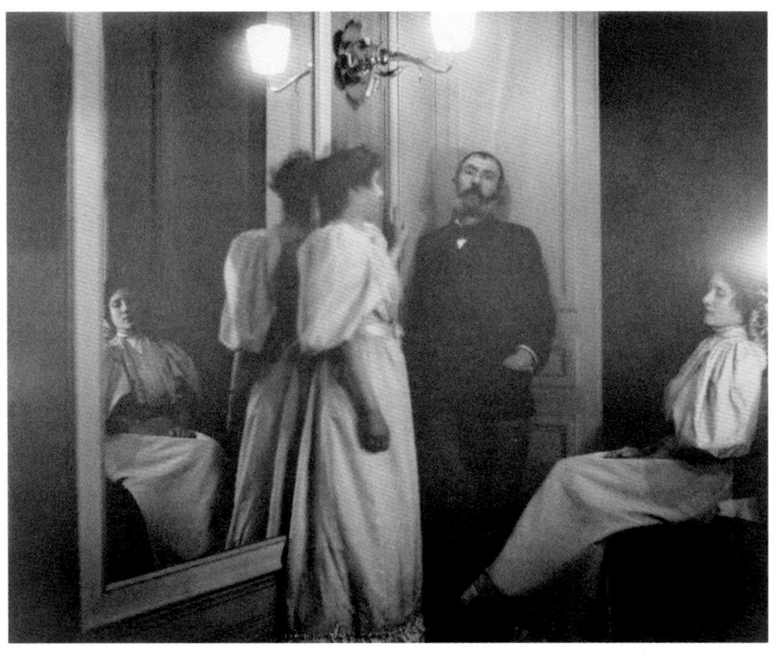

Edgar Degas
Portrait of the Painter Henry Lerolle and his Two Daughters, Yvonne and Christine, with a Mirror

Gelatin-silver print from a glass negative
11½ × 14¼ in. (29 × 36.2 cm)
Acquired in 2004

Following a course of treatment at Mont-Dore in the summer of 1895, Degas was caught up in a brief but intense passion for photography that lasted less than two years. He took pictures of his nearest and dearest, either at his place or in their respective homes. This meditative night portrait of the painter Henry Lerolle and his two eldest daughters, Yvonne and Christine, was created at their Paris address on the Avenue Lequesne.

Unlike his contemporaries, who were drawn to the snapshot, the open air, and the expressive search for movement, Degas freezes in lamplit interiors his models' bodies and expressions, which they hold still for long minutes in front of the camera lens. Through a subtle play of indirect lighting and reflections, he brings out these hieratic silhouettes from the dark field of the room, leaving the details of both the room and the faces in deep shadow. Conversely, the dresses, door, and the plinth of the mirror absorb the gleam of the lamps. In his treatment of chiaroscuro, Degas returns to the opposition of black and white that he had already experimented with in his monotypes.

In the midst of this opaque atmosphere, echoing the symbolist circles that he indeed frequented at the Lerolles's, these figures—deep in thought—definitely recall the early aesthetic of the portrait, that of the early daguerreotypes and calotypes, when the subjects, blinded by the dazzling light and turned to stone by the lengthy exposure time, were seemingly suspended.
M. R.

Henri de Toulouse-Lautrec
Panels for La Goulue's Booth:
Dance at the Moulin-Rouge

Oil on canvas,
9 ft. 9¼ in. × 10 ft. 4½ in. (2.98 × 3.16 m)
Acquired in 1929

Following on radically from his lithography work, deployed in the form of posters in the street, Toulouse-Lautrec accepted a commission to do two monumental decorative panels for La Goulue, a well-known cabaret dancer who was wishing to perform in a booth set up at the Foire du Trône. Out of loyalty to this fading star of the Moulin Rouge, he produced a work, which stood exposed to the elements at the entrance to her booth, and was only saved from a very early demise when it was bought up by the collector Viau in 1900. *Dance at the Moulin-Rouge, La Goulue and Valentin le Désossé* (left panel) commemorates the devilish acrobatic dances that brought fame to the dancer and her partner in the past. To the rear are the top representatives of this nocturnal life, including Jane Avril in the feathered hat. *The Moorish Dance* (right panel, not reproduced here) recalls the belly dance show performed by La Goulue inside her booth, loosely inspired by eastern choreographies. The audience is placed in bold perspective in the foreground, and was composed of friends of Toulouse-Lautrec such as Oscar Wilde, seen from behind, and the well-known critic and backer Félix Fénéon, in the bottom right-hand corner. The artist has also featured himself amid this colorful audience. X. R.

Émile Zola
Jacques and Denise in their house at Verneuil

Gold-toned aristotype with
glossy gelatin surface
3½ × 2½ in. (9 × 6.5 cm)
Purchased in 2017

The album entitled *Denise et Jacques. Histoire vraie par Émile Zola. Juin-septembre 1897*, which the writer compiled himself, contains snapshots of his children in various activities. In the garden of the house at Verneuil-sur-Seine, Denise and Jacques run around on the gravel, learn to ride a bicycle, sit astride a mechanical horse, blow soap bubbles, and play with shovels and watering cans.

Zola learned photography in 1888, at the time he was falling in love with Jeanne Rozerot, a laundress who worked for his wife, Alexandrine. From 1894, having almost completed his vast *Rougon-Macquart* novel saga, Zola took it up more intensively. Of the ten thousand photographs of the places where he stayed, the sites he visited, the foreign cities he explored, and his friends or staff, the most remarkable are those he took of the microcosm of his family.

In a kind of diary, his images capture all the drama of this double life. With his mistress Jeanne and their children, Zola kept himself to himself, in a "large country house enclosed by walls no stranger's gaze could penetrate," as Denise wrote in 1931 in *Émile Zola par sa fille*. Records of the emotional bond between him and his "adored darlings," these photographs are nothing less than declarations of love. Bathed in summer light, Zola captures his little ones' lives—reclusive, but full of joy. M. R.

Emmanuel Frémiet
St. Michael Slaying the Dragon

Copper
20 ft. 3 in. × 8 ft. 6½ in. × 3 ft. 11¼ in.
(6.17 × 2.60 × 1.20 m)
Gift of Mme Gabrielle Pasquier-Monduit, entrusted to
the Musée d'Orsay in 1983

While he produced monumental work such as the famous *Joan of Arc* in the Place des Pyramides, Frémiet supplied numerous models for casting, including the statuette of *St. Michael*. The work was noticed by Victor Petitgrand, the architect in charge of restoration work on the abbey on Mont Saint-Michel; in 1895, he commissioned Frémiet to produce a plaster model 7 feet (2.20 m) high for a copper work in excess of 20 feet (6 m) that was intended for the church spire. The Musée d'Orsay copy is a replica of it. Any artist portraying St. Michael has to measure up to Raphael's *St. Michael Vanquishing Satan*. While his wings are deployed, Frémiet's archangel is less ethereal: his calmly jutting hip gives him the self-assurance of one who knows himself to be invested with divine power to overcome evil. The armor, associated with St. Michael since the Middle Ages, is rendered with meticulous accuracy. Having worked on the Château de Pierrefonds with Viollet-le-Duc, the sculptor's obsession with historical truth was bound to delight someone like Petitgrand, full of the theories of the great architect and restorer. The holy protector of the French Army during the Hundred Years' War, St. Michael was taken as the symbol of national resistance following the defeat of 1870; such fervor, the eminently symbolic status of Mont Saint-Michel, and the power of the work itself explain the success of further bronzes produced from this model. O. F.

Georges Minne
The Mason

Marble
30¼ × 23½ × 9 in. (77 × 60 × 23 cm)
Acquired in 2010

The closing years of the nineteenth century were extremely fertile ones in the career of Georges Minne, working from his villa at Forest near Brussels. At the time, he was moving in Belgian avant-garde circles. Belgian architect Victor Horta and artist Henry Van de Velde both possessed copies of the *Mason*, which Minne produced the same year as his well-known *Boy Kneeling* (p. 268). The Musée d'Orsay marble comes from the collection of the tycoon Fritz Waerndorfer, a friend of Minne's and a collector of his work, who played a key role in the Vienna Secession. The original copy of the *Mason* was designed for Victor Horta's home, and the subject is undoubtedly a tribute to his profession as an architect. Leaning on a bent leg, the crafts-man is holding an imaginary plumb line over a rough-hewn block. Minne's admiration for Gothic art is noticeable both in the subject and in the setting of the figure inside a constrained frame; this decorative work was the starting point of a staircase. The craftsman's body forms a compact block with just an arm, a leg, and the head emerging. What make the composition so effective are the simple lines of force, with the powerful vertical line of the arms supporting the convex shape drawn by the right leg and the back. *The Mason*'s synthetic modeling indi-cates the influence of another fellow country-man of Georges Minne's, the sculptor Constan-tin Meunier. O. F.

Léon Frédéric
The Ages of the Worker

Oil on canvas (triptych)
5 ft. 4¼ in. × 6 ft. 1½ in. (1.63 × 1.87 m: center panel);
5 ft. 4¼ in. × 3 ft. 1¼ in. (1.63 × 0.94 m: left and right panels)
Acquired in 1898

The Brussels-based painter Léon Frédéric executed this ambitious work about the conditions and fate of contemporary working people between 1895 and 1897. At the center, children mix with a dense crowd in a working-class street in Brussels, while the lateral panels follow the "ages" all the way to old age: for the men, work; for the women, childbearing and motherhood. In the background we can make out the Saint-Gilles prison, the Saint-Pierre hospital, and the courts—reminders of the precarious life of the working man. Frédéric rendered each detail meticulously and yet, paradoxically, this heightened realism contributes to the work's symbolism. A photographic hyperrealism combines with unreal light, sharp colors, and an unlikely accumulation of figures. Above all, the painter associates a multiplicity of references, drawing on Flemish tradition (the primitives, Breughel, Rubens, Jordaens), popular prints (the theme of the "steps of life"), and religious painting (the triptych form and transpositions of the life of Christ). Like Minne, Frédéric renewed expression of the sacred and provided a spiritual backdrop to the burning social issues of the day, bestowing nobility and dignity on the poorest of the poor at a time when they were attaining their first form of political representation in Belgium. When the French state bought this painting in 1898, the artist felt he had truly arrived. S. Py.

Richard Riemerschmid
Candlestick

Brass
14 × 6¼ in. (35.8 × 16 cm)
Acquired in 2002

As of 1897, Richard Riemerschmid decided to abandon his painting career and devote all his time to design and architecture. His intention to contribute toward constructing a "modern" lifestyle involved him from his earliest days in the creation of the Vereinigte Werkstätten für Kunst im Handwerk (United Workshops for Art in Craft), intended to offer artists, craftsmen, and manufacturers a chance to work together within a structure that provided answers to questions of a technical and economic nature raised by their production. Whether their manufacturing method was craft or industry, whether or not their distribution involved a wealthy clientele, was of little importance. All that mattered was the quality of the result.

This model of candlestick features among the artist's earliest work in the field of decorative art, and also as one of the first and most representative examples of Jugendstil.
The object's shape combines suppleness and sobriety. All that remains of a possible plant model is the allusion to its development and growth. Riemerschmid is looking for suggestion and to restore the idea of biological life; and, unlike those working in contemporaneous movements in Scotland and in Vienna, he rejects straight lines. From the whirling base a stem shoots up, with no detail to hamper its vigor and dynamism up until the final budding.
Ph. T.

Giovanni Boldini
Comte Robert de Montesquiou

Oil on canvas
5 ft. 1 in. × 2 ft. 8½ in. (1.55 × 0.83 m)
Gift of Henri Pinard on behalf of
Comte Robert de Montesquiou, 1922

Robert de Monstesquiou, a man of letters and icon of aristocratic society at the turn of the twentieth century, who inspired Proust's Baron de Charlus character in *À la recherche du temps perdu* (*Remembrance of Things Past*), was extremely meticulous about his appearance. This portrait is certainly one of the most famous of the fifty-five painted and sculptural likenesses of this dandy who also had his own "Ego Imago," a set of volumes featuring some 190 photographs of himself, which he himself composed. The painter and model worked out every detail of this falsely casual image, from the dominant composition in grays, favored by the count, to the cane bought at the Goncourt sale and said to have belonged to Louis XV. The emphasis here is on the proverbial eloquence of this dandy, for whom clothing was of moral as well as aesthetic import. The portrait here functions as a controlled theatrical staging rather than as a revelation of personality. Boldini and Montesquiou could not, however, control all the effects: in 1897 critics mocked the aesthete as a Narcissus swooning in the mirror of his cane. But Montesquiou was impervious to such notions of ridicule. He appreciated the portrait and bequeathed it to the Louvre. S. Py.

Arnold Böcklin
Shield Bearing the Face of Medusa

Relief in painted papier mâché
Diam. 24 in. (61 cm)
Acquired in 2007

The work of the Swiss painter Arnold Böcklin reflects his deep and very singular fascination with ancient Greece and Rome. This interest is most strikingly shown here, in one of the artist's few three-dimensional works. Like his contemporaries, the Germans Max Klinger and Franz von Stuck, the Frenchman Jean-Léon Gérôme, and the Belgian Fernand Khnopff, Böcklin was fascinated by classical polychrome sculpture. In this he was strongly influenced by Georg Treu, an archeologist who had excavated at Olympia and was famous for the lecture he gave in 1883, "Should We Paint Our Statues?". In 1885, Treu organized an exhibition of polychrome sculpture, combining recreations of antique pieces and contemporary works, among them the first version of *Shield Bearing the Face of Medusa*, made specially by Böcklin in collaboration with his son-in-law and student, Peter Brückmann. The Orsay piece is one of several other copies made during Böcklin's lifetime. The artist offers a very personal take on the Greek myth of Perseus, the hero who managed to decapitate the hybrid monster Medusa, whose face had the power to petrify anyone who looked at it. One of Böcklin's major works, this *Shield* offers a hallucinatory symbolist vision of an already spectacular myth. É. P.

Félix Vallotton
Women at their Toilet
or The Gynaeceum

Oil on canvas
19¼ × 24 in. (48.1 × 60.2 cm)
Acquired in 2011

Called "nude women, night effect" by the artist, then "the gynaeceum" by his dealer Druet, this scene definitely depicts the interior of a richly decorated brothel. In a complex composition, the painter shows all kinds of carpets, drapes, openings, and mirrors. The models, whom we find in other paintings by Vallotton, seem to be in a hurry to get ready. Vallotton does not take a moral view of the society of his time, but there is a little irony perhaps showing through in the triviality of the ceremony presented here (washing in the tub, the woman bending over to reach her feet, as with Degas), and even in the attitude of the young woman in the foreground, with her face buried in a towel. No doubt this is also a way, as in Jean-Antoine Houdon's bronze *Winter* (or *Shivering Girl*, 1787, in the Louvre), of drawing attention to the body's full, generous curves. Vallotton does indeed exalt the sensuous power of line, notably admired in Ingres, and takes pleasure in outlining the contours of the bodies treated in flat tints, as did some of his Nabi friends, with whom he may have exhibited this painting in 1897. S. Py.

Maurice Denis
Triple Portrait of Yvonne Lerolle

Oil on canvas
5 ft. 7 in. × 3 ft. 9¼ in. (1.70 × 1.10 m)
Frame by Marthe or Maurice Denis
Acquired in 2010 with the help of Georges
D. Havas, in memory of Léo Havas, Robert
and Case Havas, as well as the Fonds du
Patrimoine and interest of an anonymous
Canadian donation in 2010

The model for this ambitious portrait was Yvonne Lerolle, the eldest daughter of the painter, collector, and music lover Henry Lerolle. A friend of Denis's since 1891, Lerolle was among the first to collect his works; in his salon he held gatherings of painters, composers, and writers, such as Degas, Renoir, Debussy, Chausson, Gide, and Valéry. There Denis met the Lerolle girls, who also sat for Renoir. In this portrait, Yvonne is twenty years old. She was to marry Eugène Rouart the following year. Nothing here gives an inkling of the girl's unhappy fate, cut off by her marriage from the brilliant and comforting environment of her childhood and youth. Through this multiple portrait featuring "three aspects" of Yvonne in the foreground, Denis uses a favorite device of his to suggest a path in life that she would take. Dressed in white, pure and—as it were—glorified, Yvonne smells a bunch of flowers, before gradually moving gracefully off into the distance toward a serene and harmonious landscape bathed in a soft, unreal twilight, and enlivened by some women dancing happily. In order to attain what he hoped would be "a more adequate Symbolism," Denis did numerous studies and sketches, making a "friend" of this portrait, the word used by his model, who kept it all her life. But most of all it is a poetic, melancholy meditation on love and passing time. S. Py.

René Lalique
Poppy

Gold, silver, diamonds, cloisonné enamel,
and openwork enamel
3 × 9¼ × 4 in. (7.5 × 23.5 × 10.5 cm)
Acquired in 1897

To overhaul the jeweler's art and rid it of the conventions that he felt were holding it back, René Lalique set great store by the design. The forms he created were taken from the world of animal and plant life. To convey them, he would pick materials whose main quality was not their commercial value but the powers of suggestion produced by their textures and their colors. This attention to shades led the jeweler, while continuing to use precious stones, to become interested in the multiple ways of using enamel, with its almost unlimited possibilities and variety of effects, through playing with its translucent and matt qualities so as to convey the feelings and impressions that the artist experienced in contact with his models from nature. Faced with so many novel features, the critics saw Lalique as the inventor of "modern jewelry," and hailed the sensitivity of his transpositions. In this example, the flower petals are made with a mesh of openwork gold, with the gaps filled with translucent enamel. The heart, crowned by a crest of brilliants, is in an opaque blue enamel, while the gold stamens have a black enamel tip on the end. One admirer enthusiastically exclaimed, "You would think this flower would crumple with a puff of wind, because each part of it seems so mobile and alive." Ph. T.

August Endell
Pedestal table

Elm
26½ × 22 in. (67.5 × 55.5 m)
Acquired in 2008

August Endell was one of the pioneering figures of the Jugendstil tendency in Munich. He studied philosophy before devoting himself to architecture and the decorative arts, and this background is evident in his 1896 essay *Um die Schönheit* (On Beauty), in which he discusses the symbolic value of studying the world of plants and establishes a theory of linear rhythms. Also in 1896 he built his first Jugendstil statement: the façade of the Elvira photography studio. He designed furniture for private clients, such as the poet Henry von Heiseler, and the owners of the sanatorium at Wyk auf Föhr, producing some of the earliest examples of what might be called organic furniture. Drawing on the branches of trees and underwater flora in his design for their frames, he gave his pieces flat, horizontal surfaces whose contours bring to mind tanned animal hides. In 1901 he left Munich for his native Berlin, where he gradually moved away from abstract, dynamic biomorphic and abstract forms to a more "functional" style, while also spending more and more of his time teaching at the Schule für Formkunst, which he founded in 1904. Ph. T.

Paul Hankar
Dining-room table

Oak and mahogany
3 ft. 6¾ in. × 6 ft. 2¾ in. × 3 ft. 7¼ in.
(0.78 × 1.90 × 1.10 m)
Gift of the newspaper *Hokkaido Shimbun*, 1998

In a career lasting less than ten years, Paul Hankar managed to create a dense and original body of work deeply marked by the rationalism of Viollet-le-Duc. This table comes from the townhouse he built in 1897-98 at 48 rue Defacqz, Brussels, for the painter Albert Ciamberlani, a Symbolist who specialized in large decorative ensembles. Period photographs give an idea of the dining room, which comes across as a perfect setting for its main piece of furniture. The squares in the oak parquet floor echo the tabletop, which also has checkers, albeit in mahogany, set in an orthogonal structure in oak. The legs and crossbars supporting the heavy top form a pattern that picks up the beams of the ceiling and cornice of the sideboards as well as the motifs crowning the wooden paneling. The legs in fact constitute an architectural "order" in their own right, being conceived as conical columns decorated with rings at their base and topped by capitals. As for the center rail, it takes the form of a riveted grid in mahogany whose perfectly Japanese-inspired style evokes much of the architectural metalwork conceived by the artist. Ph. T.

Vítězslav Karel Mašek
The Prophetess Libuse

Oil on canvas
6 ft. 4 in. × 6 ft. 4 in. (1.93 × 1.93 m)
Gift of the Jean-Claude Gaubert gallery, 1974

Doubtless inspired by the hieratic Mariannes and the heroic St. Genevièves seen in Paris, the Czech painter Mašek sought to give form to the legendary founder—in the eighth century—of Prague, and of Bohemian culture, Libuse. He focuses on evoking her divine aura as a prophetess mediating between her people and the magical powers. Standing above the River Vltava in its wild state, Libuse appears as an oracle before the heavenly vault, clothed in a long robe embroidered with the different phases of the moon, her brooch decorated with a cow; her heavy tresses evoke an Egyptian priestess of the goddess Hathor, or a Gallic druidess.

She holds out a branch from a lime, the sacred tree in Slavonic culture. Like his compatriot Mucha, Mašek borrows the decorative richness of the fabrics and headdress from Byzantine art, and the hieratic pose as well. Using the pointillist technique, the image—discovered in Paris—also recalls the mosaics of Ravenna. Despite the dreamlike blue tone, Libuse's gaze, full of foreboding, and the mysterious shadow advancing in the foreground, give this melancholy effigy a disturbing and vengeful political dimension, recalling the cultural oppression experienced by Czech art under the domination of the Austro-Hungarian empire. C. F.

Auguste Rodin
Balzac

Plaster statue
4 ft. 4 in. × 3 ft. 11¾ in. × 10¾ in. (1.32 × 1.21 × 0.27 m)
Donated by A. Rodin, 1916

In 1891, as president of the Société des Gens de Lettres, the writer Émile Zola ensured that Rodin was chosen to make a monument to Honoré de Balzac, nearly half a century after Balzac's death. The sculptor threw himself into the hunt for images of Balzac. This was the beginning of a four-year gestation period. Rodin hesitated in his choice of garment, and ended up making studies of nude figures in a variety of positions. Having finally found the structure for his figure, he began working on the drapery. According to the sculptor François Pompon, Rodin "soaked his dressing gown in a big bowl of plaster and clad his model with it. The garment became increasingly simple, the fabric looser and more voluminous. Rodin was trying for a figure with an upward, skyward thrust, and conceived what was an almost abstract symbol of the novelist's power. The head monopolizes attention, dominating a body that is arched back, the hair defining the movement. When the plaster was exhibited in 1898, the critics went to town, mocking the formless block, comparing it to a toad in a sack, a statue with the wrapping still on, or a block of salt left in the rain. The work marked a complete break with the prevailing codes and was rejected. Rodin took back the statue, returned the money, and refused any offers to buy it. It was not until 1939 that a bronze cast was unveiled in Paris. C. C.

Fernand Khnopff
Future or A Young Englishwoman

Marble, light polychromy, brass and copper laurel wreath
17¾ × 11 × 7¾ in. (45 × 28 × 20 cm)
Acquired in 2006

In 1898, the Belgian symbolist artist Fernand Khnopff was a guest of honor at the first Vienna Secession. He submitted sixteen paintings and four sculptures, including this *Young Englishwoman*, which the critic Ludwig Hevesi described. "The ideal woman in white marble … highlighted with some exquisitely subtle traces of color. … Here again, we feel the sensuality, but there is something vampiric about Khnopff's sensuality." As with certain martyrs, the statue's skull is sliced off at the forehead. It's not clear if visitors to the 1898 exhibition could see this detail. Hevesi mentions a scarf dotted with tiny blue stars. Some pictures show the marble bust wearing a crown of leaves, while the oldest photograph shows the *Young Englishwoman* without either a scarf or a crown. Nowadays her forehead is adorned with a laurel wreath. Although Khnopff has given the bust the features of his sister, Marguerite, the marble also has the artist's own pale blue eyes. It may be the expression of a myth that fascinated the symbolist artists, that of the "original androgynous man," mentioned in Plato's *Symposium*, a dual being that Zeus cuts in two in a moment of anger. This mutilation was thought to have been the cause of the lover's quest and yearning for fusion. Under a misleading title, *A Young Englishwoman* perhaps expresses the artist's dream of being united with his beloved sister Marguerite. A. P.

Fernand Khnopff
Incense

Oil on canvas
33¾ × 19¾ in. (86 × 50 cm)
Acquired through the financial backing
of the Yomiuki Shimbun Group in 2007

The artist's sister Marguerite was the model both for this painting and for the bust *Future*, also called *A Young Englishwoman*. Instead of the incense burner announced in the title, she is holding a late fifteenth-century-inspired monstrance. Khnopff makes multiple references to the Flemish primitives, through things like the careful, sumptuous treatment of the embroidered fabric, or the model, oversized in relation to the architecture, no doubt representing the church of Our Lady at "Bruges-la-Morte" (to quote the title of the novel by Rodenbach), then in vogue and Marguerite and Fernand's home city. The illusionist effect is also close to photography, which Khnopff engaged in (with his sister for a model) and used for his painting, adding to the work's strangeness and to its spiritual dimension, highlighted by the inscription "deo dei" on the frame. This refers back to the portion given to God, symbolized by the incense representing purification, prayer rising up to the Lord, sacrifice, and offering. But it is a religion all of his own that the artist stages in this picture, which was one section of an altarpiece intended for his Brussels home. Here Khnopff invites us on a mysterious ritual based on an exploration of the self, typical of Symbolism at the end of the century, in the confinement of an interior, created as a refined, protective setting by the artist in reaction to the world around him. S. Py.

Georges Minne
Boy Kneeling at the Fountain

Silver-plated bronze statue
31 × 7½ × 17¼ in. (78.5 × 19 × 43.5 cm)
Gift of Enrique Mistler, 1933

In his early works, unadorned simplification earned the Belgian symbolist sculptor Georges Minne sharp criticism for his primitivism, his awkwardness and rudimentary craftsmanship. His fellow countryman, the poet Emile Verhaeren, came to his defence, pointing out that "his characters are almost beyond what it is possible to be ... they come and go toward other worlds where only the Idea can live." In *Boy Kneeling at the Fountain*, Minne's search for sobriety led him to reject out of hand anything anecdotal or visionary; no pathos, just slow, grave rhythm, and silence turned inward. In Georges Minne's view of art, line is the key visual feature, with the contours emphasizing the statue's solidity. Whether grieving or resigned, the gaunt figure is self-absorbed and meditative. The artist is looking for volumes potentially imposing in their fullness. By constantly simplifying, he contrives to give true monumentality to his figures. The great writer Hippolyte Fierens Gevaert believed that "his sculpture would only achieve its full expressive value when combined with architecture." And true enough, in 1900 Minne produced a composition, borrowing Rodin's idea of repeating several identical figures, by placing five copies of *Boy Kneeling at the Fountain* around the edge of a circular fountain. É. P.

Paul Gauguin
The White Horse

Oil on canvas
4 ft. 7¼ × 3 ft. ¼ in. (1.40 × 0.92 m)
Acquired in 1927

On July 3, 1895, Gauguin left France for good. He went to Tahiti, then from 1901 he settled in Atuona, in the Marquesas Islands, where he died in 1903 at the age of fifty-four. Despite material hardships, failures, and later illness, these last years were fruitful ones, producing nearly a hundred completed paintings, dominated by the monumental *Where Do We Come From? What Are We? Where Are We Going?* (Museum of Fine Arts, Boston), in which the horseman motif appears, to be developed subsequently in *The White Horse*. In an Eden-like natural setting, there are two nude horsemen in the background, while a horse drinks at a pond painted in deep blue. The figures, animals, and elements of the landscape are juxtaposed in a composition devoid of depth and deployed along the vertical plane. The luxuriant vegetation forms a web of decorative lines. Gauguin includes in the mix reminiscences both classical (the Parthenon frieze by Phidias) and modern (Edgar Degas racecourse scenes). The artist emphasizes the dazzling bright colors painted in flat patches and contrasting complementary colors. This daring non-mimetic use of color passed completely over the head of the Tahitian pharmacist who commissioned the painting, and who refused to pay for it on the grounds that the white horse is … green. S. Py.

Henry Van de Velde
Writing Desk

Oak, gilt bronze, copper, and leather
4 ft. × 8 ft. 9 in. × 4 ft. 2½ in.
(1.28 × 2.68 × 1.22 m)
Acquired in 1987 thanks to the support of Crédit Lyonnais

This desk is without doubt one of the most accomplished creations of Art Nouveau in general and of Van de Velde in particular. It was the ideas of John Ruskin and William Morris that inspired him to give up his career as a painter in 1893 and concentrate on being an architect and decorator. Designed around a subtle play of abstract, dynamic lines in one, unbroken rhythm, one single pulsation, this piece impressively demonstrates his ability to merge form and decoration. Ornament here—the lithe play of molding—is not the self-contained embellishment of a surface, but a constructive or demonstrative feature. Its role is to exalt the purpose of the object which, so Van de Velde believed, should be immediately evident. This model was crafted in several different types of wood. It would appear that four were made in all, one of them gracing the offices of the famous *Revue blanche*, another the office of Berlin-based publisher Ludwig Loeffler. The Musée d'Orsay piece, the only one to have kept its electrical lighting system, featured in the study presented by Van de Velde at the Munich Secession exhibition in 1899. Ph. T.

Félix Vallotton
Misia at Her Dressing Table

Distemper on cardboard
14¼ × 11½ in. (35.9 × 29 cm)
Acquired in 2004 with the backing of Nippon Television
and the Meyer Foundation

This picture is the first appearance in Vallotton's painted work of the woman at her dressing table, a motif that crops up regularly in his output. The model is powdering her neck, with a gesture that has her arms drawing some graceful albeit anatomically unlikely arabesques. This painting is both a genre scene and a portrait of Misia Natanson. Clearly observable are the mischievous profile of this very attractive young woman, the high chignon that she was fond of at that time, and the dresses with a large bow that are seen in contemporary photographs. The work was probably commissioned by her first husband, Thadée, one of the founders of *La Revue blanche*, for which Vallotton produced the series of engravings, *Intimacies*, at around the same time. This portrait bears a few similarities to one of the plates in that set, and the painter actually makes reference to his work as an engraver by reproducing one of his woodcuts in a frame on the blue wall. That same year, 1898, the woman who had been a muse not only to Édouard Vuillard and Henri de Toulouse-Lautrec, but to Pierre Bonnard and Auguste Renoir as well, inspired two further portraits by her "dear Vallo." With its brightly colored outlined forms and its sharp contrasts of light and shade, this one is undoubtedly one of the most carefully considered and accomplished. S. Py.

Ferdinand Chanut
Project for an astronomical observatory

Watercolor, gouache, pastel, ink on
paper, 25½ × 37 in. (65 × 94 cm)
Purchase, 2024

After training at the École des Beaux-Arts, Ferdinand Chanut spent most of his career as head of the Galeries Lafayette architecture agency from 1909 to 1929. It was there that he designed the grand hall, a project for which he called upon major artists from the École de Nancy.

Unveiled at the Salon des Artistes Français in 1904, this project for an astronomical observatory garnered plaudits from the critics, winning a medal (second class).

With its poetic power, this spectacular drawing is reminiscent of the work of François Garas and Henry Provensal, whose dreamlike designs are considered exceptional examples of the symbolist quest in architecture. Chanut's plan nevertheless stands out for its manifestly futuristic idiom, of which it is a precocious instance.

This is particularly evident in the brutalist and geometric nature of the forms, accentuated by the low-angle view, the smooth surfaces, and the design of the base, distinguished by the clever interplay between parabolic and hyperbolic curves.

Devoid of all historical reference, this formal freedom was made possible by the use of reinforced concrete, a material architects had begun to use around 1900. The modernism of the project is further enhanced by its graphic representation—a singularly pictorial and poetic style far removed from the tradition of nineteenth-century architectural drawing. The lunar atmosphere pervading this almost monochrome night scene gives the construction a fantastical character, hovering between earth and sky. C. R.

François Garas

Temple of Thought, Dedicated to Beethoven, Moonlight

Oil on canvas
4 ft. 6 in. × 3 ft. 5¼ in. (1.37 × 1.05 m)
Acquired in 2002

"On the Champ-de-Mars, there are hardly any really novel works except the fantastic and powerful temple project by M. Garas," wrote Arsène Alexandre, a journalist with *Le Figaro* newspaper, in 1899. François Garas, with his impetuous and lively imagination, sought to transpose ideas, feelings, or musical rhythms into architecture. This odd, mysterious architect studied at the École des Beaux-Arts; graduating in 1894, he refused to become a practicing architect, being too pragmatic for that. From 1897 to 1914, he presented his increasingly dreamy projects at the Salon of the Société Nationale des Beaux-Arts, *Artists' Interiors* evoking alchemists' laboratories and, most notably, *Temples for Future Religions*, dedicated to Beethoven, Wagner, Life, Death, and Thought. "The exterior of my temple is made up of three parts that define the evolution of thought: 1° uneasiness before the mystery represented by the huge barely sketched sphinx guarding the entrance; 2° the meditative state represented by the extra low dome, like a giant skull; 3° the effort of thought on the infinite represented by the soaring tower." A devoted worshipper of Beauty, Art, and the Absolute, he disappeared from the architectural scene in 1913, caught up by the materiality of the world, as he took over his father's brickworks. C. M.

Heinrich Vogeler
Sunday Walk

Wool and cotton
1 ft. 11½ in. × 3 ft. 3¼ in. (0.60 × 1.00 m)
Acquired in 1987

When a group of enlightened amateurs decided to revive a local industry, they set up the Kunstwebschule in Scherrebek (Schleswig-Holstein); this weaving school opened in 1896. Seven years later it went into liquidation, though not before producing some of the most representative creations of the Jugendstil. Wools were spun and dyed on the spot using plant-based processes. Weaving was done on a conventional upright loom, with no instrument or shuttle apart from nimble fingers. When the Kunstwebschule called upon the painter Heinrich Vogeler, Vogeler had already been part of a colony of artists based in Worpswede since 1894, and had already designed several items of furniture and everyday items. His tapestry cartoons deploy a whole world of legend; thanks to an intimate mix of the strange and the everyday, they exude an inimitable poetic flavor. The layout of the compositions, with no perspective, and an economy of means and colors, demonstrates the dual impact of the Japanese print and of folk art. The motif of the medieval warrior and his beloved passing against a backdrop of a landscape in spring is frequent in the artist's work. This design was presented at the Exposition Universelle in Paris in 1900, with great success, receiving some thirty orders.
Ph. T.

Paul Cézanne
Apples and Oranges

Oil on canvas
29¼ × 36½ in. (74 × 93 cm)
Bequeathed by Comte Isaac de Camondo, 1911

The still life was an essential aspect of Cézanne's painting. In the tradition of the Dutch masters of the seventeenth century, of Jean-Baptiste-Siméon Chardin in the eighteenth, and of his elder, Manet, he was fascinated by the poetic nobility of everyday objects. Toward the end of his career, Cézanne worked to reduce form to its quintessence, as is evident from these *Apples and Oranges*. This painting also features ceramics and rich decorative cloths draped in the background, which make the space highly ambiguous. The composition, enlivened by the bright white cloth with its upward dynamic, imparts a distinctive rhythm to this study of the play of light over the fruit, the positioning of which suggests a certain instability. In this work Cézanne continued to work with multiple viewpoints, a technique that would be taken up by the proponents of cubism some ten years later. Thanks to his lively, allusive brush, Cézanne manages to endow these modest objects with the same kind of monumentality as his portraits. The time-lessness of the subject is conducive to the lyrical use of color, which is especially compelling in the modulation of browns and oranges, which structures the overall composition and adds to its mysterious beauty. X. R.

Lucien Bonvallet
Tea fountain

Solid cast, chiseled, and chased silver,
carved and tinted ivory
16¼ × 12½ in. (41 × 32 cm)
Acceptance in lieu, 1994

Founded in 1804, the Cardeilhac gold and silver firm reached its apogee under Ernest Cardeilhac. Lucien Bonvallet began working for the firm in 1885 and became their accredited draftsman during preparations for the Exposition Universelle of 1900. Between 1894 and 1899 he designed a significant number of models in gold or silver, including this sumptuous "tea fountain"—part of the "Art moderne" service. The pieces made after his designs met with an enthusiastic response both from the international jury and from critics. From the numerous commentaries it appears that Bonvallet's work with Cardeilhac was seen as the quintessence of the French style, thoroughly but discreetly assimilating the grand tradition of the eighteenth century while refreshing the ornamental repertoire with studies done directly after nature, offering a restrained range of plants taken from the humble flora of fields and gardens with refined stylization which kept all the grace and spontaneity of the motifs, perfectly merging decoration and form, and fluid and balanced curves and contours. In 1902 Bonvallet set up independently, specializing, among other items, in copper vases. The Musée d'Orsay has some magnificent examples of these, bequeathed by the artist's daughter. Ph. T.

Léopold Chauveau
Monster

Plaster treated with linseed oil and shellac
4¾ × 2 × 2¼ in. (12 × 5 × 5.5 cm)
Restricted lifetime gift from Marc Chauveau,
through the Société des Amis du Musée d'Orsay
et de l'Orangerie, 2019

A surgeon by training, Léopold Chauveau became a self-taught artist in his thirties, when he met the sculptor Georges Lacombe in 1904 (p. 242). After trying his hand at drawing and sculpture, Chauveau modeled his first monster in 1905. Exploring the morphological frontier between the animal and the human, he dreamt up hybrid beings that fill the letters he sent to his children. He drew inspiration from childhood memories, and from his knowledge of medicine, anatomy, and zoology—his father was a veterinarian and professor of comparative pathology at the Muséum National d'Histoire Naturelle. He also drew on his life experience, World War I in particular, during the course of which he treated the wounded and lost several loved ones, including his wife, two of their sons, and his friend Lacombe. Solidly constructed and powerfully expressive, his sculptures of monsters fuse the strange with the familiar, the tender with the disturbing.

In 1922, Chauveau abandoned sculpture to devote himself to writing and illustrating children's stories. "I draw monsters—very kind, very gentle, very harmless—quite ridiculous compared to the real, living monsters that are today turning the world upside down," he noted in a notebook in September 1939 toward the end of his life. His works remained in the care of his family and little known until a significant donation to the Musée d'Orsay by his grandson in 2019. F. B.

Félix Vallotton
The Dinner, Lamp Effect

Oil on cardboard mounted on wood
22¾ × 35½ in. (58 × 90 cm)
Acquired in 1947

Vallotton returns to the theme, commonplace in the painting of his day, of the meal in a modern interior. But what might have been a banal and peaceful homely ritual seems to be a grating echo of André Gide's famous 1897 comment: "Families, I hate you … shut-in homes, closed doors." Squeezing the guests—his own family members—into a cramped space, the Paris apartment in the Rue de Milan, Vallotton caricatures the faces, up to and including the disturbing wild-eyed look of the little girl, Madeleine, born to the painter's wife Gabrielle from her first marriage (on the right of the composition). Being an excellent woodcutter, the artist heightens the contrasts between the shaded areas and others, such as the tablecloth, which receives the light from a lamp decorated by the painter. Clear forms are outlined, dominated, as in a cinema shot, by the massive and oppressive silhouette of the painter seen from behind. Despite the intimate dimension of this family drama in which the well-nigh obsessive hostility between the painter and his stepdaughter is plain to see, the painting was put on show in 1900. Vallotton made a second version (Kirov Museum, St. Petersburg) of this dinner scene which, like the scenes of couples that he was painting around the same time, cast a cruel glance at relations within the modern family, or between lovers. S. Py.

Bruno Paul
Armchair

Oak, modern upholstery
33½ × 28 × 26 in. (85.5 × 71 × 66 cm)
Acquired in 1999

This armchair comes from one of the large sets presented by Germany at the Exposition Universelle held in Paris in 1900, in the category described as "Fixed decoration of public buildings and housing." It was intended to furnish a hunting lodge. Its designer, Bruno Paul, trained as a painter. He soon became interested in the decorative arts and at Munich in 1897 was involved in the founding of the Vereinigte Werkstätten für Kunst im Handwerk (United Workshops for Art in Craft). The armchair was in fact manufactured at those workshops.

Primarily there is a determination not to conceal the construction but, on the contrary, to draw attention to its component elements. Whether part of the backrest, the legs, or the armrests, they are actually just cutout planes with no relief or modeling.

Such a trend reflects a dual influence—first, that of Henry Van de Velde, who was highly reputed in Germany since the Dresden International Exhibition in 1897; and secondly that of Chinese and Japanese furniture made of sober assemblages of uprights and cross-pieces. This rigor was tempered, however, at least in the early days of his creative work in Munich, by a touch of fantasy, anthropomorphic in origin: here the ends of the seat's armrests recall a clenched fist. Ph. T.

Pierre Bonnard
Marthe Standing in the Sun

Aristotype from negative on soft film coated
with gelatin-silver bromide
1½ × 2 in. (3.8 × 5 cm)
Donation subject to usufruct by M. Antoine
Terrasse, 1992

This naked body in broad daylight, among some dark, luxuriant vegetation, belongs to Pierre Bonnard's companion Marthe, whom he met in 1893 and who became his ever-present muse. In a photographic variation on a bathing scene, she engages in a game of love in the gardens of an estate rented out at Montval (Yvelines), alternating with Bonnard in the role of model and operator as they pose for each other in front of the camera. A first series of photographic nudes created in the Paris apartment would serve as a basis for the illustration of Verlaine's collection of free verse *Parallèlement*—a commission Bonnard received from the publisher Ambroise Vollard. This time Marthe literally lent her silhouette to Chloe in one of the lithographed plates of Longus's *Daphnis and Chloe* (1902). During the Nabi period, the opportunities Bonnard had for directly combining his photographic and his painted work were few and far between. This print, recording a fleeting pose, does however fall within the tradition of the photographic sketch. But while it is entirely constructed around the contrast between the white of the flesh and the tree trunk with the black of the shaded areas, in his lithograph Bonnard derived a line drawing from it, rendering Marthe's graceful movement of the hips and playing on the voluptuous line, rather than on tonal contrasts. M. R.

Pierre Bonnard
Man and Woman

Oil on canvas
3 ft. 7¼ in. × 2 ft. 4½ in. (1.15 × 0.72 m)
Acquired in 1948

After first meeting Marthe in 1893, Bonnard made the young woman his favorite model: her slender silhouette is a regular feature of both the artist's painting and his photographic work, in which Marthe is idealized and unaffected by time, and generally portrayed alone. This painting is an exception to that rule. Bonnard paints himself by her side through a complex device whereby the scene is a reflection viewed in a mirror. In the full light, Marthe is engrossed by the sight of cats playing, a new take on the evocative association with female sexuality that had contributed to the scandal caused by Manet's *Olympia* of 1863 (p. 83). Through an uncompromising self-portrait, foreshadowing the ones he was to paint at the end of his life, the artist uncovers himself in the half-sha-dow. Although sold and exhibited, the work is strikingly intimate and autobiographical in tone. In addition to the eroticism of Marthe's pose, already noted in *Woman Dozing on a Bed* or *The Indolent Woman* (1899) and the *Blue Nude* (between 1899 and 1900, both in the Musée d'Orsay), we have the realistic rendering of the male nude occupied with the more mundane task of dressing or undressing. "The flesh is sad," Bonnard seems to be saying, after Mallarmé, confining the lovers in this disturbing scene behind closed doors, like a modern Adam and Eve, firmly separated by a folded screen dividing the composition into a diptych and seemingly forming an insurmountable barrier between two experiences of loneliness. S. Py.

Lars Kinsarvik
Armchair

Carved and painted wood
3 ft. × 1 ft. 7 in. × 1 ft. 9 in. (95 × 49.5 × 55 cm)
Acquired in 2003

This model of armchair, devised by Lars Kinsarvik and presented at the Paris Exposition Universelle in 1900, is a fine example of what was known as the "Dragon" or "Viking" style. In a bid to promote a national style that asserted their culture's difference from Sweden's (the dissolution of the union between Norway and Sweden was promulgated in 1905), during the final third of the nineteenth century, Norwegian artists made numerous references to their nation's past, both in technical and in formal terms. Lars Kinsarvik gained his reputation as one of the champions of the revival of the carved and painted wood technique, whose qualities and profound originality were vaunted by the historian Lorenz Dietrichson, whether his animal heads on Viking ships, or the bas-reliefs decorating the doors of medieval churches. Mixing history and popular culture, the cabinetmaker, who mostly worked to commission, especially when completely decorating beer halls and hotels, devised generally straightforward, robust forms. The elements composing this armchair's structure—backrest stiles and back rail, armrests, and leg stretchers—are literally turned into totems and bas-reliefs from which there springs a whole world of legend, with figures of witches and masks alternating with tendrils and running foliage decorations in a polychromy based on green and yellow tones, dotted here and there with touches of blue. Ph. T.

Peter Behrens
Bench

White lacquered poplar, red leather upholstery
3 ft. 6¼ in. × 3 ft. 11½ in. × 1 ft. 8 in.
(1.07 × 1.20 × 0.51 m)
Acquired with the help of the Société des Amis du Musée d'Orsay, 1999

In 1898 the Grand Duke of Hesse, Ernst-Ludwig, founded an artists' colony in Darmstadt under the direction of the Viennese architect Joseph Maria Olbrich. His aim was to make the city an economic and artistic capital, and the members of the colony were tasked with building a new quarter on unused land constituted by prototypes of new kinds of dwellings. Everything, from the general plan to the smallest interior details, was to be realized by the artists themselves. One of the seven individual houses inaugurated in 1901 was built by Peter Behrens. This bench comes from the dining room, in which the dominant white color was punctuated by touches of ruby red. This was echoed by an identical linear rhythm that ran across the furniture, woodwork, lighting, porcelain, and silver. The firm design of the openwork backs, the rigor of the construction, and articulation of the framing, all suggest affinities with the work of the Belgian Van de Velde, which was abundantly reproduced and discussed in Germany. But the gentle subtlety of the curves reflects the striving for elegance and urbanity shared by all the colony's designs. Ph. T.

Odilon Redon
Green Plant in an Urn

Oil on canvas
33½ × 23½ in. (85 × 60 cm)
Bequeathed by Mme Arï Redon, 1984

Flowers only became a predominant feature of Redon's work during the 1890s, and most of all after 1900, when the artist received a number of commissions for large decorations mostly comprising floral and plant motifs. From the outset, these bouquets were seen from a symbolic, sentimental standpoint, here visible in the ambiguity of the shift between the plant itself and the flowers decorating the urn. The dreamlike quality of this plant against a flamboyant yellow ground, where the stylization, the layout, and the ceramic decoration all belong to the *japonisme* of the time, fits into the broader ornamental context of Art Nouveau. However, this composition lacks the bright, metaphorical colors that earned Redon the admiration of the public for other flower works. The plant featured here is doubtless a fruit of the artist's own imagination, painted with a tonal freedom defended by his friend Gauguin, whom he admired. With such virulent colors, Redon was viewed as one who inspired the Fauvists' work in praise of pure color at the Salon d'Automne of 1905. Emblematic of the artist's return to color after his work on black, marking the belated launch of his commercial success, this piece comes from the large collection bequeathed to the State by his son's widow in 1984. X. R.

Paul Gauguin
House of Pleasure:
Nude Woman and Small Dog
Nude Woman and Tree with Red Fruit

Polychrome *Sequoia gigantea* wood
5 ft. 2½ in. × 1 ft. 3¾ in. × 1 in. (1.59 × 0.40 × 0.25 m)
6 ft. 6¾ in. × 1 ft. 3¼ in. × 1 in. (2.00 × 0.39 × 0.25 m)
Acquired in 1953

"Madagascar is still too close to the civilized world. I am going to leave for Tahiti and hopefully for the rest of my life," Gauguin wrote to Odilon Redon before his first voyage in 1891-93. After returning to France, he sailed off again for Tahiti, and in 1901 settled at Atuona, in the Marquesas Islands. His hut on the island of Hivaoa was on two levels: a ground floor with rooms open to visitors, and an upper floor reserved for close friends, along with his bedroom and studio. Gauguin took great care over decorating this space, turning it into a total work of art that he called the "House of Pleasure." Carved with lines showing different planes and heightened with polychrome, these wood panels framed the door into the bedroom, which was the only way through to the studio. Polynesian inscriptions and figures are combined with motifs of luxuriant plant life, following the artist's personal primitivist aesthetic. The lintel is marked "Maison du Jouir" between two profiles with aquiline noses evoking the figure of the Polynesian god Taaroa. On the uprights (shown here) are two nude Polynesian women. The plinths each bear a motto of Gauguin's, "Soyez mystérieuses" (Be mysterious), and "Soyez amoureuses et vous serez heureuses" (Be loving and you will be happy), along with faces and busts quoting motifs from his paintings. In praise of love and lightheartedness, the Maison du Jouir panels stand as a testament, as Gauguin died just a year after completing them. O. F.

Odilon Redon

Decoration for the dining room at the Château de Domecy:
Tree against a Yellow Ground; Trees against a Yellow Ground; Yellow Branch in Blossom

Charcoal, oil, and tempera on canvas
8 ft. 1½ in. × 5 ft. 4¼ in. (2.47 × 1.63 m)
8 ft. 2¼ in. × 6 ft. ¾ in. (2.49 × 1.85 m)
8 ft. 1½ in. × 5 ft. 8 in. (2.47 × 1.73 m)
Acceptance in lieu, 1988

Tree against a Yellow Ground is one of the eighteen panels (fourteen of which are held at the Musée d'Orsay) that decorated the dining room in the Château de Domecy in Yonne (northern Burgundy). This decorative painting, Redon's first real venture into that form—he was over sixty years old—was commissioned by Robert de Domecy, who had been one of his main collectors since the early 1890s. The baron did not stipulate an iconographic program, but expressed the wish that yellow and red be the dominant colors. Redon, who executed this major piece of work in his Parisian studio between June 1900 and April 1901, chose, as he put it, to paint "flowers, dream flowers, imaginary animals," which he completed with two panels: a Buddha and a poet. All these were themes that he adapted from earlier works. Here, the motifs seem to have been put randomly into the composition, in which empty space and dissymmetry play an essential role, as they do on Japanese screens. Like a number of his Nabi friends, Redon experimented with a mixture of media, combining oil and tempera on a fine canvas, achieving a matt, textured surface. In short, the painter created a refined, poetic, and dreamlike world. Its almost abstract indeterminacy is conducive to contemplation. S. Py.

Camille Claudel
The Age of Maturity

Three-part bronze group
45 × 64¼ × 28¼ in.
(1.14 × 1.63 × 0.72 m), acquired in 1982

The dramatic subject of *The Age of Maturity* has its roots in the love affair Camille Claudel had with Auguste Rodin, which proved as torrid as it was painful for both artists.

Twenty-four years Claudel's senior, Rodin eventually broke off with her to stay with Rose Beuret, his lifelong companion. Transfiguring this personal experience into a symbolic work of universal import, the artist divests her figures of all reference to any specific era or identity, just as Rodin had done in his famous *Kiss*. Exacerbated by their nakedness, the powerful modeling of the surfaces highlights the effects of time on all three bodies.

On her knees, a young woman stretches out her hands to an older man she still loves, begging him not to leave her; turning his back on his former lover, he is pulled away by a woman of a certain age. Her body is only partially concealed beneath a large swirling piece of drapery, reinforcing the general movement of a composition that travels upward from right to left. Similarly, the hollows and eddies on the base seem to reflect the inner turmoil of figures caught up in the maelstrom of life.

Exhibiting it as a large plaster group at the 1899 Salon, Camille Claudel was commissioned by a collector to have it cast in bronze. A few smaller copies were then produced, while the isolated figure of *The Implorer* became singularly successful. F. B.

Céline Laguarde
The Gauze Dress

Gum bichromate print
6 × 7¾ in. (15.2 × 19.6 cm)
Purchased in 2017

By the beginning of the twentieth century, Céline Laguarde had established herself as a leading figure in Pictorialism, attaining an exceptional degree of national and international recognition unprecedented for a woman photographer in France. The artist and her work have recently emerged from a century of oblivion thanks to the gradual coming to light of her personal collection, most of which had remained unpublished. Patiently rebuilt in the Musée d'Orsay's collections, it has been enriched in parallel by other works from various sources to form a unique ensemble of portraits, figure studies, and landscapes.

Rejecting conventional imagery, then devoted to depicting the spontaneity and innocent charm of childhood, Laguarde incorporates her young model into her rather severe art of the figure, in which solemnity and grace take precedence over expressiveness. Her grasp of the psyche of children inspired *The Gauze Dress*—an subtle tribute to the imagination of that stage of life, and that is nourished here by the pleasures of dressing up and dreaming of being an adult woman or a princess by wearing clothes that are patently too big.

Laguarde's highly personal approach was rooted in a daily intimacy with Marie Irigoin-Guichandut. The latter developed from an ever-willing little doll into Laguarde's favorite muse and her most astute collaborator and interpreter. Through this relationship of mutual loyalty, the artist was able to magnify the blossoming of femininity as it unfolds in the transition from childhood to adulthood. Produced over a period of fifteen years, Laguarde's corpus is unparalleled in turn-of-the-century French art photography. T. G.

Carlo Bugatti
Chair

Wood sheathed in parchment, painted
and gilt highlights, embossed copper
3 ft. 2¼ × 1 ft. 2¾ × 1 ft. 8¾ in. (97 × 37.2 × 53 cm)
Acquired in 1922

The model for this chair was designed by Carlo Bugatti for the "games and conversation room" at the first International Exhibition of Modern Decorative Arts in Turin in 1902. This room reproduced the form of a snail's shell, on a human scale. Soon nicknamed the *camera a chiocciola* (snail room), it was both a variation on the morphology of that creature and a meditation on the theme of the spiral. It marked the high point of Bugatti's work as a furniture designer. To magnify the curves he created, Bugatti had the idea of completely cladding these new forms with a satiny skin of parchment-covered leather, which adhered perfectly to the wooden structure. This skin was further illuminated by a light decoration of slender red and gold insects. Having "provoked within the jury, as well as among the public, the liveliest debate … the most passionate arguments," Carlo Bugatti won the highest award, the diploma of honor, for having been "the first person in Italy to successfully create, and not just dream of, modern furniture." Ph. T.

Paul Signac
The Demolisher

Oil on canvas
8 ft. 2½ in × 4 ft. 11¾ in. (2.51 × 1.50 m)
Gift of Ginette Signac, 1947

The Demolisher is one of a series of large decorative figures on the theme of laboring, to which Signac gave much thought, starting in 1896. Here the painter expresses his anarchist convictions, wishing to take a "firm pickaxe to the old social edifice" so as to usher in a new golden age, represented in his large canvas, *In the Time of Harmony* (1893-95). The description of the workers against a backdrop of an urban landscape clearly is coupled with an allegorical and prophetic dimension. These demolishers recall the "fellows" "who, in a single grunt, will grind the heaps/Of old hopes and deceased powers," celebrated by the Belgian poet Verhaeren, who was then close to Signac. Exalting the strength and nobility of the proletarian, the rendering of the bodies is sculptural and monumental. Their attitudes are dramatized, as it were, in a choreography; they draw a dynamic line that contributes to the decorative power of a composition that is more than eight feet (2.51 m) high. Signac gave this "panel" to the Maison du Peuple, built by Victor Horta in Brussels (later demolished). The architect neglected this gift, so the painter abandoned the decoration project, which also included "haulers" and "builders," and shortly thereafter renounced his large-figure compositions in favor of landscapes. S. Py.

Bernhard Hoetger
Human Machine

Bronze
17¼ × 14½ × 7 in. (44 × 37 × 18 cm)
Gift of Mme Marcel Duchamp, 1977

Human Machine may be seen as Bernhard Hoetger's first modern torso. Here he combines the influence of Auguste Rodin with realism, this torso emerging from a frame of the pit props that hold up mine shafts. The artist portrays the powerful contrast between the straight timbers and the organic motif of the body effectively. Bronze is the ideal medium for such tense and tortured anatomies. The title refers to the world of industry as the human meat grinder. With the exaggerated expression of his effort, a strapping, almost faceless and armless miner becomes an icon of the plight and the human tragedy of the working classes. Like Jules Dalou in France or Constantin Meunier in Belgium, the German sculptor Hoetger is another poet of the working-man's world, its grandeur and its miseries. É. P.

Odilon Redon
The Buddha

Pastel on beige paper
35½ × 28¾ in. (90 × 73 cm)
Purchased in 1971

Buddhist themes recur in Redon's oeuvre, appearing as early as 1895 in lithographs and accompanied by a quotation from *The Temptation of Saint Anthony* by Gustave Flaubert: "They brought me to the schools. I knew more than the doctors." In this pastel, radiant with color and teeming with plants and organisms typical of Redon's imaginative world, the artist frees himself from all literary baggage. As Redon specialist Dario Gamboni has pointed out, the "circular shapes" above the Buddha "hint at embryology." Off-center and to the left of the composition, the Buddha's sturdy form echoes that of the tree on the right. Showing no fear, his gesture adds to the sense of peace emanating from the work.

Although professing no specific faith, in Redon's oeuvre, the Buddha, with eyes closed, becomes, like the artist's Christ-like and Druidic figures, an image of meditation. To avoid all misunderstanding, the artist reminds us that his art is meant to be open and indeterminate: "I have sometimes painted Venus or Apollo without pagan intentions; I have also painted the Buddha; and this image, as a symbol, still moves the hearts of countless members of humanity, and these subjects (if subjects they are) are as sacred to me as any others." (*Le Mystère et l'Éclat. Pastels du musée d'Orsay*, exh. cat., Paris: Musée d'Orsay/RMN, 2008, p. 103) C. C.-P.

Victor Horta
Wall light

Brass and dichroic glass
19¾ × 8¼ × 8½ in. (50 × 21 × 21.5 cm)
Acquired in 2006

The invention of electric lighting gave Victor Horta new ways of expressing his taste for the play of serpentine lines, and his skill at composing metal arabesques and giving them a role in the general rhythm of the interiors for which they were designed. He worked with existing typologies—candlesticks, chandeliers, wall lights, floor lamps—but also incorporated lighting into fixed architectural structures. In his designs, girandoles thus become part of mantelpieces, sprays of light emerge from staircases or become joined to the pillars supporting glass ceilings. The inspiration here comes from the plant world: a vertical stem, neither too stiff nor too limp, is redoubled in the middle, giving rise to two arms of light of unequal length, bending under the weight of their corollas in dichroic glass while two tendrils intertwine freely. This ensemble no doubt comes from the townhouse built and decorated in Brussels between 1899 and 1904 for the industrialist Octave Aubecq. The building was demolished in 1950, but the museum acquired a significant ensemble of its woodwork and furniture in 1980. Ph. T.

Émile Gallé
Hand with Seaweed and Shells

Modeled glass, metal oxides, marbling,
low and high-relief appliqué work, wheel-engraved
13¼ × 5¼ in. (33.4 × 13.4 cm)
Gift of the artist's heirs, 1990

Gallé's last creation in glass, *Hand with Seaweed and Shells*, represents what was a significant part of his decorative repertoire, inspired by the marine world. He began working with this theme in the 1880s, but it was particularly prominent in the sumptuous group of works he presented at the Exposition Universelle of 1900 under the generic title *The Soul of Water*. In October 1904, a month after the master glassmaker's death, this *Hand* was displayed at a decorative arts exhibition in Nancy in a remarkable vitrine, *The Sea Floor*, the structure of which was inspired by the morphology of the octopus. Its strange, ambiguous character makes the piece endlessly intriguing. Is the hand emerging from the wave or being pulled under? And does it symbolize life or death? Is it an allusion to Aphrodite being born from the spray of the Ionian Sea or to Ophelia drowning in the stream? Also, the formal references embrace Buddhism, sailors' ex-votos from antiquity, and medieval reliquaries. But perhaps this life-death duality is due most of all to the artist's own situation: he knew that he was condemned, the sickness eating away at him having been diagnosed as "progressive pernicious anemia." Ph. T.

Jean-Léon Gérôme
Corinth

Polychrome plaster, wax, and metal wires
18¾ × 13 × 11¾ in. (47.5 × 33 × 30 cm)
Acquired in 2008

Gérôme, leader of the neo-Greek movement, was fascinated by Greco-Latin antiquity, as his work shows. In the 1870s, at the apogee of his career as a painter, he tried his hand at sculpture, exhibiting the results for the first time at the Salon of 1878. He was soon taking an interest in polychrome sculpture, in keeping with his taste for archeological precision. He loved to paint marble in an illusionist manner: "I began by concerning myself with the coloring of the marbles," he wrote, "because I have always been frightened by the coldness of statues." *Corinth*, an original painted plaster, heightened with jewelry in colored wax, was the last polychrome sculpture Gérôme worked on in the year of his death. One of the artist's major works, the piece was found in his studio after his death—he had been completing a version in colored marble. *Corinth* plays on the Greek idea of the *tykhe*, a statue personifying the protective or allegorical divinity of a city, but also evokes a luxuriant, erotic Orient. A hieratic idol and a prostitute, disturbingly excessive in its representation of the real, *Corinth* constitutes the perfect synthesis of the femme fatale favored by Symbolism and Art Nouveau, while showing, with a degree of rawness, an unveiled, distanced allegory of the Parisian *demi-monde* contemporaneous with its creation. É. P.

Osman Hamdi Bey
Dervish at the Children's Tomb

Oil on canvas
79½ × 59½ in. (2.02 × 1.51 m)
Unknown acquisition method, n.d.

The son of a high-ranking official in the Ottoman Empire, Osman Hamdi Bey was not destined for a career in the arts. Arriving in Paris in 1857 to study law, he took up painting in Gustave Boulanger's studio. Obliged to return to Istanbul in 1869, he held various administrative positions before becoming director of the Imperial Museum (now Archaeological Museum). At the same time, he produced genre scenes with Ottoman subjects inspired by the compositional methods and styles of French painting, Jean-Léon Gérôme in particular. The first director of the Imperial School of Fine Arts in Istanbul, today Hamdi is considered one of the fathers of modern painting in Turkey.

The tombs depicted here are those of the son and daughter of Grand Vizier Ibrahim Pasha (c. 1550–1601), in their father's mausoleum (*türbe*) in Istanbul, within the complex dedicated to Prince Mehmed, son of Sultan Suleiman the Magnificent. In depicting the interior decoration of the *türbe*, however, Hamdi took a number of liberties. The man coming to pray in the half-imaginary site, for instance, was painted from a photograph of the artist himself striking the same pose. Since Hamdi was a supporter of the Tanzimat, a reform movement in the Empire under the influence of the European powers, the spiders' webs clearly visible in the corners and the chipped tiles may be interpreted as symbolizing the decline of traditional Ottoman civilization. In Paris, where this painting was exhibited in 1903, Hamdi's pictures owed their popularity to their supposedly authentic character. The composition and significance of the scene, however, are more complex than might initially appear. L. C.

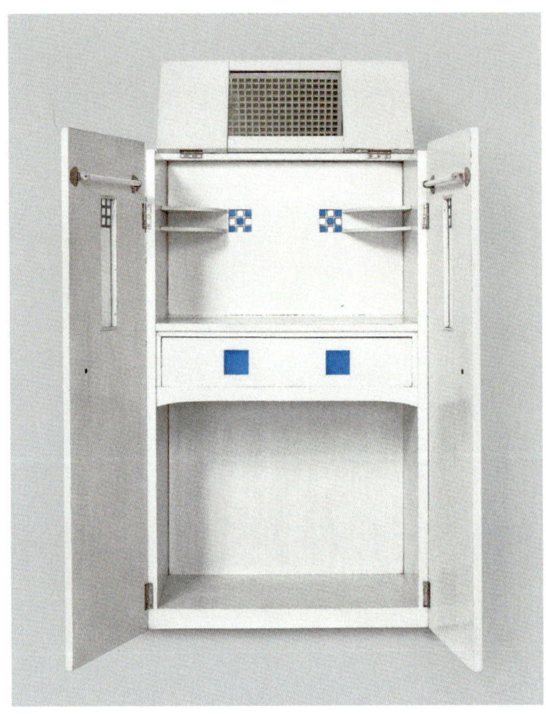

Charles Rennie Mackintosh
Bathroom cabinet

White lacquered wood, mother-of-pearl and
ebony, colorless and colored glass, lead
silver-plated brass
4 ft. × 2 ft. 4½ in. × 1 ft. 4½ in.
(1.22 × 0.72 × 0.42 m)
Gift of Mr David Weill, through
the Fondation Lutèce, 1985

This piece of furniture was part of an ensemble for two bedrooms at Hous'hill, a house near Glasgow that Mackintosh refurbished and modernized in 1903-04 for Mrs. Catherine (or Kate) Cranston, a famous patron who had commissioned Mackintosh to decorate the interiors of several tea rooms in Glasgow between 1896 and 1904 (Buchanan Street Tea Rooms, Argyle Street Tea Rooms, Ingram Street Tea Rooms, The Willow Tea Rooms). The furniture of Hous'hill remained in place until 1926 and was finally sold off at auction in 1933. Today, only the furniture of the two bedrooms has been recovered as a complete ensemble. It is shared between the Musée d'Orsay and the Royal Onta-

rio Museum in Toronto. This was the last occasion on which Mackintosh used a technique that he had greatly favored since 1998, namely, the uniform application of white paint to the wood. The furniture for Hous'hill saw Mackintosh taking his search for formal purity to new lengths. The white lacquered surfaces, broken up by touches of color in small squares, highlight the radical, abstract quality of the furniture construction while also providing light and clarity. The formal rigor was further heightened by the perfectly symmetrical layout of the various identical elements, the beds, commodes, mirrors, and bathroom furniture. Ph. T.

Cuno Amiet
Snowy Landscape
or Deep Winter

Oil on canvas
5 ft. 10 in. × 7 ft. 6½ in. (1.78 × 2.35 m)
Acquired in 1999 with the help of the Meyer
Foundation and private sponsorship, in memory of
Maurice and Betty Robin

Just a thin strip of gray sky marking the horizon bounds this inordinately vast expanse of snow. Lost in this immensity is the outline of a skier, leaving the white thread of his trail behind him. *Snowy Landscape* is astonishing for its daring and for the radical nature of its chromatic range. Yet this is a far cry from the monochrome: the dazzling white of snow is suggested by the juxtaposition of tiny touches of color, in a technique akin to Post-Impressionism. This broad, almost metaphysical land-scape is as unusual as the figure and the career of its creator, the Swiss painter Cuno Amiet. For a time linked to the Pont-Aven school of painters, which he joined in 1892–93, and from the late 1890s heavily influenced by the art of his famous compatriot, Ferdinand Hodler, he moved on to further stylistic experimentation during the years 1903–04. Thus, as a "manifesto" of a new painting style, this picture is exactly contemporaneous with the painter's early expressionist experiments, before he went on to meet and join the Die Brücke group in Dresden in 1905. Perhaps it was because of the singularity of his multifaceted career ("multifaceted is the world, multifaceted is my painting" he said himself) that this artist long remained unknown. C. B.

Hector Guimard
Armchair

Pear wood, original upholstery
in chased repoussé leather
41¾ × 30 × 22 in. (106 × 76 cm × 56 cm)
Acquired in 1989

Guimard's early furniture was designed with slender, curving lines that were both architectonic and decorative, branching out or intersecting at vigorous nodal clusters. These pieces, often made to blend in with the wall, lack both density and volume. As of 1902–03, however, Guimard began to take an interest in spatial presence: the unity of his furniture was no longer just about fluidity of line, but also came from the overall rhythm of the curving profiles. This chair, from a villa in Chaponval, Castel Val, is a fine illustration of this new direction. The lining is reduced to simple leather panels, highlighting the "functional" structure enlivened by the subtle ribbing along the wood. The slightly concave seat and back as well as the open arms, their ends inviting the hands to rest, make the chair welcoming. The decoration, a tangle of carefully and precisely carved abstract motifs, is concentrated at the end of the arm boards. The anthropomorphic quality of the chair brings to mind other contemporary designs, such as those of the Catalan Gaudí and of Pankok in Munich. Ph. T.

Josef Hoffmann
Revolving bookshelf

Bleached oak, black varnish,
and silvered metal
31½ × 19½ × 19½ in. (80 × 50 × 50 cm)
Acquired in 1997

The architect and decorator Hoffmann was one of the founders of the Vienna Secession. His goal was to bring a boldly modern style of architecture to turn-of-the-century Vienna, and in keeping with this he advocated a rigorous and simple style of furniture based on orthogonal forms. In 1903 he founded the Wiener Werkstätte with Koloman Moser, which proved to be a veritable laboratory for this new aesthetic.

This small bookcase, reminiscent of certain English designs, has a spare, geometrical form perfectly devoid of ornament, and may disconcert by its simplicity. Its construction, however, is extremely refined: each side is ordered differently. Its subtle elegance also comes from the use of oak treated with white lead and then a coat of black varnish, as in ancient techniques developed by Japanese cabinetmakers.

The first clients of the Wiener Werkstätte belonged to the small circle of Hoffmann's and Moser's friends. This bookcase was made for the Berlin apartment of Margaret Stonborough-Wittgenstein, sister of the pianist Paul Wittgenstein and the philosopher Ludwig Wittgenstein. It was the Werkstätte's first order from outside Austria. Ph. T.

Victor Laloux
Cross Section of the Gare d'Orsay

Print on blue paper
26¾ × 38½ in. (68 × 98 cm)
Gift of the SNCF, 1986

At the end of the nineteenth century, the Compagnie du chemin de fer d'Orléans sought to remedy the peripheral location of the Gare d'Austerlitz by building a more central terminus. The French state, which gave it the land of the Palais d'Orsay, demanded that a competition be held in order to guarantee the architectural quality of the building, which would stand opposite the Palais du Louvre. In 1898, the company named as the winning candidate a laureate of the Prix de Rome, the architect Victor Laloux. Laloux had just been working for them on the station at Tours. The station and its hotel were built in two years, the opening timed to coincide with the Exposition Universelle on July 14, 1900. To help the station blend in with its prestigious surroundings, he concealed the metal structure and the two large glass canopies of the train arrival hall behind stone frontages. The Rue de Lille and Rue de Bellechasse were the hotel sides. On the platform side were the porch and vestibule, which were the way in for passengers. The station saw less traffic after 1939 when longer trains were introduced, and it was under threat after World War II, until it finally won a reprieve from the government which decided to transform it into a museum in 1971. A. T.-B.

Frédéric Marin and Joseph Graf

M. B.'s Villa in the Parc Saint-Maur: plans, elevations, cross section

Ink, wash, and watercolors
26½ × 35¼ in. (67.3 × 89.5 cm)
Acquired in 2006

Toward the mid-nineteenth century, the town of Saint-Maur-des-Fossés, southeast of Paris, saw something of a population explosion, further amplified by the advent of the railroad. The availability of cheap land attracted businessmen, traders, and industrialists, who also liked the calm, green setting. The gradual dividing up of the former castle grounds provided them with land to build on. The demand was so great that the building trades really came into their own. Many architects set up in business there, including Joseph Graf, a graduate of the École des Arts Décoratifs, who joined forces with Frédéric Marin to found a firm of architects there. Graf, held to be one of "the top architects in the Paris suburbs," proposed for the housing in this area a neo-Norman style very popular at the time for vacation homes. He gave the building a certain picturesqueness, obtained with the use of brick and half-timbering, the presence of the turret, and the enameled ceramic decoration. The large glass canopy on the top floor suggests that the villa might have been designed for an artist. The frame around the drawing, carefully composed in the spirit of Art Nouveau, is evidence of the care the architect took in what is ultimately a fairly unimposing building, one which did not survive subsequent redevelopment in the town. A. T.-B. – C. M.

Odilon Redon
Paul Gauguin

Oil and gold metal paint on canvas
26 × 21½ in. (66 × 54.5 cm)
Acquired in 1950

This portrait of Gauguin was in all likelihood inspired by the artist's death in the Marquesas Islands on May 8, 1903. That November, Redon published an article in praise of the "refined, savage, grandiose and delicate" Gauguin. For the only time in his work, he devoted several tributes to the painter, whom he likely met in 1886. During the 1890s, the two artists were hailed as masters of Symbolism, of the art of suggestion. Here Gauguin's dark profile stands out against a medallion in the manner of funerary reliefs or ancient medals. Redon has made no attempt to portray a likeness, being content to feature the "Inca" nose and long hair that Gauguin was so proud of. He saw in them the sign of his Peruvian bloodline, that part of the "savage" that he struggled tirelessly to become. Neither time nor suffering leave any mark on this juvenile, androgynous countenance, which is surrounded by "dream flowers." The features are barely visible, being seen—as it were—against the light, bathing in mystery a profile that seems to be about to disappear. The golden ground heightens the sacred, precious character of what is a gloriously evanescent apparition rather than a flesh-and-blood face. Thus, far from conventional solemnity, with this apotheosis of a glorified friend, Redon also celebrates their shared belief in the transcendence of art. S. Py.

Medardo Rosso
Ecce Puer

Bronze
17¼ × 14½ × 10½ in. (44 × 37 × 27 cm)
Gift of Francesco Rosso, 1928

Medardo Rosso's artistic testament, *Ecce Puer*, was created while the artist was staying in London, in 1906. He had been commissioned to do a bust of the industrialist Emil Mond's son, but Rosso could not get the modeling right. During a reception at the Monds' home, the artist caught a glimpse of young Alfred William through a drawn curtain and was struck by the effect. So he depicted the child's face covered with a thin veil, which transfigures and reveals it. The theme of the veiled figure had already received virtuoso treatment in the eighteenth century, but Rosso's exploration is more concerned with the effect than with the technical feat. The portrait is not a likeness; instead it renders a "vision of purity in a banal world." The changes of title are evidence of this shift from the portrait to a disembodied representation of childhood: after calling it *Portrait of the Child Alfred Mond*, then *Impression of a Child*, he opted for *Ecce Puer* in 1910. This last title refers to Pontius Pilate's "Ecce homo" as he points to Christ, and also to Nietzsche's autobiography. Rosso is the only artist who manages to create truly impressionist sculptures, a particularly complex affair; only Rodin attempts to come close in his *Balzac* (p. 265), which led to a falling-out between the two men. Served by an imprecise, *non finito* type of modeling, Rosso's works deny the materiality of sculpture in order to capture a fleeting glimpse, an impression. O. F.

Lewis Hine
Hazerville, Interior of Tobacco Shed, Hawthorn Farm

Gelatin-silver print
5 × 5 in. (12.5 × 17.7 cm)
Gift of M. Harry Lunn, 1986

Fifty years after Victor Hugo's poem "Melancholia" (*Les Contemplations*, 1856), Lewis Hine's photographs tackle the issue of child labor, which in 1910 involved an estimated two million young boys and girls in the United States. Between 1908 and 1918, Hine—who trained as a sociologist—inspected mines, factories, fields, hidden workshops, and streets around the country in order to document the exploitation of underage workers for the National Child Labor Committee. Hine photographed without the employers' knowledge, thanks to a small hand-held camera, often getting his young subjects to stare into the lens, the bet-ter to confront the shocked or moved spectator with his responsibilities as a citizen. A key instrument in the committee's information campaigns, Hine's images were later exhibited in touring shows, projected during talks, or used as posters and as illustrations in publications. Thus the photographer, who was close to the protagonists of the emerging social reform movement in the USA, was an innovator in his approach to the medium, which he used as a vehicle for his progressive vision of society, thereby establishing himself as one of the pioneers of engaged, humanist photography. T. G.

Edward Steichen
In Memoriam

Gum on a platinum print
(photograph taken in 1901)
18¾ × 14¼ in. (47.6 × 36 cm)
Acquired in 1999 with funding from the Fonds du Patrimoine
and the support of the Commission Nationale de Photographie

Trained as a lithographer, Steichen conceived *In Memoriam* when he was still hesitating between careers in painting and photography. His dedication to the latter was decisively influenced by his friendship with Alfred Stieglitz, founder of the Photo Secession group in 1902. Steichen became one of the leading figures of this American elite of Pictorialism, the first artistic movement in the history of photography. In order to prove that the camera did not just mechanically record reality but could also interpret it, the pictorialists produced a whole arsenal of theories and practices which, paradoxically, almost negated its basic imitative function. In addition to the use of blurring and pigment prints—in this case, gum bichromate print—which allowed manual intervention in the photographic process, pictorialism further distanced the raw visual reality by playing aesthetically on the qualities of engraving, drawing, and painting. Evincing Steichen's admiration for Rodin, Carrière, and Whistler, this large-format print belongs to a series of symbolist-style nudes that, according to George Bernard Shaw, "look as though they were taken in coal cellars." This lugubrious quality was grimly echoed by stories—corroborated by the title—that the model killed herself out of love for the photographer. T. G.

Mackay Hugh Baillie Scott
Armchair

Solid blackened profiled and carved pear wood,
mother-of-pearl and ivory inlays, painted highlights
3 ft. 8 in. × 2 ft. 2 in. × 2 ft. ½ in. (1.88 × 0.66 × 0.62 m)
Acquired in 2005

This ceremonial chair, one of a pair, was commissioned from the English architect Baillie Scott by Hans Bacmeister, then the director at the Dresden Opera, for the theater's most important guests. Typifying the work of the arts and crafts movement, in which Scott played a major role, the chair also illustrates the dialogue that existed between the major centers of Art Nouveau. Black furniture was made mainly by arts and crafts designers, but can also be found in the work of artists concerned with creating rectilinear geometrical forms emphasizing the orthogonal architecture of the furniture and the opposition between full and empty

(Charles Rennie Mackintosh in Scotland, Josef Hoffmann and Koloman Moser in Vienna).
The neo-Gothic heritage is much to the fore in the arrangement of small columns, which give the upper part a rib-like profile, and in the sculpture on the side panels. This influence combines with that of masters in Munich and Darmstadt (Richard Riemerschmid, Peter Behrens, Joseph Maria Olbrich), evident in the curved profiles at the base of the chair which straighten as they rise upward. As for the mother-of-pearl rosette decorating the back, it was one of Scott's signature touches. Ph. T.

Edward Burne-Jones and William Morris
The Adoration of the Magi

Tapestry, wool, and silk on cotton weft
8 ft. 5½ in. × 12 ft. 4½ in. (2.58 × 3.77 m)
Gift of M. Pierre Bergé, 2009

In 1886 the rector of Exeter College, Oxford, commissioned William Morris, the heart and soul of the arts and crafts movement, to do a tapestry intended for the college chapel. The proposed subject—the Adoration of the Magi—was immediately approved by William Morris and Edward Burne-Jones. Two years later, the painter, who had been working with Morris & Company for about ten years, most notably in the field of stained-glass work, delivered the cartoon of the tapestry, today kept at the Victoria & Albert Museum in London. In actual fact, only the figures are by him, the greenery and architecture having been entrusted to his colleague, John Henry Dearle. This is the first composition that Burne-Jones specifically designed for tapestry. Up till then, pieces woven to his designs by the weavers at the workshops set up by Morris at Merton Abbey in 1881 were adaptations of stained-glass window cartoons. Completed in 1890, *The Adoration of the Magi* fulfilled Morris's wildest dreams as a lover of fine work and the atmosphere of the medieval guilds. His enthusiasm was shared by critics and art lovers alike. In fact, nine versions were commissioned from 1890 to 1907. This one, ordered by the banker Guillaume Mallet, was produced in 1904. Ph. T.

Koloman Moser
Inkwell and tray

Silver and glass
Inkwell: 2¾ × 3½ × 2¼ in. (6.7 × 9.2 × 5.5 cm)
Tray: 6 × 9 × 6 in. (15 × 22.7 × 15.4 cm)
Acquired in 1986

The use of perforated metal as at once module, decorative surface, and envelope of a volume undoubtedly represents the birth of modern design. Josef Hoffmann and Koloman Moser were the men behind these objects. These two members of the Vienna Secession, founded in 1897 with the aim, among others, of rehabilitating the decorative arts, founded the Wiener Werkstätte in 1903 with the help of a banker and textile industrialist, Fritz Waerndorfer. This was a crafts association inspired by British groups such as C. R. Ashbee's Guild of Handicraft and Mackmurdo's Century Guild. Published in spring 1905, its manifesto listed the group's activities as gold and silver work, jewelry, leather, and cabinetmaking. Ceramic and glass pieces were produced by independent industrial firms. The Wiener Werkstätte provided Hoffmann and Moser with a vehicle for disseminating their aesthetic based on extremely rigorous geometry and the most inventive abstraction, and underpinned by the insistence on impeccable quality of execution and the beauty of flawless materials. Conceived as miniature architecture, the perforated objects could be produced in either lacquered metal or, as here, silver. Ph. T.

Maurice de Vlaminck
Restaurant de la Machine at Bougival

Oil on canvas
23½ × 32 in. (60 × 81.5 cm)
Gift of Max and Rosy Kaganovitch, 1973

Vlaminck's career was very unusual: a self-taught painter full of anarchist ideals, he authored a few pamphlets and bawdy novels. The vehemence of his convictions was matched by the flamboyance of the landscapes he painted during the few years when he was the most "barbaric" of the fauves. His encounter with Derain was a seminal event. As early as 1901, they were sharing a studio at Chatou, and painting side by side, at Rueil, Argenteuil, Bougival, etc. At these locations, made famous by the Impressionists, they released color from its mimetic function, restoring its full expressive power. Vlaminck was doubtless the most radical in the search for chromatic intensity: "I wanted to burn the École des Beaux-Arts with my cobalts and my vermilions," he later stated. A second encounter left a lasting mark on his painting—that was with the art of Van Gogh, which he discovered at a retrospective mounted at the Galerie Bernheim-Jeune in 1901. It was a "soul-rending" experience for him. His influence is perceptible in the dynamic brushstrokes, in the impasto, and in the palette of pure colors for this canvas. It was painted in 1905, the year of the Salon d'Automne that featured Vlaminck alongside Matisse, Marquet, and Derain in the famous room 7, soon to be known as the *cage aux fauves* (the wild beasts' cage). C. B.

Victor Segoffin
War Dance

Marble
8 ft. 2½ in. × 4 ft. 7 in. × 2 ft. 7½ in.
(2.50 × 1.40 × 0.80 m)
Acquired in 1905

"If this is the sacred dance, whatever will the profane one be like?" the critic Gillet anxiously wondered in 1905 on seeing this dancer, singing full-throatedly, with her very manly physique—square jaw, bushy eyebrows, and small bosom. The dance theme—moving away from the conventional setting of classical ballet—had already been treated in a sensuous, bacchanalian way by Jean-Baptiste Carpeaux (p. 96) for the façade of the Paris Opéra. Segoffin's dancer reverts to this freedom of movement and an off-balanced stance suggesting drunkenness. As decoration for the dance foyer, also at the Opéra, Gustave Boulanger painted a *Bacchic Dance* and a male *War Dance* that Segoffin was no doubt familiar with. Although warlike, his *Dance* is not, contrary to expectations, barbarous, and has an ancient flavor; it is influenced by the *Titeux Dancer*, a famous work from antiquity that entered the Louvre in 1891, her trance suggestive of a Bacchante's, and her tunic adorned with a Gorgon's head. The dance step beginning with the raised leg and the veil covering the cymbals echo the free, light, and airy choreographies of Loïe Fuller and Isadora Duncan, who were very popular at this time.
O. F.

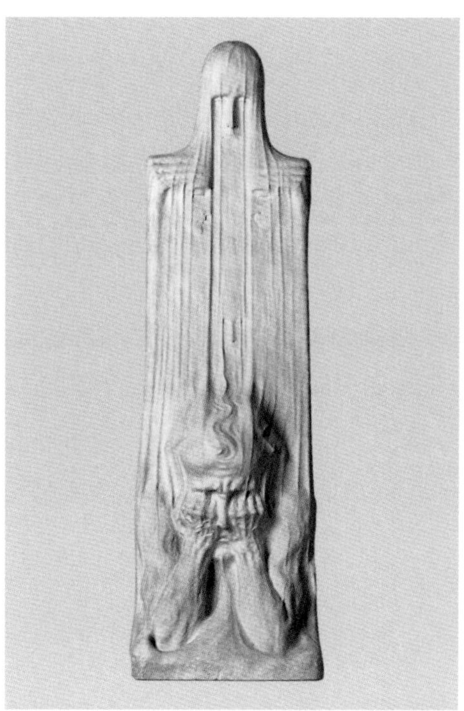

Boleslas Biegas
The Poor Man's Despair

Plaster
5 ft. 7 in. × 1 ft. 7¼ in. × 1 ft. ¼ in.
(1.7 × 0.49 × 0.31 m)
On loan from the Société Historique et
Littéraire Polonaise since 2009

The Polish sculptor Boleslas Biegas came to live in Paris in 1901, where he developed a style all his own, populated with dreamlike visions. He aspired to "create new, sincere works, derived from the mystery of the Eternal Being." *The Poor Man's Despair* takes the form of a primitive stela: the way the upper section is carved out and the treatment of the face in planes indicates the influence of pre-Christian Slavic art, most notably its iconic Zbrucz Idol. Emerging from the lower section is the bust of a man with bulging muscles, the artist's double. His existential malaise is palpable, with his palms leaning firmly on his tormented face. The hydrocephalic forehead illustrates the power of his inner world, and also the genius of the artist whose art did not always enjoy favor among buyers—for Biegas, creators, the "Elect," "suffer terribly." Standing over the man is a long, veiled silhouette forming the outline of the stela. At once protective and disturbing, this androgynous apparition with impassive features is akin to the symbolist figure of the sphinx. Its mask is repeated three times in very low relief on the stela. The fantastical dimension is heightened by the syncretism of the forms: the apparition's shoulders become hands, the despairing man's blend in with the face, and the bones in the hands become cheekbones. For Émile Verhaeren, Biegas gets the "block of clay to speak and shudder as if the whole human organism were imprisoned inside it." O. F.

Auguste Rodin
The Walking Man

Bronze, 6 ft. 11¾ in. × 5 ft. 3¼ in. × 2 ft. 4¼ in.
(2.13 × 1.61 × 0.72 m)
Donated by Maurice Fenaille, Victor de Goloubeff,
Johanny Peytel, and Léon Grunbaum to mark
the fiftieth anniversary of the proclamation
of the kingdom of Italy, 1911

Using the layering process, Rodin composed *The Walking Man* from two separate studies for *St. John the Baptist*: legs and an incomplete and cracked torso that the artist decided to leave as it was. So the fragmented figure of *The Walking Man* is not a preparatory study for *St. John the Baptist*, but very much the end result of his research into movement. Rodin was struck by the pose adopted spontaneously by his model Pignatelli, crying out: "But it is a man walking!" Without the head and eloquent hands, the *St. John the Baptist* loses its identity, only keeping the anatomical elements involved in the walking action. Exhibited in 1900, the first small-size model went unnoticed. It was not until the work was enlarged in 1905-06 that it took on all its broad expressiveness and was given the title *The Walking Man*. What particularly interested Rodin was the essential impulse behind movement, and not the exactness of the halted pose; the two feet are both on the ground, a position never found in the action of walking. For Rodin, "the artist is telling the truth and photography lies; because in real life, time never stops." O. F.

Vilhelm Hammershøi
Rest

Oil on canvas
19½ × 18¼ in. (49.5 × 46.5 cm)
Acquired in 1996

This intimate work by the Danish painter Hammershøi, painted no doubt in his apartment in Copenhagen with his wife Ida as model, was inspired by the silent world of seventeenth-century Dutch interiors, as painted by Vermeer and Terborch. However, it also displays an indeterminacy of meaning that is wholly modern. One can appreciate it for its formal rigor, the construction of its lines and surface in a harmony of grey, white, and black, following the example of Whistler, the only contemporary Hammershøi actually admired. One can also read it as a hymn to conjugal love, composed on the blazon that is the back of the woman's neck, caressed by a soft, hazy light.

And yet this work is not without its uncanny side. It is a portrait from behind, which not only makes the model anonymous, inaccessible, and enigmatic for those around her, but also puts her face to face with the empty, cold wall, in a situation of noncommunication, mental confinement, in the spirit of Hopper. The title "Rest" may thus designate an avant-gardist formal composure, a felicitous doziness on the part of the model, depicted in the realist vein, or the incommunicative exhaustion of a symbolist sphinx. The artist thus leaves it up to the viewer to complete the painting, in keeping with Duchamp's later adage that "it is the beholder who makes the painting." C. F.

Louis Majorelle
"Orchids" display case

Mahogany, rosewood, and gilt bronze
7 ft. 2¼ in. × 4 ft. 6¾ in. × 1 ft. 10¾ in.
(2.19 × 1.39 × 0.58 m)
Donated by Mme Antonin Rispal, 2005

This piece is characteristic of the stylistic options that earned Majorelle general approval, both from the critics and from his clientele, and made him the leading exponent of the "modern" French furniture of his day. This model illustrates the language devised by the artist on the eve of the Paris Exposition Universelle of 1900. Freeing himself from the influence of Gallé, who had enabled him to shake off the weight of styles of the past by studying plant models, he then placed the emphasis on structure and began restricting his ornamentation, which nonetheless remained naturalist in spirit—the plants are readily recognizable and form the structure of the modeling. This large semi-circular display case, decorated with gilt bronzes ornamented with orchids, is representative of the luxury furniture produced by Majorelle. It is a luxury that neither the gilt bronze nor the warm, rich mahogany make ostentatious, thanks to the elegant simplicity of the architectural lines, which never become lost in excessive sinuousness. Here the tradition of the fifteenth century is clear, and we also find it in the use of gilded wood, which Majorelle, for a time pursuing a path opened up by his father Auguste, whom he succeeded in 1879, had long before made a specialty. Ph. T.

Akseli Gallen-Kallela
Flame

Tapestry and wool
11 ft. 1¾ in. × 6 ft. 2¾ in. (3.40 × 1.90 m)
Acquired in 2006

In Paris, during the 1900 Exposition Universelle, Finland's pavilion was unanimously hailed. What was amazing and captivating was certainly the facility with which the national spirit was integrated within the quest for contemporary forms, more concerned with responding to the new requirements of "modern" man in the early twentieth century than with offering novelty for the sake of novelty. Inside the building, the architect Eliel Saarinen stepped aside to make way for another master builder: Akseli Gallen-Kallela. Although a painter, he is the man who designed a certain number of decorative art models—wood paneling, furniture, drapes, carpets, materials, fireplace—presented in the pavilion. The textile products are from the workshops of the Suomen Käsityön Ystävät (Friends of Finnish Crafts), created in Helsinki in 1879 for the purpose of perpetuating national traditions and rural expertise. This special quality encouraged the exhibition panel of judges to award the manufacturer a gold medal. Its attention had been "most of all ... caught by one drape of a highly original composition produced by the artist Mr. Gallen." This composition, which nowadays has attained status as an icon of Scandinavian design, was none other than this *Flame*. The copy at the Musée d'Orsay corresponds to a later version. The flames are the same as in the 1900 version, decorated with a geometric pattern with a folk inspiration. On the other hand, a fern pattern running through the entire tapestry has disappeared, making room for green tongues against which the red flames stand out. Thus the upper part of the piece presents a uniform beige-cream color, giving rise to a particularly dynamic asymmetrical effect and to a feeling of robust simplicity. Ph. T.

André Derain
Charing Cross Bridge
or **Westminster Bridge**

Oil on canvas
2 ft. 8 in. × 3 ft. 3 in. (0.81 × 1.00 m)
Gift of Max and Rosy Kaganovitch, 1973

Charing Cross Bridge is one of twenty-nine familiar London landscapes that Derain painted in 1906-07, at the height of the fauvist years. His art dealer, Ambroise Vollard, funded these trips following in the footsteps of Monet, whose views of London the artist had admired at the art dealer Paul Durand-Ruel's in 1904. This picture is both a tribute to the master, who also painted this bridge, and Derain's different take on it: "I will be looking for something else, which on the contrary will be something fixed, eternal and complex," wrote Derain, who was working in both London and Paris. While the adopted viewpoint and layout are true to the topography, the accelerating perspective of Victoria Embankment conveys the feeling of speed and of the bustle of modern urban life. Derain outlines and separates the different elements with a blue ring. Applied in flat tones or in vibrant strokes, the colors really hit the eye through the effect of this intensification of colorful contrasts that Derain called his "intentional disharmonies." The work is defined by its expressive power, gradually revealed as he labored alongside Matisse at Collioure in the summer of 1905, and echoes those "alarmingly expressive" Oceanic arts that Derain admired at the British Museum around this time. S. Py.

Frank Lloyd Wright
Chair

Stained and varnished oak,
modern leather upholstery
4 ft. 1¼ in. × 1 ft. 5¾ in. × 1 ft. 8 in.
(1.25 × 0.45 × 0.51 m)
Acquired in 1982

This chair comes from the house built by Wright in 1908 in River Forest, a suburb west of Chicago, for his collaborator Isabel Roberts: one of the "Prairie Houses" Wright designed between 1887 and 1910. Demonstrating, in the words of architectural historian Nikolaus Pevsner, the way in which "abstract art can be used to sculpt volumes in space," these individual houses evinced a strong Japanese influence, not only in their form but also in the spiritual and aesthetic values that shaped them: union with nature, respect for materials, the primacy of light and transparency, fluidity of space. Furniture such as this chair perfectly embodied its maker's concern to "incorporate as organic architecture ... furnishings, making them all one with the building and designing them in simple terms for machine work." Indeed, the internal functional division of the house is to a large extent determined by the furniture. For example, the chair backs formed by regularly spaced vertical bars set up a play of screens and partitions that delimits a functional space within the overall space—in this instance, the dining area. Ph. T.

Henri Rousseau,
also known as le Douanier Rousseau
The Snake Charmer

Oil on canvas
5 ft. 6½ in. × 6 ft. 2½ in.
(1.69 × 1.89 m)
Bequeathed by Jacques Doucet,
1936

The silhouette of a woman with hypnotic eyes, bright black and white iris against an ebony black skin, seems to have stopped time with the enchanting sound of her flute. The river and the luxuriant vegetation in this imaginary jungle, including the snakes and that odd-looking bird with the spatula-shaped beak—the entire scene seems to be frozen in an unknown time and unknown place. *The Snake Charmer* reigns over this primitive Garden of Eden, just as *War* (p. 239)—a vengeful woman with a dress as white as the body of this new Eve is black—flies dominantly over a landscape ravaged by fighting. With hardly a mention from the critics when it was first shown at the Salon d'Automne of 1907, *The Snake Charmer* was the first painting by Henri Rousseau to enter the Louvre, where it was hung alongside the great masters in 1937. The road from indifference to consecration took all of thirty years, although a small circle of friends, avant-garde painters and poets did not wait for this official recognition. The banquet held in his honor by the young Picasso in 1908 was symbolic in this regard: among the attendees were the writers Alfred Jarry and Guillaume Apollinaire, and the artist Robert Delaunay. It was actually Mme Berthe Delaunay who, on her son's recommendation, commissioned this exotic-looking scene from Le Douanier—and later the surrealists would celebrate the dreamlike beauty of these strange jungles. C. B.

Aristide Maillol
The Cyclist

Bronze
3 ft. 2¾ in. × 11 in. × 8¾ in. (98.5 × 28 × 22.5 cm)
Acquired in 1923

Virtually all of Maillol's work is devoted to the female body, and *The Cyclist*, made in 1907, is without doubt one of the finest male nudes the sculptor from Banyuls ever produced. The statue depicts the racing cyclist Gaston Colin, and like *The Mediterranean* and *Desire*, this is a work commissioned by Maillol's first patron, the German count Harry Kessler. As is his wont, the artist proceeds by simplification of his forms, and refocusing on the work's composition. The cycling champion's slim, muscular body, seemingly captured in a moment of private introspection before making his determinedly modern effort, is given an almost naturalist treatment, although still clearly very freely inspired by ancient statuary. It was Count Kessler who took Maillol to Greece in 1908, a trip during which the sculptor became very keen on pre-classical Greek art: "This is the most beautiful art I have seen in the world. It is an art of synthesis, an art superior to the work of the flesh that we moderns are seeking." É. P.

Joseph Bernard
Straining toward Nature

Lens stone
2½ × 11½ × 12½ in. (32 × 29 × 31.5 cm)
Gift of Jean Bernard, 1980

The son of a stonecutter, Joseph Bernard learnt how to cut his material at a young age. After an academic training, and having made several works for the Salon, he returned to direct cutting with *Straining toward Nature*. Paul Gauguin, Aristide Maillol, and Georges Lacombe had already practiced this technique on wood, but Bernard was the first to revive it for stone. He drew directly on the block before roughing out the form and proceeding by successive stages, regularly retracing the features in order to refine the cutting. A veritable manifesto, this seminal work lays the foundation of Bernard's aesthetic and technique. The sculptor cut a round, archaic-style face of a young woman with simplified features, whose form still recalls that of the block of stone. The title denotes his desire to get back to the deep nature of the material and to reveal it: "This, clearly put, is my ideal and my goal: realization as close as possible to the guiding thought of the conceiving brain and, for that reason, the material must be directly worked, one must know its soul and its flesh through and through, nothing about the elements used to make the work is banal … everything is sensitivity, everything is worthy of the artist." This conception contrasts with Rodin's, who used a number of assistants to produce his marble pieces. *Straining toward Nature* drew an immediate response from the new generation of sculptors. O. F.

Léon Spilliaert
Dyke at Night

Ink wash and watercolor on paper
18¾ × 15½ in. (47.8 × 39.5 cm)
Purchase, 2011

This drawing by Spilliaert was made some ten years after the one by József Rippl-Rónai, but both exploit the spellbinding pathos of nocturnal landscapes. Born in Ostend, on the Belgian coast, Spilliaert was a highly introverted, almost completely self-taught artist. He is known for his works on paper in which the black is rendered with a precision and virtuosity highlighted by the use of pencil, pen, India ink, or pastel. The drawing is part of series made between 1900 and 1920. On a sheet of exceptional size, he represents the dyke running along the beach with an immense sky above the dense, disturbing silhouettes of the big seaside hotels that seem to be clinging to the jetty. The image is dotted with surprising, bewitching rings of light that endow the composition with depth. The elongated, twinkling light falls vertically from the streetlamps and creates a composition that verges on abstraction. The presence of the sea is suggested more by the clammy fog in the play of light than by any direct reference. The fascination of the composition derives from the subtle rhythm of the marks of vertical light on the darkness, which floods the image and seeps into the soul of the beholder. I. J.

Émile Antoine Bourdelle
Hercules Killing the Birds of Lake Stymphalis or Hercules the Archer

Gilt bronze
8 ft. 1½ in. × 8 ft. 1¼ in. × 4 ft. ¼ in.
(2.48 × 2.47 × 1.23 m)
Acquired in 1924

Training first in Montauban and later in Toulouse, Bourdelle went on to work as an assistant with Rodin. There was a bond of mutual admiration between the two men, although before long Bourdelle's desire for synthesis and construction in planes clashed with Rodin's analytical modeling. From 1905, Bourdelle was aiming for simpler lines: "To contain, maintain, and control, these are the tasks of the constructor," he liked to say. He now took many of his subjects from mythology, including *Hercules the Archer*, which enabled him to scale up his work. As he himself explains, it was "undertaken with a view to mastering the purest aspect of my deeper vision; going way beyond all previous flights, more than just human blood,

bone, cartilage and muscle, I brought to the form the structure of the forces surrounding it." This work, which depicts the hero's victory over monsters, and likewise Bourdelle's over his own impetuous inspiration, is remarkable both for its tension and for its balanced construction. The dynamic comes from the interaction between the filled and empty areas, between brute force and balance. The nude denotes power, high-strung energy, straining between two opposite efforts, with the arm bending the bow and the foot leaning against the rock. References to primitive Greek sculpture and to Roman art are used as a kind of catalyst for his modernity. É. P.

Marcel Kammerer
Function Room of the Wiesler Hotel in Graz

Pencil, pen, ink, watercolor, gouache,
and gold highlights
15 × 12¼ in. (37.8 × 31.2 cm)
Acquired in 1997

Like most of the Art Nouveau artists, the protagonists of the Vienna Secession defended the idea of total art, a global aesthetic approach intended to revive the applied arts and lifestyles. A student and later colleague of Otto Wagner, one of the best-known architects in this movement, Marcel Kammerer provides magnificent evidence of this with this view of the entrance to the function room of the big Wiesler Hotel in Graz, Austria. After working on the hotel layout in a Renaissance building (1903–04), in the years 1906–09 Kammerer was put in charge of extending it, and designing the interior decorations and the furniture. During this second stage of the work, his style dropped the fancy aspects of Art Nouveau to adopt a more pure, stylized decorative language, as can be seen from this drawing. Combining aesthetics and functionality, the decorations are reduced to some sober and very harmonious geometric patterns of classical inspiration. The human figure that the architect inserts in his scene, as in a picture, is far from trivial: the elegant, slender young lady in light colors, perfectly in tune with the aesthetics of the piece, seems to be responsible for convincing us of the necessary harmony between art and utility.
A. T.-B.

Ferdinand Hodler
The Woodcutter

Oil on canvas
4 ft. 3¼ in. × 3 ft. ¾ in. (1.30 × 1.01 m)
Acquired in 2005

In 1908, Hodler was commissioned to design the second set of banknotes issued by the Swiss National Bank, which had been founded the previous year. Since the late 1880s, Hodler had been hailed as the herald of the independent Swiss art that the young Confederation was seeking to define and promote. He submitted three projects, one of them being this *Woodcutter*. These banknotes were in circulation from 1911 until 1958, disseminating compositions that he had transposed to a large format back in 1910. They were so successful that he made a few replicas, like the one in the Musée d'Orsay. Through his work of observation and synthesis, Hodler, in his own words, "brings out the forms of the human body. He shows us nature enlarged, simplified and stripped of all her insignificant details. He shows us a work that is commensurate with his experience, his heart and his mind." Above and beyond the national icon, heroically exalting physical strength, *The Woodcutter* is a meditation on man's place in the cosmos, the rhythm and ordering of which the artist has to draw from the source of beauty. Thus *The Woodcutter* is a further addition to the symbolist compositions that saw Hodler break through at the turn of the twentieth century as a leading exponent of the European avant-gardes, and whose melodious, abstract, and expressive painting influenced artists like Gustav Klimt, Paul Klee, and Wassily Kandinsky. S. Py.

Baron Adolphe de Meyer
Nijinski Lying on his Stomach, his Face Pressed against the Floor

Photomechanical print (collotype)
6¼ × 9 in. (16 × 22.7 cm), sheet taken from
the album *Sur le Prélude à l'après-midi
d'un faune*, produced by Paul Iribe in 1914
(pl. XXX), photographed in 1912
Gift of Michel de Bry, 1988

A total artistic masterpiece, the ballet with choreography by Nijinski, to music composed by Debussy in 1894 and freely inspired by the poem by Mallarmé, was staged in Paris in May 1912. The finale of this short performance caused an instant furor among the audience, reported in the press the very next day. The Faun, played by Nijinski, dressed in a bold costume designed by Léon Bakst—leotard and horns set on a curly-haired wig—lay voluptuously on the veil left by the Grand Nymph and openly mimed orgasm.

The ballet was performed in London in June and July 1912. Diaghilev, who skillfully orchestrated the promotion of his company, then commissioned a set of pictures from his friend de Meyer, a German-born member of the Linked Ring, a circle that included English pictorialist photographers. Being unable to capture the show live, de Meyer separated out, in front of a curtain, the main features of the choreography as a sequence of still postures, like a frieze on an ancient Greek urn, while underscoring the expressive powers of the peripheral parts of the dancers' bodies. Scratching streaks on his glass plates, touching up the prints with a brush, and highlighting in white, he toned down the shadows, creating veiled effects, and thus softened the original theater stage set. This invaluable album, designed like a book, with texts by Jean Cocteau, Jacques-Émile Blanche, and Auguste Rodin, was published by Paul Iribe in 1914, thereby offering a visual and literary interpretation of this choreographic poem.
M. R.

Raoul Brandon
Apartment Building, 199–201 rue de Charenton, Paris 12

Pencil, pen, and watercolor
2 ft. 8¼ in. × 3 ft. 5¼ in. (0.82 × 1.05 m)
Acquired in 2002

Breaking with the classical uniformity imposed by Haussmann, the decree of August 13, 1902 on the buildings of Paris gave architects greater freedom by allowing the curves and overhangs formed by balconies and bow windows. Specializing in the construction of apartment buildings, Raoul Brandon took full advantage of this legislation, as evidenced by this one at 199-201 rue de Charenton. The façade shows its volumes accentuated by the two buildings in the foreground, the cantilevered balconies on the second floor, and the open loggia on the fifth. The upper stories are set back, which was another possibility afforded under the decree, allowing for the construction of high, set-back roof areas. These changes keep to a symmetrical composition, testifying to the classical revival of architecture in the decade after 1910. Although the building was intended for a modest clientele, it was richly decorated, comprising some imposing caryatids as supports for the projecting bow windows. This simple yet pleasing building won the 1912 *Concours de façade* awarded to promote architectural originality. This perspective view, where the presence of people, an automobile, and a streetcar emphasize a busy neighborhood, then seeing great transformation, demonstrates the gifted draftsmanship of the architect, careful to make sure that his output received good publicity. A. T.-B.

Édouard Vuillard
The Library

Tempera on canvas
13 ft. 1½ in. × 9 ft. 10 in. (4.00 × 3.00 m)
Acquired in 1935

This monumental picture was commissioned by Marguerite Chapin for her Paris apartment, for which Pierre Bonnard also painted *In a Boat* (Musée d'Orsay). Having connections with both artists and writers, this beautiful American woman, who after her marriage became Princess of Bassiano, and was a driving force behind numerous literary journals in France and Italy, had asked Vuillard for a portrait and a folding partition. In this setting, she is featured in profile and, as it were, against the golden light in a lavishly decorated interior. Vuillard indeed includes many references, whether it be the frieze, copied from a well-known ancient sarcophagus in the Louvre, the Renaissance medallions and pilasters, or the central tapestry,

quoting both Titian and Rubens. He thus introduces a set of pictures within the picture, structuring a compartmentalized, centered composition while saturating the painted surface in this all-over effect that the painter likes so much. But instead of the stifling and sometimes threatening closed doors of the 1890s, *The Library* brings together the gentleness and majesty of the skillful arrangement. Vuillard fuses the painting of modern life with the grand manner. The princess seems to have remained somewhat unconvinced by this original contribution to the classicism of the decade after 1910, since she did not keep this decorative work, nor did she keep the Bonnard. S. Py.

Paul Auscher
Dressing table

Birch and oil paint
4 ft. 8¾ in. × 2 ft. 9 in. × 1 ft. 9¼ in.
(1.45 × 0.84 × 0.54 m)
Donated by Mme Antonin Rispal, 2005

Architect to the retailers Les Nouvelles Galeries and Félix Potin, designer of the first two big movie theaters to be built in Paris, the Batignolles-Cinéma (1913) and Marcadet-Cinéma-Palace (1919), Paul Auscher also built a number of private homes, including the one he had constructed for his own use at 5 rue de Talleyrand, Paris, in 1910-11. On this occasion he also designed the furniture. This was made by a firm in Le Havre, Établissements Doré, and decorated, under his direction, by Jean Kern, a painter and engraver of Swiss origin. The ornamentation consists of a combination of geometrical motifs—fillets, squares, hexagons, triangles, and lozenges—which play an architectural role insofar as they underscore the vertical dynamism and orthogonal character of the forms. This furniture shows affinities with a number of other pieces from the same period, notably those of the Vienna Secession and the Belgian Gustave Serrurier-Bovy. Not that tradition was totally eliminated here: the proportions and delicacy of the dressing table for Mme Auscher's bedroom evoke the Louis XVI style, a reference underscored by the elegant *profil perdu* of the marquise with the high coiffure inscribed in a medallion painted on the back of the mirror's lateral sections. Ph. T.

Herbert Ward
Aruwimi Native

Bronze
21½ × 10¼ × 9 in. (54.5 × 26.5 × 23 cm)
Acquired in 1911

Originally a colonial agent, traveler, and explorer, who later published the story of his expeditions (*Five Years with the Congo Cannibals*, 1890), Herbert Ward joined Stanley's expedition to the Congo in 1887. He was deeply moved by the dignity of the oppressed African populations that he met, and brought home many study drawings with the idea of one day producing a set of ethnographic works. After studying in Paris at the Académie Julian and at the Royal Academy in London, he decided to learn modeling in 1899, and exhibited this bust at the 1911 Salon des Orientalistes in Paris, two years after displaying at that same Salon his bust of the *Bâ Congo Girl*, also kept at the Musée d'Orsay. This warrior depicted by Ward is thought to have belonged to a tribe living on the banks of the Aruwimi, a tribe of the Congo in the northwest of the country. Like his writings, Ward's sculptures show genuine empathy for his models, who nicknamed him "the Eagle-winged White Man." Faithful depictions, with no simplistic attempt at the picturesque, and carefully chosen bronze patina (like those of Charles Cordier two generations earlier), these busts are among the finest portraits of Africans in European sculpture in the second half of the nineteenth century. É. P.

Ker-Xavier Roussel
The Abduction of the Daughters of Leucippus

Oil on canvas
14 ft. 2 in. × 7 ft. 10½ in.
(4.31 × 2.40 m)
Acquired in 1935

This large rounded panel is one of the decorations that the dealers Josse and Gaston Bernheim had requested from Édouard Vuillard and Roussel for their private mansion on the Avenue Henri-Martin in Paris. Roussel was Vuillard's brother-in-law and close to him, and had joined the Nabi group. From 1900 on, he had a preference for subjects taken from mythology in brightly colored landscapes, here the abduction of the daughters of Leucippus by the Dioscuri, Castor and Pollux at the time of their marriage. Taking the opposite line to the well-known painting by Rubens (c. 1617), which highlighted the violence of the episode, Roussel portrays the young women covering themselves up as the horsemen approach through some luxuriant spring vegetation. The figures are vigorously painted and seem to float amid a landscape constructed in patches and touches of impasto color, with a matt finish and tones recalling fresco and the art of tapestry. The garland going round the frame increases this effect and shows how much, even after the group of Nabis split up, they tried to make "imaginations conform to the eternal laws of decoration," as Denis put it. But here it is a decoration conceived as an escape from the modern world and as an evocation of a golden age, an idyll in tune with the classical feeling that permeated French painting in the period around 1910. S. Py.

Paul Follot
Chair

Maple, marquetry in kingwood and ebony,
original leather upholstery
36¼ × 19¼ × 18¼ in. (92 × 49 × 46 cm)
Acquired in 2011

On the eve of World War I, French furniture production witnessed a reaction against the purportedly internationalist and individualist nature of Art Nouveau and its asymmetrical, unstable forms. Young designers were urged to return to national traditions—not those of the classical age, but the style of the Empire, Restoration, and Louis-Philippe periods. The great theoretician of this new departure was André Véra. Published in 1912 by the journal *L'Art décoratif*, his manifesto for "The New Style" argued that the new generation should turn away from Art Nouveau and instead seek reason and symmetrical and geometrical form. It was to revive a French tradition defined by the unsurpassable qualities of "order, clarity, and harmony." Véra specified the kinds of motifs that decorators could use: "It is thus that the basket and garland of flowers and fruits will come to constitute the signature of the new style, as was the case, for example, with the torch, quiver, and arrows in the eighteenth century."

This design was presented at the 1912 Salon d'Automne by Paul Follot who, as a student of Eugène Grasset, was trained in a very Art Nouveau atmosphere. Its back formed by a wickerwork basket brimming with fruit, a motif totally devoid of Naturalism but highly stylized and strictly geometrical, it constitutes a perfect response to Véra's exhortations. Ph. T.

Auguste Renoir
Madame Renoir

Polychromed mortar bust
32½ × 20¾ × 13½ in. (82.4 × 53 × 34.5 cm)
Gift of M. Blot, 1955

Renoir came to sculpture very late in life. He seems to have tried his hand at this art form in around 1875, doing portraits of his family, and of his son Claude. In 1913, he was prompted by Ambroise Vollard to undertake some full-blown compositions. As his hands were virtually paralyzed with rheumatism, Vollard found him a young sculptor to help him, and Richard Guino did the modeling from the painter's drawings or even paintings. The bust of his wife was executed after she died in 1915, for her grave near Cagnes-sur-Mer. Renoir initially wanted to place a seated statue of Aline feeding their first son there. For this bust, which was ultimately cast in bronze, Guino worked from an oil painting Renoir did of her twenty years earlier. He has kept the same sedate figure, showing a "healthy robustness." This copy was made in hydraulic lime and sand mortar, and polychromed using the fresco method, i.e. while the mortar was still wet. É. P.

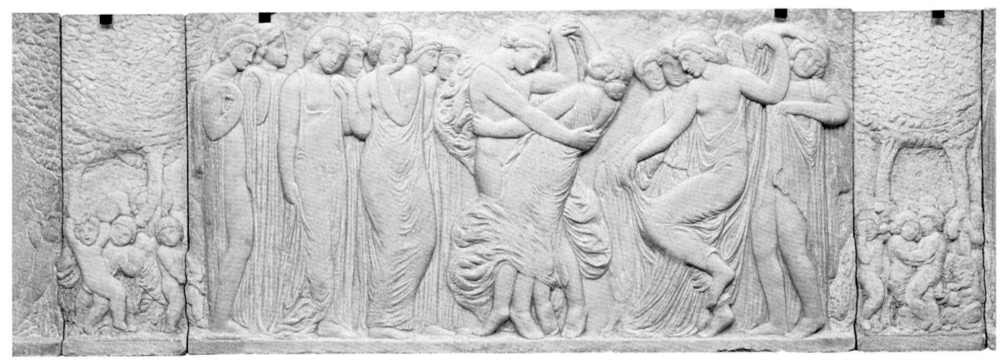

Joseph Bernard
The Dance

Marble
14 ft. 2 in. × 7 ft. 10½ in. (0.85 × 5.25 m)
Gift of Jean Bernard, 1980

Made for the music room of Paul Nocard's townhouse in Neuilly, this frieze of *The Dance* ran along the back of a stage surmounted by an organ. Bernard began with the idea of three independent panels, then had two little reliefs of *putti* cut after his own design to link the scenes, constituting a continuous band. Dance, one of the artist's favorite themes, enabled him to pursue his exploration of rhythm. The relief presents an opposition between the static, vertical lines of the musicians, singers, and spectators, and the aerial figures of the dancers, often balancing on tiptoe. The positions of the dancers standing in a group illustrate the variety of their dances: in the central panel, an entwined couple stands alongside three young women whose pose is repeated by the planes of the relief. The disorderly group playing cymbals on the left side is answered by the dancers on the right; they perform the same step but at different moments. Bernard gives his figures impassive, impersonal faces, dresses them in light, very simple veils, and positions them in an Arcadian antiquity. Doing away with superfluous details, he tends "toward an art that would be the most intense expression of Beauty in its most characteristic lines." O. F.

Anne Wardrope Brigman
The Heart of the Storm

Silver bromide gelatin print mounted
on three pieces of cardboard
9¾ × 7¾ in. (24.8 × 19.7 cm)
Purchased in 2017

"Like one in the calm that is the center of a cyclone–guarded by the very tornado around," run the lines by the American poet Edward Carpenter that Anne Wardrope Brigman inscribed on the back of this photograph.

In *The Heart of the Storm*, two female figures huddling together in the hollow of a California juniper are enshrouded by a mass of dark clouds. One, naked, raises her right hand in a protective gesture, her head ringed by a halo of light, while her legs remain bound to the tree from which she emerges. Like a nymph or a dryad, the other woman, her body draped in a transparent veil, rests her head on the breast of her companion, who offers her comfort. To make this fantastical composition, Brigman worked on the negative: drawing a circle in pencil for the halo, she inscribed lines with a burin to represent the translucent fabric swept by the wind and brushed out details in the background with gouache.

After experimenting with painting, as a photographer, Brigman took the mountains of the Sierra Nevada as her chief subject, showing women friends in osmosis with their granite rocks, pines and cedars, waterfalls and springs. By exalting the symbiosis between nature and humanity and embracing a liberated, frontal nudity, Brigman presents a vision of the photographic nude at odds with that which men practiced in their studios.

Retouching the negative, cropping, and making alterations when printing, Brigman delighted in manipulating the image at a time modernism was reaching its acme in the United States.

M. R.

Pierre Bonnard
The Pastoral Symphony or The Country

Oil on canvas
4 ft. 3¼ in. × 5 ft. 3 in. (1.30 × 1.60 m)
Donated by M. Philippe Meyer, 2009

This painting belonged to a set of four panels all the same size, now separated, and originally intended for the private mansion of the brothers Josse and Gaston Bernheim, on the Avenue Henri-Martin in Paris. The Bernheims had been Bonnard's dealers since 1906. To decorate their home, they also called in Ker-Xavier Roussel (p. 333). With *The Pastoral Symphony* Bonnard seems to bring an answer to something his friend Vuillard said: "Golden age, brightness, gaiety." Inspired by the countryside around Vernon in Normandy, Bonnard uses bright, luminous colors to celebrate a pastoral scene in which man lives in harmony with a generous nature, effortlessly delivering its fruits.

A woman milks a cow, while a man leads a horse. Some young, nymph-like women and naked children playing add to the serenity and innocence of the scene. The composition is deployed lengthwise and, using a method Bonnard was fond of, gives the spectator a broad vista over a verdant landscape and a sky with vibrant, saturated colors. In many ways, *The Pastoral Symphony* can be viewed as the culmination of the direction that the painter embarked upon at the start of the 1910s, and shows his classical feeling working toward the invention of a new Arcadia, an aspiration then shared by other artists such as Matisse. S. Py.

Auguste Renoir
The Bathers or Women Bathing

Oil on canvas
3 ft. 7¼ in. × 5 ft. 3 in. (1.10 × 1.60 m)
Gift of the artist's sons, 1923

From 1900 on, Renoir had more and more time for the female nude, which he described as an "indispensable art form." Defying illness, he painted *The Bathers* (or *Women Bathing*) during the final months of his life, at Les Collettes, his property in Cagnes (Provence). The painting is of some women bathing, a traditional subject close to Renoir's heart, being a way of treating the nude in the open air. This is the last monumental nude by the artist, who, according to his son, the filmmaker Jean Renoir, viewed this painting as a "culmination" and a "good starting-point for his future research." Renoir invites us to an idyllic setting featuring these timeless, sensual bathers enjoying heavenly nature bathed in light. With great freedom and a highly personal technique, Renoir draws with his brush, diluting the pigments, leaving the drips to show, and looking for the fluidity of a work in progress. This painting is also a resounding homage to the masters the painter admired, like Boucher, Titian or Rubens, as well as ancient statuary. Lastly, it sums up his conception of the nude and of painting, the key elements being the exalting of color, the artist's fantasy, and the inventing of a world "in which there was no place for death," as emphasized by Henri Matisse, who saw this picture, partly painted in front of him, as "the painter's masterpiece." S. Py.

Claude Monet
Weeping Willow

Oil on canvas
3 ft. 7¼ in. × 3 ft. 3¼ in. (1.1 × 1.0 m)
Donated by M. Philippe Meyer, 2000

In 1890 Monet bought the house at Giverny where he had been living since 1883. He was now free to lay it out in accordance with his vision as a painter. The "water garden" in particular kept him busy until his death in 1926. He dug a pond over which he built a bridge, recalling once more his interest in Japan. Five works on the walls of the Musée d'Orsay evoke the artist's world at Giverny: a painting of the irises in *The Artist's Garden at Giverny* (1900) and four canvases showing the "water garden" that he began to create in 1893, influenced by Japanese art (*The Water-Lily Pond, Green Harmony*, 1899; *The Water-Lily Pond, Symphony in Rose*, 1900; *Blue Water Lilies*, c. 1916-19 [p. 342]; *Weeping Willow*, 1920-22). In this large, almost square canvas representing one of the weeping willows by the pond, Monet's brush imparts an undulating movement to the branches and leaves. In the 1920s, it was no doubt an ensemble of paintings on this and the *Japanese Bridge* and *Path* themes that provided some of the "great, disconcerting studies" (like this canvas), mentioned as early as 1920 by the Duc de Trévise, which the painter kept in his studio. These compositions culminated in the set of *Grandes Décorations* that the artist donated to the French state, and which were placed in the Orangerie in the Tuileries in 1927, the year after Monet's death. S. P.

Eugène Atget
La Villette, Rue Asselin, Prostitute Waiting in Front of her Door

Albumen paper print from glass negative coated with gelatin-silver bromide
8¾ × 7 in. (22.5 × 17.8 cm)
Gift of Marie-Thérèse and André Jammes through the Société des Amis du Musée d'Orsay, 1990

In spring 1921, probably at the request of André Dignimont, a painter and collector of erotic images, Atget made a series of a dozen photographs of prostitutes and brothels for a publication that never reached the shelves. He positioned his imposing bellows camera in Versailles and, in Paris, in the Fort-Monjol area of the nineteenth arrondissement where the Rues Monjol and Asselin (now Rue Turot) had a number of bawdyhouses that were permanently open to clients. Sitting on a straw chair, a woman is frozen in a waiting posture, as emphasized by Atget's title. The finesse of the details and the violent contrast obtained in developing the print make this woman of the streets one with her stone-dominated environment, which bears the scars of both urban development and social marginality. The slightly off-center composition, the checkerboard pattern of the stones, and the subtle play of lines all heighten the sense of depth and draw the gaze in toward the black hole of the door.

This image, which Man Ray collected with others by Atget in an album published shortly after Atget's death, soon achieved iconic status in the history of the medium, helping to elevate the conscientious, dogged artisan who archived Old Paris to the status of founding father of modernism. M. R.

Aristide Maillol
Mediterranean

Marble
3 ft. 7½ in. × 3 ft. 10¼ in. × 2 ft. 3 in.
(1.10 × 1.17 × 0.68 m)
Acquired in 1923

The first major sculpture by Aristide Maillol, *Mediterranean* made a considerable impact in 1905 when its plaster version was presented at the Salon d'Automne. Its calm simplicity contrasted with the works by Rodin exhibited in the neighboring room. Using geometrical forms—in this case, the square—Maillol sought a perfect equilibrium of masses. For him, "sculpture is architecture," freed of any accessory details and dominated by simple lines of force. This sculpture constitutes a culmination of Maillol's research around the figure of a seated woman, legs crossed and leaning on one arm. He began by treating the theme in painting and tapestry, then moved on to sculpture. Maillol tried several different positions for the left arm,

folding it, resting the elbow on the leg and the fist against the head in the definitive version, thus achieving the "perfect square" he was looking for. Although he worked with a model (his own wife), Maillol gradually moved away from anatomical exactitude, making his volumes more dense and pure: "Art does not consist in copying nature," he said. This quest for pure form pre-exists the subject: "It is beautiful, it signifies nothing. It is a silent work" (André Gide). In fact, it was only in 1923, when making this version in marble, that Maillol baptized the work *Mediterranean*. This title is an homage to the sculptor's home region and to his favorite physical type, the powerfully built, voluptuous Mediterranean woman. O. F.

Claude Monet
Blue Water Lilies

Oil on canvas
6 ft. 8¼ in. × 6 ft. 6¾ in. (2.04 × 2.00 m)
Acquired in 1981

Some ten versions of the *Water-Lily Pond*, their format almost a perfect square, featured in Monet's exhibitions at Galerie Durand-Ruel, Paris, in 1900, and the following year in New York. From 1904 onward, the scenery and vegetation around the pond at Giverny increasingly disappeared from the canvas, its last manifestation being a strip at the top of the painting, before the surface of the water took over completely. "You must know that I'm entirely absorbed by my work. These landscapes of water and reflections have become an obsession. It's quite beyond my powers at my age, and yet I want to succeed in expressing what I feel," Monet wrote the novelist and critic Gustave Geffroy on August 11, 1908. Focusing his gaze on the reflections of the cloudy sky in the water at his feet, with its luxuriant floating world of vegetation, the painter played on the contrasts between the water lilies and water of the pond, between zones that absorbed light and others that reflected it. In 1916 his canvases started becoming bigger: the "water landscape" of the *Blue Water Lilies*, with its handsome shadows, was part of the collection belonging to Tériade, a publisher and editor of the artistic and literary review *Verve*. S. P.

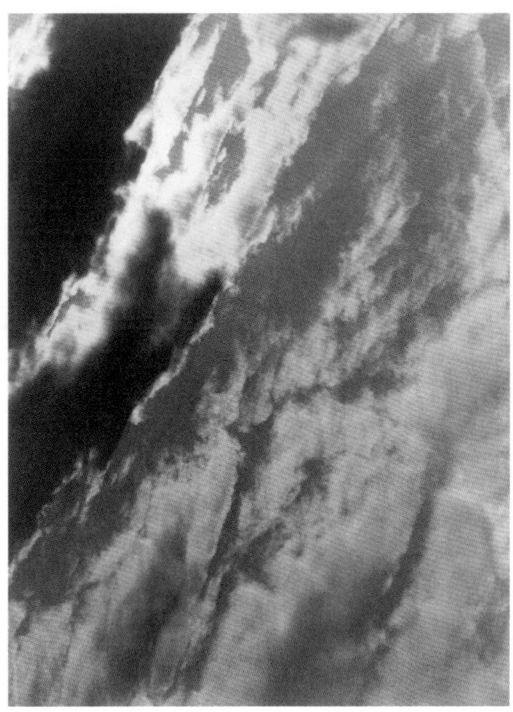

Alfred Stieglitz
Equivalent

Gelatin-silver bromide print
4½ × 3¼ in. (11.6 × 8.6 cm)
Gift of the Georgia O'Keefe Foundation, 2003

This frame—from the infinite continuity of cloudy skies, the field of which, with its subtle shades of gray, is divided into dark and light masses—was taken by Stieglitz with a Graflex camera pointed at the firmament from his summer house at Lake George (New York), in 1925. Deprived of any reference to the earth, this small-format, vertical picture, which can be viewed any way up, offers no orientation or anchoring in space. It is one of a series of cloud studies he began in 1922 and carried on until the start of the following decade, a subject that had by then become a central preoccupation for this champion of modernity in photogra-phy. After giving his first set of views the title *Music—A Sequence of Ten Cloud Photographs*, seeking to establish correspondences with music, Stieglitz titled the next several hundred studies he went on to produce *Songs of the Sky*, and then *Equivalents*, in the sure knowledge that their deeper meaning lay beyond the trans-cription of their apparent subject matter. Equi-valents of his feelings, "of the chaos of the world and his relationship to that chaos," these cloud fragments form, through the practice of photo-graphy, a masterly metaphysical exploration, and equally a radical aesthetic experiment.
M. R.

INDEX OF NAMES

The page numbers in bold correspond to the entries for the works.

LIST OF AUTHORS

Anaïs Alchus (A. A.)
Curator

Yves Badetz (Y. B.)
Curator

Claire Bernardi (C. B.)
Curator

François Blanchetière (F. B.)
Curator

Joëlle Bolloch (J. B.)
Documentary Research Officer

Laure Chabanne (L. C.)
Curator

Catherine Chevillot (C. C.)
Senior Curator

Caroline Corbeau-Parsons (C. C.-P.)
Curator

Élise Dubreuil (É. D.)
Curator

Côme Fabre (C. F.)
Curator

Ophélie Ferlier (O. F.)
Curator

Thomas Galifot (T. G.)
Curator

Leïla Jerbouai (L. J.)
Curator

Isabelle Julia (I. J.)
Senior Curator

Martine Kaufmann (M. K.)
Art Historian

Jérôme Legrand (J. L.)
Documentary Research Officer

Laure de Margerie (L. d M.)
Documentary Research Officer

Caroline Mathieu (C. M.)
Chief Curator

Édouard Papet (É. P.)
Chief Curator

Sylvie Patin (S. P.)
Senior Curator

Sylvie Patry (S. Py.)
Senior Curator

Paul Perrin (P. P.)
Head of Curatorial and Director of Collections

Anne Pingeot (A. P.)
Senior Curator

Isolde Pludermacher (I. P.)
Curator

Clémence Raynaud (C. R.)
Curator

Xavier Rey (X. R.)
Curator

Anne Robbins (A. R.)
Curator

Marie Robert (M. R.)
Curator

Philippe Thiébaut (Ph. T.)
Senior Curator

Alice Thomine-Berrada (A. T.-B.)
Curator

Jean-Rémi Touzet (J.-R. T.)
Curator

ACKNOWLEDGEMENTS

The authors would like to express their gratitude to all those who contributed directly or indirectly to the production of this book, and in particular to the team of documentary researchers at the Musée d'Orsay, Elsa Badie-Modiri, Isabelle Gaétan, Sylvie Gohel, Nadège Horner, Véronique Kiensy, Jérôme Legrand, Dominique Lobstein, Philippe Mariot, Annabelle Mathias, as well as Charlotte Cachin-Liébert, Raphaël Dupouy, Marina Ferretti-Bocquillon, Éric Jouvenaux and Patrice Schmidt.

PHOTO CREDITS

COLOPHON

MUSÉE D'ORSAY

Publishing Director
Marie-Caroline Dufayet

Editorial supervision and iconographic research
Virginie Berri, assisted by Rachel Scrivo for
the first edition and by Irène Egan and Manon
Morgand for the second edition

SKIRA

General Manager
Nathalie Prat

Editorial supervision
Juliette Chambon
Irène Rodriguez
Roxanne Rebours

Copyediting and proofreading
Mark Nathan

Graphic design
Diane de Noyelle
Mathis Bécard

Layout
Anouk Chambon

PHOTOENGRAVING
Les Artisans du Regard, Paris (1st edition)
Litho Art New (2nd édition)

© Éditions Skira Paris, 2025
ISBN 978-2-37074-270-4

© Musée d'Orsay
ISBN 978-2-37074-285-8
Legal deposit: November 2025
Printed by Graphius in Ghent, October 2025

Cover:
Auguste Renoir, *The Swing*, 1876, oil on canvas,
3 ft. ¼ in. × 2 ft. 4¾ in. (92 × 73 cm), bequeathed by
Gustave Caillebotte, 1894